GOD'S ITINERARY

GOD'S ITINERARY

Where Epic Faith Meets Priceless Peace

A MEMOIR

Kara Washington &
Charles Washington III

Inquiries may be sent to GodsItinerary@gmail.com.

Some names and identifying details have been changed to protect the privacy of individuals.

Printed by CreateSpace, an Amazon.com Company • CreateSpace, Charleston SC

For Worldwide Distribution, Printed in the United States of America

ISBN 10: 1723042536
ISBN 13: 978-1723042539

Library of Congress Control Number: 2018908645

Cover Photo & Pieces of a New Puzzle p. 260: Julien Le Bars, Pic my Trip Paris
Cover Design: Olivia Pro Design & Cesar Graphics
SuperChad Drawing p. 256: William Malbury
All other photos from the author's personal collection.

This book is dedicated to:
Amare Charles Washington

You are, without a shadow of a doubt, the best thing that happened to Daddy and me. We both love you to infinity and beyond, and please always remember that the sky is the limit son, in terms of what you can accomplish in this world as long as you keep God at the center of your life. You have absolutely inherited the strength, courage, and resiliency of your father. I am incredibly proud of the way that you have accepted and embraced the life God has seen fit for us. Although we have our share of daily struggles, there has not been one day along this five-year journey of grief, that you have not given me something to smile or laugh about. You truly light up my world ACW! I love you. - Mommy

Introduction

Itinerary: a Detailed Plan For a Journey

They always say if you want to make God laugh, tell Him your plans. I never knew how true this was until recently. That's what happens when you survive two detached retinas in your one good eye, you have a miscarriage after two years of trying to conceive, your first child needs open heart surgery before age one, and as a family, you embark upon a heart transplant journey not once, but twice in a sixteen-month window. Over the last few years, I've discovered that God does have a plan, and to accept *God's Itinerary* for our life, we need two ingredients: FAITH and LOVE. To gracefully endure His plans, we need crazy faith, unheard-of faith, relentless faith, EPIC FAITH.

It was around the three-year mark of our heart transplant journey that Charles "Chad" and I decided to write this book. Every time we took a step in the direction of progress and thought we had our timeline figured out, another headwind would come and everything changed again. We had the wind knock us out on multiple occasions and we seemed to discover a new rock bottom each time. But when we realized that our faith in God and love for each other allowed us to make the best out of even the craziest situations, we both agreed that our tests and trials were clearly bigger than us and would have to be shared.

When Chad passed away, our book naturally took on a whole new meaning. It now represents Chad's legacy of endurance, gratefulness and Epic Faith. Chad was a quiet warrior whose courageous actions spoke volumes to many. This memoir is divided into parts that Chad wrote and parts that I wrote. Since the project's inception, it has been our sincere prayer that our story of triumph, defeat, fear, joy, hope and determination can serve as motivation and encouragement for whatever you may be facing in your life today.

Prologue

Please, let me not be too late, was all I could think as I navigated the traffic through Los Angeles on that Saturday afternoon. I'd been such a coward to stay away for so long. I knew that now. My hands shook as I steered the car into the hospital parking lot. How do you say goodbye to the person you love more than life itself? I didn't want to say goodbye.

I parked the car and rushed to the unit. I hit the buzzer and the doors opened right away. A nurse was standing outside of Chad's room, motioning for me to hurry. I ran into the room, skipped the yellow gown protocol and rushed to Chad's side.

"I'm so sorry, Chad," I said, not caring who was listening. "I didn't come sooner because I was scared." I swallowed hard. "But, that's not the way we handle things, so here I am. I love you. You're the best thing that's ever happened to me." Tears stung my eyes, but I soldiered on. "I could not have asked God for a better husband for myself and father for our son. Amare will be just fine because he is as strong as you are."

I swallowed the lump in my throat as I stood beside the love of my life who was once five foot eight, one hundred and sixty plus pounds and full of life and laughter. "You look at me now," I said to the less than one hundred pound version of Chad as his pain-ridden gaze pierced my soul. "Don't you dare try to act like you don't know me when I get to heaven."

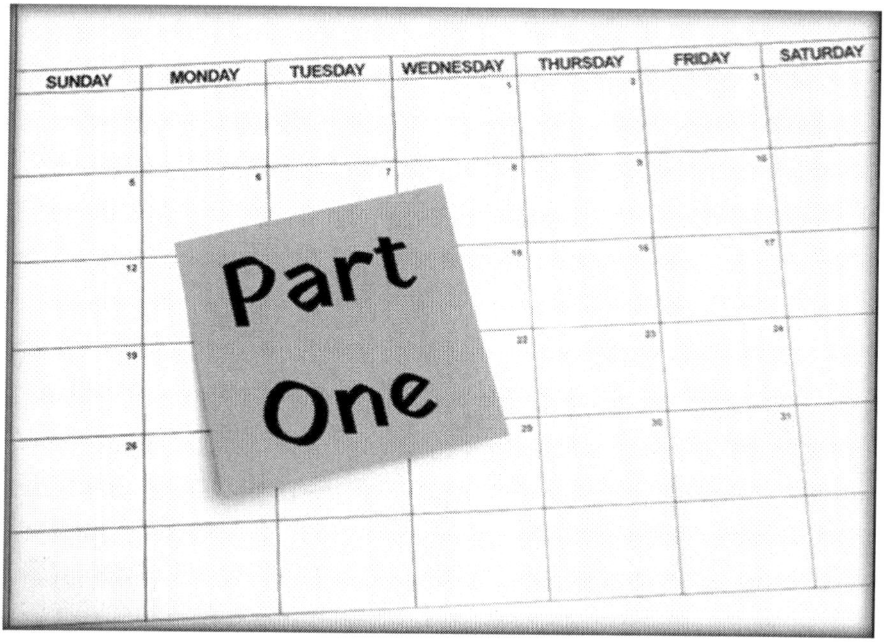
SUNDAY
MONDAY
TUESDAY
WEDNESDAY
THURSDAY
FRIDAY
SATURDAY
Part One

MEET CHAD

Chad

Against All Odds

The task ahead of you is never as great as the power behind you! I was born May 26, 1977, three months earlier than scheduled. At birth, I weighed two pounds and one ounce. I am the surviving child of a set of premature triplets. We three all had major health issues: kidney, heart, and lung defects. My two brothers did not live past the first seventy-two hours of our birth, and the doctors told my parents to prepare themselves for my death as well. God, however, had other plans for my life.

Initially, the doctors thought I needed a patent ductus repair, a congenital disorder that results in failure of a fetal blood vessel to close after birth. When I was just ten days old, they attempted the repair and discovered I had Tetralogy of Fallot instead. This meant that my heart had four anatomical abnormalities, one per chamber. Doctors couldn't repair this until I was older, so I was age four when I returned to the hospital for another surgery. The operation was performed at Kaiser Sunset Hospital. My pediatric cardiologist at the time was Dr. Trace. I remember being in an oxygen tent a lot. I recall a rather long and heated disagreement with my father on the day of my discharge. I, not being a huge fan of eggs at the time, didn't want to eat the gross hospital eggs that were on my tray, while my father protested that they were good for me and were just what I needed to help my currently frail body grow strong and vibrant. I was told, rather vehemently, that we were not leaving until I ate all of my eggs. We didn't, and I did.

My first pacemaker, there have been about six, was implanted at age ten at UCLA Medical Center. The hospital rooms had paid cable television. I remember watching *Jacobs Ladder*, at least as much of it as I could, before I got too scared. The procedure took place in December of '89 right around Christmas. I distinctly recall driving my new remote-controlled, battery-operated Porsche 911 up and down the hallway outside my room. There are also memories of a New Year's Eve celebration with apple cider. Little did I know, roughly thirty years later, I would be back in the same hallways, but this time with a virtually remote-controlled heart.

Elementary School

In sixth grade, I had the bright idea to share part of my cardiac experience with my classmates. This was partly to address schoolhouse rumors, and also to fulfill an oral science project requirement. I think my thought process at this point was that this was a scientific subject in which I had a unique perspective and expertise to share. In other words, I knew I'd get top marks and I could simultaneously silence the haters. I did an excellent presentation. I had two visual aids: a poster board with a drawing/mock-up of a cross-section of a human torso. The mock-up had a model of a pacemaker and its leads in relation to the human anatomy. The second visual aid was me. I took off my shirt and proceeded to show what each scar was and why it was made. I explained what a pacemaker was, what it did, why I needed it, and how it was connected inside of me.

"For I know the plans that I have for you," declares the Lord, "plans to prosper you and not to harm you, plans to give you hope and a future." Jeremiah 29:11 NIV

When I finished my stellar report, I opened the floor for questions. The questions ran the gamut from can you be outside when it rains, how long does the battery lasts, and are you surprised you're still alive? I received an A on the project and also was able to educate some children about a rather complex subject in the process. I was, and still am pleased about being able to do that to this day. There were a few kids that started teasing me as a result of the presentation, and while it was only a few kids doing the teasing, they were harsh and relentless. Unfortunately, I didn't learn my lesson about children's capacity to inflict cruelty.

I repeated a similar presentation the following year at the Catholic school I was newly enrolled in at the time. The presentation went well, academically speaking. Unfortunately, I had given some of my schoolyard nemesis fresh ammo. The result was that they would trip me and while I was on the ground, another one would straddle me with two hands in the air as if holding a defibrillator and yell out "clear!" As a result of this, I became extremely private about my condition. I would not shower or change in public if I could avoid it. I wore a shirt whenever I went swimming, and I certainly didn't talk about it publicly again.

"For I know the plans that I have for you," declares the Lord, "plans to prosper you and not to harm you, plans to give you hope and a future." Jeremiah 29:11 NIV

HOW WE MET

Kara

I attended First Church of God Christian School in Inglewood, California from kindergarten through the eighth grade. There were twenty-four people in my graduating class and the school was predominantly African American. My first day as a freshman at Alexander Hamilton Academy of Music in West Los Angeles, introduced me to a whole new world. My new classmates no longer doubled as my Sunday school buddies and my new principal and teachers did not sing in the choir at my church. Instead of having twenty-four classmates, I now had more than two hundred and twenty-five from all different walks of life.

On a hot first day of school in August of 1992, I met Chad. After a twenty minute walk from home to the bus stop, my sister Tiffany and I joined at least fifteen other students waiting for the school bus. Tiffany was two years ahead of me so she already had a set group of high school friends. I boarded the bus and walked about halfway down the aisle to an empty seat. Just moments after I had slid over to the window, per the rather scary bus driver's instructions, a young freshman-looking boy asked, "Do you mind if I join you?" It was obvious that he was just as nervous as I was about the first day of high school. We both stumbled on our words on the twenty-five minute ride, but we did manage to introduce ourselves before the awkward silence settled in. By the end of the first week, we were official school bus buddies with a couple of classes together and a number of mutual friends. I found myself looking forward to my morning chats with Chad, as I had never really conversed one-on-one with a peer of the opposite sex on a regular basis like this.

Somehow Tiffany and I were always rushing to get to the bus stop on time, which meant that my jewelry was thrown in my pocket to be put on later. I was notorious for wearing the little charm bracelets that were nearly impossible to clasp without assistance. After a few mornings of watching me struggle, Chad graciously offered to help me. In many ways, those bracelets acted as ice breakers to our relationship. As we rode along in the bumpy yellow bus, we would chat about our families or any upcoming weekend plans. We had great conversations and enjoyed each other's company.

As the year went on, Chad began to express an interest in being more than just friends. He would bring me the most endearing presents, often times coordinating with my locker partner and leaving surprises for me. My all-time favorite gift was the life-size Kerokee stuffed pillow from the Hello Kitty Store. Just when I thought I had every Kerokee product available, Chad surprised me with this adorable pillow that eventually accompanied me across the country as my built-in college roommate.

On one particular Valentine's Day, Chad met me outside of my algebra class with a bouquet of roses. Although it was a grand gesture on his part, I was mortified. I was extremely shy back then, especially when it came to dealing with guys, so while many girls would have loved to walk the campus with flowers on Valentine's Day, the last thing I wanted to do was draw attention to myself or indicate that there was a relationship brewing. I thanked Chad for the flowers and successfully hid my unease with the gesture. Then, when no longer in his presence, I stuffed the flowers in my backpack where they remained until I got home later that day. Throughout high school, our friendship continued

Yes, if a person continues asking, he will receive. If he continues searching, he will find. And if he continues knocking, the door will open for him. Luke 11:10 ICB

to flourish. At one point, Chad even slid "The Note" to me. You know the one stating: "Will you go with me? Circle: Yes, No or Maybe." Despite his best efforts, I elected to keep our relationship platonic. At the end of the day, I was a nerd at heart and saw young "love" as nothing but drama and a distraction from school.

Upon graduation in 1996, I went away to school in Chicago and Chad attended an in-state college. This was pre-email and Internet days, so we were good ole' fashioned pen pals. We would occasionally talk on the phone, but more frequently, we sent letters to one another about various topics including school, family and our feelings. Over the course of our friendship, Chad alluded to the fact that he had health issues but had never gone into any detail. The topic seemed to be one that he preferred to keep private so I never pressed the issue. At one point, after our friendship had further developed via phone calls and snail mail, the matter of his medical condition resurfaced. I think it was then that I officially entered Chad's circle of trust and he decided to bridge the gap between what I thought I knew or had heard, and the truth. "So what have you heard about my condition?" Chad asked me in a nonchalant manner during one of our typical evening phone calls. "I really don't know much," I said. "I have just vaguely heard that it is something pertaining to your heart." Chad's reply was that instead of talking about it or trying to explain it, he preferred to send me his college application essay. Chad said this essay would reveal everything from his condition to his position in life.

Anxious to finally put a rest to the rumors and speculation, I checked the mail every single day. It was a Wednesday evening when the tell-all letter arrived. I could not get to my dorm room fast enough. Thankfully, my roommate was not home so I had the small space to myself. As I meticulously read the letter, I realized that I previously had no clue about Chad's true condition. As promised, in the letter, Chad described the circumstances surrounding his birth, including his heart defects and the fate of his brothers. The essay culminated with the way in which Chad's medical battles had trained him to handle life's various adversities.

Yes, if a person continues asking, he will receive. If he continues searching, he will find. And if he continues knocking, the door will open for him. Luke 11:10 ICB

My life has been like that of a Sequoia tree. When I was born, I was a 3-month premature seedling, weighing some mere 2 pounds, 1 ounce. I was the sole-survivor of triplets. Because of my early birth, I suffered from a condition called Tetralogy of Fallot. This condition is characterized by four defects of the heart. In addition to the Tetralogy of Fallot, they also diagnosed me with congenital heart disease. This is an incurable ailment that has steadily been a nuisance to me throughout my life. Fortunately, the Tetralogy *is* repairable.

At a tender ten days old, I underwent my first operation, an attempted Patent Ductus repair. As it turned out, I didn't need that particular operation. In addition to being the victim of an unnecessary operation, I spent the first three months of my life in and out of incubators and oxygen tents. At age four, I had my second operation. This one was to repair the Tetralogy of Fallot. The operation was a very delicate one and due to complications, I wasn't expected to live through the night. Obviously I did, but not without obstacles.

When I was ten, I had a cardiac pacemaker implanted. This changed my life. I finally began growing and my energy level skyrocketed. With my new found vitality, I realized that I possessed an extremely strong will for survival that would allow me to prevail when faced with adversities. One such time was when my grandfather, whom I was extremely close with, died. At his funeral my sister was supposed to give a tribute to him, but she wasn't able to. My father asked if I could do it. Of course I did it. Yet, to this day, I don't know how.

My most recent adversity came in the form of yet another surgery. This one, in July of 1995, was a Tetralogy of Fallot re-repair. The thought of having any surgical procedure is a scary one for most people, including me. Yet I feel the thing that separates me from most people, is that I look forward to the second chance, a resurrection if you will. For with it comes the chance to grow stronger both mentally and physically. The chance to express love and concern, and the chance to examine your outlook on life, and make any necessary changes.

Much like the towering Sequoia tree needs to face and overcome obstacles to grow and flourish in the forest, I too have faced and will continue to overcome obstacles in my life. I only hope that my life can continue to flourish as I overcome the challenges that are presented.

CHAD'S COLLEGE ESSAY

I called Chad as soon as I was done reading the letter. "Hi there," I said trying to be as delicate as possible before approaching the previously inaccessible topic. "Hey," he said, with a slight hint of hesitation in his voice. Given that we had been friends for over five years now, and this would be our first in-depth discussion on the topic, I knew it was imperative that I tread lightly. "So, I got mail from a certain someone today," I said. "Oh really," Chad responded. "And did you read said mail?" Chad asked. "Multiple times," I answered, and went on to explain that I really had no clue about what his heart condition truly was. Still not exactly an open book, Chad simply asked me if I had any questions for him. I honestly did not know where to begin. I admitted that my biggest shock was that he was a triplet, and I asked Chad if he thought about his brothers often. Not being a medical or science-minded person, I did not press too hard for further detail regarding his actual condition, but instead we talked about Chad's feelings and how he coped with everything. It was then that Chad explained how after being teased in elementary school, he had made a conscious decision to keep his medical condition private.

Outside of that evening, the topic of Chad's health never really came up again over the course of our ever flourishing relationship. From the outside looking in, Chad seemed perfectly fine and with the exception of significant scars on his chest and back, which no one ever saw, there were no other physical indicators of his condition. The average person would have never known that Chad was not in perfect health. Between the "appearance" of good health and the absence of this topic in our on-going conversations, I concluded in my young head that Chad was fine and had survived the worst of his ailments.

During the summer between our college freshman and sophomore year, Chad and I, along with our mutual high school friends, hung out quite frequently. It was during this time that I began to develop a significant interest and attraction to Chad. I had never been in a serious relationship before, but having been away from home for a year now, I could definitely tell that there was something different and unique about

Yes, if a person continues asking, he will receive. If he continues searching, he will find. And if he continues knocking, the door will open for him. Luke 11:10 ICB

Chad that I did not see in other guys. He was a true gentleman and it was obvious that he genuinely cared about me.

As the summer came to an end, I had finally decided that I was ready to try our friendship at the next level, a real bonafide relationship. Still being shy and lacking confidence on emotional matters, I decided to write Chad a letter revealing my feelings. In my head, the thought of having this conversation in person seemed as impossible as walking on the moon. I had spent some time that week drafting the letter which would divulge my true feelings to Chad. The note was not particularly long but of course formatted very colorfully with buzz words such as "feelings" and "friendship" in pink and purple. It had all the signs and indicators of young, nervous love. The overall tone of the letter was that I had finally come to my senses and realized what we had far exceeded simple friendship. I let Chad know that I would like to finally try our relationship at the next level. My note was prefaced with tons of disclaimers such as: "I understand if it is too late and you no longer feel this way" and "I hope that this does not jeopardize our friendship." I knew that my timing could very well be off and perhaps Chad's initial interest had lapsed. I anticipated that after multiple past attempts, it was highly unlikely that Chad would be initiating this conversation with me again. So the risk of rejection had by default, been transferred to me.

Our typical summer hang-out days consisted of me, two or three of my girlfriends and Chad, along with his friend Aaron, all going out to eat or catching a movie. The plan for one specific day was for me to slip Chad the letter just as we were parting ways for the evening. Needless to say, I walked around the entire day with the letter in my pocket and butterflies in my stomach. I was so nervous about sharing my true feelings after all this time. What if he no longer felt this way? What if he didn't take me serious? What if??? So as the evening came to a close, I had just about talked myself out of it. The only problem was talking my girlfriends, Jessica and Janice out of it. These two very strong-willed ladies who I love dearly, were in no shape, form or fashion going to let me chicken out on delivering the letter. By the end of the night,

Yes, if a person continues asking, he will receive. If he continues searching, he will find. And if he continues knocking, the door will open for him. Luke 11:10 ICB

according to their version of the story, I practically threw the letter towards Chad and sped off in my mom's minivan nearly running over his feet! When I got home, all of five minutes away, Chad called me. I could tell that he had found my level of nervousness quite comical. I clearly heard the smirk plastered across his face. He was not letting me off easy. I was still his girl, but I'd tortured him for years, insisting we be platonic friends. As if in disbelief, Chad refused to let me off the phone until I told him why I'd had this sudden change of heart. I explained to Chad that the change had not been sudden and that I had been wrestling with the concept for quite a while. I admitted that the possibility of our friendship being ruined if things didn't work out, seemed like an awfully big risk to me. But I had finally come to the realization that the potential of missing out on something great, seemed like a bigger risk. And this is where it all began…

Yes, if a person continues asking, he will receive. If he continues searching, he will find. And if he continues knocking, the door will open for him. Luke 11:10 ICB

DATING YEARS

Kara

In May 2000, I graduated from Loyola University Chicago. With the exception of my brother Kevin who was in Japan on tour with the Navy, all of my immediate family flew in. Aunt Margaret, my dad's sister flew in as well. Having been a couple for almost two solid years at this point, Chad had no intention of missing this day either so he too flew in. My mom being originally from Chicago, still had tons of family in town. In fact, during my last semester, which was more heavily focused on an accounting internship than actual classes, I lived with my mom's sister, Aunt Adrienne and her husband, Uncle Evan. This was the first time that Chad would meet my extended family in Chicago. Having lived with Aunt Adrienne and had many heart-to-heart conversations over the past six months, a small portion of anxiety began to build up in anticipation of her officially meeting Chad. In her eyes, would he live up to all that I had described?

Well, of course he did! Chad with his ever-cool, subdued yet witty personality, hit it off with my Aunt Adrienne right away. It was as if they had known each other for years. It took no time for Chad to have my Aunt Adrienne laughing in her famously contagious way. He just blended in so well with our entire group. It did not take a rocket scientist to see that Chad was definitely a part of our family. After the main graduation that Saturday, we all headed to the Signature Room in the John Hancock Building. This restaurant, on the 95th floor of one of Chicago's tallest skyscrapers, overlooked beautiful Lake Michigan and Lake Shore Drive. It was the perfect day. I felt like my past met my future and I loved every minute of it.

After all of the graduation festivities were over, Chad headed back to California and my sisters Robyn, Tiffany and I, went on a week-long celebratory Caribbean cruise. When we returned from the cruise, my dad and I loaded up my car and headed back to Los Angeles. I was moving home with my parents to save money and start my accounting career. Having only known long-distance love to this point, Chad and I were beyond thrilled to be permanently back in the same town again. We had a great time dating in Los Angeles. We hung out with each other's families and my nieces and nephews even called him "Uncle Chad" and me, just "Kara." We went on numerous double dates with his parents, seeing premiers through their movie club, dining all around the city and playing cards (even though they cheated). Chad and I were the best of friends; and outside of work hours and overnight, we were rarely apart.

We both loved to travel, so although living with our parents had its challenges, it at least afforded us the extra funds for side trips here and there. Our trips were far from extravagant, yet we always had a fantastic time together. Some of the more memorable trips from our dating years included a few Memorial Day Weekend trips to Las Vegas for Chad's birthday. One particular year, my sister, Robyn, and her future husband, Carl, went, along with Kevin and his wife Nichole. Tiffany stayed back in Los Angeles and helped my mom keep all of their kids. The highlights of that trip to me were Chad and my brother hanging out and really bonding for the first time; as well as the look on Chad's face when I surprised him with front row seats to the Blue Man Group. On another memorable Las Vegas trip, I surprised Chad with tickets to see Dave Chappelle, who he absolutely loved at the time. He had no idea that we were going to see him until we pulled up to the MGM Casino and Dave's

So these three things continue forever: faith, hope and love. And the greatest of these is love.
1 Corinthians 13:13 ICB

face was in bright lights. We loved to surprise each other and genuinely enjoyed doing whatever we could to bring happiness to one another.

In addition to Las Vegas, we also frequented Chicago almost every summer. Chicago trips always delivered big fun, and on one particular trip, we must have connected with every friend that I had in the city. We watched the 4th of July Fireworks in Grant Park with a group of friends from Loyola, went to the Taste of Chicago multiple times, attended a family barbecue at my cousin's house, and even went on an impromptu Lake Michigan dinner cruise with my college friend Alicia, and her future husband Jeffery. Chicago was our favorite city to visit and always felt like our second home.

The absolute most memorable trip from our dating years was our group vacation to Puerto Vallarta, Mexico. This trip included me and Chad, Tiffany and her future husband Shawn, my girlfriend from high school Rachel, and Chad's best friend Aaron. We were just six vivacious young adults enjoying life. Chad, being the adventurous and fearless person that he was, even went parasailing with a two-men-and-a-rope operation that he ran into on the beach. We did everything on this trip from snorkeling, party boat rides, sunset dinners, to riding ponies and partying in the club until the wee hours of the morning. I can almost still hear some of the phenomenal laughs that we shared on that trip.

We returned from Puerto Vallarta on Labor Day of 2001 (August 30th), just twelve days before the tragedy of 9/11. Given the extreme state of despair that this event left our country in, it was impossible not to re-evaluate life at that point, and consider just how precious it really was. This was the year that Chad and I began to toss around the idea of marriage and whether or not we were headed in that direction. We were both on the same page and confident that we wanted to spend the rest of our lives together. However, we were foggy on the timeline. Naturally, we were just trying to navigate our way through life as young adults and marriage always seemed like the step that people took once they were established professionals knowing exactly what they wanted out of life.

So these three things continue forever: faith, hope and love. And the greatest of these is love.
1 Corinthians 13:13 ICB

By November 2001, both of our immediate and extended families had met and gotten to know each other over the years since Chad and I had attended the same high school. It had become my family tradition to spend Thanksgiving in Palm Desert, California. My Aunt Evelyn would host the actual holiday dinner and for the rest of the weekend, we would just hang out as a family. On this particular year, I rode out to the desert with Chad and his parents. They had invited me to stay at their condo for the weekend. The day after Thanksgiving, the Washingtons had extended an invitation to my family for brunch. For some reason, I remember waking up kind of irritable that morning. Being one who does not fare well socially when sleep-deprived, I struggled to shake my snappy mood. Chad was acting kind of strange that day too but I could not put my finger on it, nor did I spend a ton of energy trying. At some point during the day, while preparing for the brunch, I had teased him about the "to-do list" that his mom often made for him and his dad. Chad admitted that he had long grown accustomed to the list and had no problems completing the tasks. He teased me and said that I could make him a list as well. So being the young dreamer that I was, I fell right into his trap. I quickly jotted down some things that I would have liked him to complete. The three items on the list were: 1) buy Kara a diamond necklace, 2) buy Kara diamond earrings, and 3) buy Kara a diamond ring. While I had no doubt that we were headed in the direction of marriage, I was totally joking with Chad regarding all three of the requests.

By the time my family and all of the guests arrived, my mood had begun to lighten but Chad's demeanor was getting stranger. We were all gathered around in the living room just casually mingling. I was sitting at the end of the couch and Chad was sitting on the floor next to me. I remember looking down and noticing that he was sweating profusely. "Are you OK?" I asked, and at this moment, Chad pulled out the "to-do" list that I had created earlier. Before anyone else caught sight of it, I snatched it out of Chad's hand and balled it up with a quickness. He laughed and told me to open it. Still reluctant and trying to be discreet,

So these three things continue forever: faith, hope and love. And the greatest of these is love.
1 Corinthians 13:13 ICB

I slowly unraveled the paper. Once I noticed that number three had a check mark next to it, I quickly looked up.

"Quit playing," I said. I hadn't even noticed that the chatter amongst our relatives had stopped and all eyes were on us. It was then that I discovered that this was far from a joke. Chad was on one knee with a velvet black box in his hand, and a rock the size of Mount Everest was glaring back at me. I distinctly remember my Aunt Evelyn saying, "Oh, my gosh! Is he proposing?"

Chad had caught me by complete and utter surprise. I had absolutely no idea that we were so close to engagement, no idea that he had gone ring shopping, and I certainly had no clue that he had asked my parents for my hand in marriage. What a wonderful surprise this was and in the presence of both of our families. How many people get to marry their best friend!?! Of course, I said, "Yes!" After the engagement was official, we found ourselves in a circle surrounded by our family, while they each proposed a congratulatory toast and made remarks regarding Chad and me. This weekend had instantly graduated from unpredictable mood swings, to an over-the-moon experience. I spent the entire next day outside on my cell phone, telling everyone that I knew the great news. I was going to be Mrs. Kara Nicole Washington!

So these three things continue forever: faith, hope and love. And the greatest of these is love.
1 Corinthians 13:13 ICB

IN SICKNESS & IN HEALTH

Kara

Wedding Woes

Once I was done informing the world of our engagement, I immediately began to execute on a vision that had been replaying in my head for quite some time. On one hand, the timing of Chad's proposal was the surprise of the century to me; yet the fact that Chad and I were getting married was like a dream that I already knew would come true. Over the course of the next eighteen months, Chad and I hit some hurdles for sure, the first one being agreeing on a date for the wedding. Poor Chad had not been made privy to the fact that he had a festering Bridezilla on his hands. He was under the impression that post-engagement, we could just play it by ear and set a date as he got closer to finishing school. Meanwhile, wanting to reap the employee benefit of the Farmer's Insurance Tuition Assistance Program, I had enrolled to pursue my MBA at California State University, Long Beach. As an adult student now myself, I could certainly respect the fact that Chad wanted to complete school prior to getting married. I was not however, on board with the unknown aspect of the timeline. In fact, I felt that getting married and eliminating the distraction of dating would actually help accelerate Chad's quest for a degree.

Chad and I "discussed" the topic of setting a date as often as I could manage to work it into a conversation. If we were not careful, the celebratory event that was designed to draw us closer, was beginning to drive a wedge between us. One week night in February, as Chad was leaving my parents' home, I had allowed my frustrations to bubble up. "Are we ever really going to get married?" I asked Chad. For a moment, he just looked at me and shook his head, as if to say, *are we really doing this again?* Although it was obvious that Chad was annoyed with my question, I used his silence as an open invitation to proceed with my thoughts. As if he didn't know, I reminded Chad that we had gotten engaged in November and here it was February and we had not set a date. Chad's response was, "But you already know that I want to finish school first." At that point, I had to fight back the tears of frustration. "Are you crying?" Chad asked in a tone of disbelief and borderline irritation. "No," I lied. "I'm just frustrated," I said, "And disappointed that you do not seem to want this as bad as I do." Clearly insulted by my last statement, Chad shook his head, said he had to go and started walking towards his car.

We did not speak again that evening, and the next morning in a very melodramatic fashion, I decided to leave my engagement ring at my parents' house and went to work without it. I figured with no wedding in the near future, why even bother claiming to be engaged. One of my friends at work (who had been married for years) noticed almost immediately that something was wrong. After describing the previous evening to her, she explained to me that men and women are different in so many ways. She pointed out to me how we ladies tend to get caught up in the magic of the wedding day, while men are thinking about the responsibility and how they want to be able to provide for their

Love is patient and kind. Love is not jealous, it does not brag, and is not proud. Love is not rude, it is not selfish, and does not become angry easily. Love does not remember wrongs done against it. Love takes no pleasure in evil, but rejoices over the truth. Love patiently accepts all things. It always trusts, always hopes, and always continues strong. Love never ends.
1 Corinthians 13:4-8(partial) ICB

household. This conversation left me feeling so guilty and childish, that by lunch time I went back home to recover my engagement ring and I also called Chad to apologize.

Finally, around Easter (March 2002), Chad and I had agreed on a wedding date. After much "discussion" and debate, we had compromised on a still longer than average engagement. We wanted to save money to pay for the wedding in cash, and allow more time for Chad to make progress in school; and we wanted a summer wedding. I also had the brilliant idea of wanting to get married on a holiday weekend so that we would always have an extra vacation day to travel for our anniversary. Unfortunately, my "brilliant" idea did not include consideration for the fact that the one-day guaranteed extension, would be accompanied by a premium price to travel during a holiday weekend. Nevertheless, July 5, 2003 was the chosen date. From then on out, I had a laser beam focus on this date. I imagine like most brides, the year of their wedding did not consist of three hundred and sixty-five days, but instead, just one.

The next big dilemma was determining the wedding party. Through much thought and difficult consideration, I had narrowed down my bridal party to ten. The ten ladies were my two sisters, Robyn and Tiffany; my best friend, Jessica; Chad's sister, Elena; my cousin, Katrina; my childhood friend, Tara; and four of my girlfriends from college, Tracey, Eva, Sidney and Cheryl. In addition to the many challenges that inherently come with a wedding party of this size, the biggest and most immediate one was that Chad did not have enough friends to accompany the ladies down the aisle. After analyzing the situation and pondering every possible configuration, Chad selected eight men to support him on this special day. These men included his father, Michael; Chad's best friend, Aaron; two pseudo uncles, Joseph and Gregg; two future brother-in-laws, Shawn and Carl; his cousin Corey; and his childhood friend, Bobby. The eight-versus-ten configuration worked out perfectly since

Love is patient and kind. Love is not jealous, it does not brag, and is not proud. Love is not rude, it is not selfish, and does not become angry easily. Love does not remember wrongs done against it. Love takes no pleasure in evil, but rejoices over the truth. Love patiently accepts all things. It always trusts, always hopes, and always continues strong. Love never ends.
1 Corinthians 13:4-8(partial) ICB

Robyn and Tiffany were honorary maids of honor and walked down the aisle solo; followed by Jessica, the acting maid of honor, who in the exiting processional was matched up with Aaron, the best man. Including our flower girl, two ring bearers, two junior bridesmaids/candle-lighters and four ushers/hostesses, our twenty-seven-person wedding party was all set! Clearly small and intimate was not the theme of this extravaganza for after-all, we were planning to do this one time and one time only, so it was all or nothing, go big or go home.

With the date and bridal party selected, over the next year and a half, we planned the wedding that I had always dreamed of. Chad was a very gracious groom who allowed me free reign on many facets of the wedding, yet he was willing to help and wanting to contribute wherever the opportunity arose. There were, however, two areas where Chad put his foot down regarding his input. This was when it came to selecting a DJ and the reception music, as well as the attire to be worn by Chad and the groomsmen. I had full confidence in Chad for these areas so he received no resistance from me on his requests. In fact, prior to the wedding day, I had no idea what the groomsmen were wearing but I knew that it would be stylish and appropriate, just like the man that I was marrying.

During the eighteen-month planning period, we learned a lot about ourselves as a couple. We took a six-week premarital class through our church, where we discussed the biblical principles of marriage. Consequential to planning a large wedding and deciding where to live, we by default quickly began to witness the nature in which we made big and small decisions together. We also began to see how we operated in the realm of family and managing expectations and personalities. At the end of the day, we always respectfully had each other's backs and it was evident that nothing and no one could tear us apart.

Love is patient and kind. Love is not jealous, it does not brag, and is not proud. Love is not rude, it is not selfish, and does not become angry easily. Love does not remember wrongs done against it. Love takes no pleasure in evil, but rejoices over the truth. Love patiently accepts all things. It always trusts, always hopes, and always continues strong. Love never ends.
1 Corinthians 13:4-8(partial) ICB

A Sneak Peak Beyond the Altar

During our extended engagement, joint decisions and managing family expectations was not the only preview I received. I also got a behind-the-scene glimpse of the productions that took place before, during and after one of Chad's medical procedures. Both of us lived with our parents at the time, so after work during the week, if we had no special plans, our normal routine was to either hang out at my parents' house, Chad's parents' house or my sisters' house, as Tiffany and Robyn shared a condo at the time. Our subliminal goal for the evenings was to spend time together and find food in the process. Once our nightly aspirations became blatantly obvious, we were labeled the "crumb-snatchers."

One evening in April 2002 I headed over to Chad's parents' house to hang out, but when I arrived, there were other relatives there like his aunt and uncle, grandparents and a few cousins. Hors d'oeuvres were nicely laid out and there appeared to be a small party in progress on this random weekday night. Gauging the confused look on my face, Chad immediately pulled me aside into an empty room and said, "Don't panic, but I went to the doctor today and my pacemaker battery is low." "Okay," was the only response that I could come up with as my brain was processing a mile a minute. Chad proceeded to explain that he was going in to have the pacemaker replaced the next day. He quickly followed up with the disclaimer that it was a routine procedure, done on an outpatient basis. I had read in Chad's college essay that he had a major heart condition and had undergone open heart surgeries. Yet, all of that was in the past and I had never been a participant in this part of his life, real-time, as it unfolded.

As a newbie to the scene, I found this news to be highly alarming; yet, having been supportive of Chad since birth, the rest of his family appeared totally calm and not the least bit frazzled. Later, as we said

Love is patient and kind. Love is not jealous, it does not brag, and is not proud. Love is not rude, it is not selfish, and does not become angry easily. Love does not remember wrongs done against it. Love takes no pleasure in evil, but rejoices over the truth. Love patiently accepts all things. It always trusts, always hopes, and always continues strong. Love never ends.
1 Corinthians 13:4-8(partial) ICB

goodnight, Chad assured me there was nothing to be worried about and that he would be just fine. Nevertheless, I went home that evening and cried myself to sleep. I woke up the next morning still numb to the idea that Chad was going in for surgery. My fear kept me in the bed far longer than usual and by 6:30am, my mom stuck her head in my room to check on me, as I had clearly altered my normal morning routine. I informed her of the events scheduled for the day and she encouraged me not to worry and said that Chad would be okay. I left the house that day physically dressed for work, but when I got in my car, the wheels immediately headed in the direction of my heart.

I drove out to Kaiser Bellflower Hospital and met Chad and his parents as they were checking in. What a relief it was just being there with him, instead of in my cube at work with my imagination running wild. Chad and his parents were totally at ease with the situation and spoke very calmly and candidly with the doctor before Chad headed back to the operating room. The procedure took significantly longer than the average time that had been quoted to us, but later I would learn that there was no average time when it came to Chad. Once the procedure was complete, the doctor came out to talk to us. "Mr. Washington could not have come in a moment too soon," the doctor said. She kept a calm and collective demeanor but seemed a little astonished as she described the old pacemaker completely dying on the table, mere moments after being removed from Chad's chest.

I instantly had a greater appreciation for how precious life really was, and more specifically in this case, how precious Chad's life was. God had spared him, yet another time. So I decided to take an intermission from the wedding hoopla and plan a surprise 25th birthday party for Chad. Tomorrow is not promised to any of us. However, for someone who had already far surpassed the doctor's expectations at birth, celebrating twenty-five years of life was not only a good idea, in my mind, it was mandatory.

Love is patient and kind. Love is not jealous, it does not brag, and is not proud. Love is not rude, it is not selfish, and does not become angry easily. Love does not remember wrongs done against it. Love takes no pleasure in evil, but rejoices over the truth. Love patiently accepts all things. It always trusts, always hopes, and always continues strong. Love never ends.
1 Corinthians 13:4-8(partial) ICB

For the next six weeks, I removed my bridal tiara and replaced it with my simply-wanting-to-make-my-fiancé-happy hat. Dave & Busters (an adult version of Chuck E. Cheese) was one of our all-time favorite places. We even frequented this place when we visited our second home city, Chicago. Our favorite D&B in Southern California was in Irvine, about a fifty-minute drive from Los Angeles. This did not stop me from wanting to throw a party there, because like many things, once the idea was in my head, there was no turning back. After communicating with the D&B Event Coordinator and selecting the private room that would be most appropriate for a group our size, it was time to decide on the menu. Chad's favorite cuisines were Italian and Mexican. Since Chad and I were connected at the hip outside of work, it would have been impossible for me to break away for any length of time to pay a planning visit to Dave & Busters on the weekend. So instead, I took one afternoon off from work and my girlfriend Tara and I drove out to Irvine for a food tasting. "Where were you this afternoon, I tried to call you at work?" Chad asked later that evening as we started our crumb-snatcher adventures. "Oh, we had meetings all afternoon," I said and quickly changed the subject, asking him about his day.

Tara and I had a fantastic time that afternoon eating and planning. The Italian food resonated with us the most so that was an easy decision. I also had the opportunity to see the actual banquet room that had been reserved for our party. Although I had seen the photos advertised online, viewing the room in person was a huge win for me. I instantly took mental pictures and was off and running from there. The next day, I drew the layout of the room as I remembered it. I began to plan where the food buffet would be set up, where Chad would sit, the birthday cake corner and the strategic placement of the happy face balloon decor. In order for the surprise to seem natural and unsuspicious, I would not be able to participate in the actual event-day room preparations. Relinquishing control of this prime piece in the surprise puzzle definitely

Love is patient and kind. Love is not jealous, it does not brag, and is not proud. Love is not rude, it is not selfish, and does not become angry easily. Love does not remember wrongs done against it. Love takes no pleasure in evil, but rejoices over the truth. Love patiently accepts all things. It always trusts, always hopes, and always continues strong. Love never ends.
1 Corinthians 13:4-8(partial) ICB

triggered a release from my anxiety tank. Fortunately, I have sisters and friends who had grown accustomed to my "issues" so they were not the least bit surprised nor offended when I delivered my computer-generated excel spreadsheet, complete with clip-art tables and very specific instructions on the desired room configuration.

Having spent the majority of our recreational time with my immediate family and friends, I wanted to branch out and include more of Chad's family for this special occasion. I worked with his mom to gather the email addresses of some of his close cousins and created an Evite. Everyone was very responsive and it took no time at all to land a party of thirty. Next, my biggest worry was whether all twenty-nine people (excluding Chad) would be able to hold the secret. Chad's actual birthday was May 26, which typically landed during the Memorial Day holiday weekend. Chad's cousins were going to be out of town that weekend so the initial date would have eliminated a good portion of the guest list. I decided instead to go with the following weekend. The party date was set for June 1, 2002. This definitely worked in favor of the surprise, since it was highly unlikely for Chad to suspect a party one full week after his birthday.

June first was also the birthday of one of my friends, Tracey, who I worked with at the time. She and Chad would always jokingly call each other birthday buddies, so Chad never thought twice when I told him that we were headed to D&B that evening to celebrate Tracey's birthday. My stomach was in knots all day long. I was extremely nervous that the surprise would get spoiled at the last minute. The closer we got to Irvine, the more anxious I grew. When we finally reached Dave & Busters, I was practically shaking with nerves. Somehow I managed to casually walk in with Chad who again, thought we were just meeting up with Tracey and friends. I slowly wondered off to the side where the banquet room was and nonchalantly said, "I think they are in here." As I opened the door and we entered, everyone yelled, "SURPRISE!" Chad was

Love is patient and kind. Love is not jealous, it does not brag, and is not proud. Love is not rude, it is not selfish, and does not become angry easily. Love does not remember wrongs done against it. Love takes no pleasure in evil, but rejoices over the truth. Love patiently accepts all things. It always trusts, always hopes, and always continues strong. Love never ends.
1 Corinthians 13:4-8(partial) ICB

speechless! Quite frankly, he looked almost too surprised for a moment and his mom rushed to his side to make sure he was okay. He was definitely okay, just totally taken aback. Here we were an hour outside of LA, a week past his birthday, and gathered with his family and friends from both sides who had all come to celebrate him. Mission accomplished. Chad's twenty-fifth birthday was a huge success! For years to come, we would continue to elaborately celebrate this gift of life that God kept graciously sustaining.

Wedding Bells

While the break from wedding-mania had been refreshing, it was short-lived. Soon after the surprise party was over, the wedding planning ramped back up and never ceased. By the time the actual wedding weekend rolled around, we were both just ready to officially be husband and wife, live under the same roof and start our married life together. Our wedding colors were lavender and gray, and by the end of the eighteen-month planning period, I think my eyes had retrained themselves to only see these two colors. No matter where I went, there was always an item, idea or something that would be just perfect for our special day. In the end, while our extended engagement had allotted for a heftier budget, it had also made way for substantially more spending opportunities. Nevertheless, after what seemed like the world's longest engagement, the Fourth of July holiday of 2003 was finally upon us.

Tuesday of that week was my last day at work and my friends from out of town began to arrive that evening. By Wednesday night, the majority of the wedding party was in town and for some guests, it was their first time visiting Los Angeles. In terms of where Chad and I would live once married, we were fortunate enough to rent the duplex that Chad's parents owned, and also where Chad had lived as a very young

---

Love is patient and kind. Love is not jealous, it does not brag, and is not proud. Love is not rude, it is not selfish, and does not become angry easily. Love does not remember wrongs done against it. Love takes no pleasure in evil, but rejoices over the truth. Love patiently accepts all things. It always trusts, always hopes, and always continues strong. Love never ends.
1 Corinthians 13:4-8(partial) ICB

child. We had agreed to host some of the bridal party until our wedding night and then everyone was on their own. My girlfriends and I had a great time catching up, looking through old pictures and reminiscing. We also hit some tourist spots like Pinks Hotdogs, Hollywood Blvd, and Roscoe's Chicken & Waffles. And of course, we paid an extended visit to the nail shop for a pre-wedding mani/pedi session.

Thursday, the 3rd of July, was the wedding rehearsal day. This would be the first and only time before the wedding that all twenty-seven members of the bridal party would gather to practice and discuss last minute wedding day details. At last, the big day was swiftly approaching and in less than seventy-two hours, Chad and I would be officially married. To say that excitement was running high would be an understatement. After all of the debating, saving, planning and hard work, the beginning of our beautiful weekend was just moments away— well, a few frustrating moments away if you consider the afternoon traffic in Los Angeles. With five females sharing one and a half bathrooms and a very small window of time to get dolled up for the rehearsal, we left the duplex a tad later than planned. As we sat on Sepulveda Boulevard in bumper-to-bumper traffic, I utilized the convenience of Nextel and began a chirping session with Chad. It turned out that while Chad was close, he was not exactly in route to the church. He was actually at the Fox Hills Mall, squaring away a tux for my nephew and brother who had flown in from Japan earlier that day. While at the mall, Chad, in his ever-brewing excitement, had gotten the notion to purchase a linen suit to wear that evening. Not initially realizing the time, or the fact that the suit would need to be altered, after our chirp session, Chad aborted operation linen suit and headed out for the rehearsal instead.

While there was some chaos naturally with a wedding party of our size, the rehearsal went over extremely well. Against some traditions, I did a practice walk down the aisle with my dad. The second I put my

Love is patient and kind. Love is not jealous, it does not brag, and is not proud. Love is not rude, it is not selfish, and does not become angry easily. Love does not remember wrongs done against it. Love takes no pleasure in evil, but rejoices over the truth. Love patiently accepts all things. It always trusts, always hopes, and always continues strong. Love never ends.
1 Corinthians 13:4-8(partial) ICB

arm around his and the music was queued up, the emotions began to creep up inside of me and I did all I could to play it cool. Looking around and seeing my closest friends and family who had traveled from near and far, all in the name of our love for each other was simply beautiful.

When the rehearsal was over, the bridal party along with any out-of-town guests, headed to Chad's parents' house which was less than ten minutes away. The atmosphere when we arrived could have been likened to a classic Hollywood movie. My soon-to-be in-laws had really outdone themselves and everything was just perfect. The silver and lavender wrapped gifts that I had dropped off for the bridal party earlier that week were symmetrically lined up on the mantel. There was light jazz and R&B playing in the background. The outdoor patio was beautifully lit to perfection. The overall mood was celebratory and bursting at the seams with love and excitement. We ate, mingled, toasted and thanked our parents, as well as all of our wedding participants. This was the start of our wedding weekend and it was fabulous.

The next day was the actual Fourth of July holiday. Having stayed up late the night before chatting about the rehearsal, my girlfriends and I did not have a particularly early start. After breakfast at Roscoe's Chicken & Waffles (me barely eating a thing as the nerves began to settle in), I dropped my friends off in Hollywood for a day of sightseeing. Already packed for the hotel that we would check into later that day, I headed over to my parents' house to hang out and relax for a minute. My dad and my Aunt Margaret were working on our wedding cake and I was pleasantly surprised that my request for love words sporadically written around the cake was being incorporated. With a house full of company, I snuck up to my parents' room for just a moment of silence and rest. Soon after, I headed out to pick up my friends and check into the Marina Marriott where I would be spending the next two nights, the first being with my friends and the second with my husband!

Love is patient and kind. Love is not jealous, it does not brag, and is not proud. Love is not rude, it is not selfish, and does not become angry easily. Love does not remember wrongs done against it. Love takes no pleasure in evil, but rejoices over the truth. Love patiently accepts all things. It always trusts, always hopes, and always continues strong. Love never ends.
1 Corinthians 13:4-8 (partial) ICB

GOD'S ITINERARY | 27

I knew there had been talks of a bachelorette party but I hadn't heard anything in a while and had very early on been instructed not to ask. I was pretty sure that the girls were up to something, but I just went with the flow for a change. At some point after checking in, I got a call from my sister, Robyn, saying that she was going to swing by the hotel to pick us up and take us to dinner. After we got in the car, she said that she just needed to make a quick stop at Elena's and we would be on our way. Of course, when we got to Elena's, I was fed another story to get me out of the car, and when Elena opened the door to her home, there were about thirty women yelling, "SURPRISE!" Turns out, there were even more friends and family from Chicago that I didn't even know I would see before the wedding.

The theme was Hawaiian and everything was decorated to a tcc. The evening was an absolute blast and the sisterhood that I felt, having my girlfriends from all different chapters in my life together in one room, was incredible. In addition to Hawaiian, the theme was also lingerie. That evening, I received enough lingerie to last for what seemed like a lifetime. Some was downright gorgeous, some was safe, and some I would have never purchased for myself, yet none of it went unworn. After all of the presents were opened and the embarrassment of receiving intimate apparel in such an open setting had subsided, my girlfriends and I packed back into Robyn's car and headed to the hotel.

Due to the fireworks show at the Marina, we ran into a number of road closures. By the time we reached the hotel, we were well past the curfew that I had written in my very elaborate weekend itinerary, yet I didn't care. After getting ready for bed, I remember my girlfriend Tracey and me chatting about how many times we had chatted about this very weekend, this day, this moment. For some reason, my excitement began to manifest itself through laughter. As we replayed the wedding events that had already taken place, particularly the bachelorette party that had

Love is patient and kind. Love is not jealous, it does not brag, and is not proud. Love is not rude, it is not selfish, and does not become angry easily. Love does not remember wrongs done against it. Love takes no pleasure in evil, but rejoices over the truth. Love patiently accepts all things. It always trusts, always hopes, and always continues strong. Love never ends.
1 Corinthians 13:4-8(partial) ICB

just ended, we literally laughed uncontrollably. This was truly the happiest time of my life thus far.

Finally, sometime after 11PM that evening, Tracey and I had laughed ourselves to sleep. We woke up the next morning bright and early and headed out for my hair appointment, leaving the other ladies fast asleep in the adjoining room. I remember initially waking up thinking: *wow, I wish I would have gotten more rest,* but then wedding day adrenaline kicked in and I never looked back. Having both the curse and benefits of a Type-A personality, I was very much known amongst my family and friends to have an itinerary for every event in my life, both big and small alike. So one could only imagine the itinerary that I had prepared for the biggest, most anticipated day of my life. This itinerary covered everything from the time I would wake up and leave the hotel, who would be driving, my hair and makeup appointments, down to the type of sandwich that I would eat from Subway prior to getting dressed. I remember being so anxious to get the day started that I had proceeded to jump in the driver's seat of my car as we headed to the beauty shop. Tracey looked at me like I had lost it, and quickly informed me that I was in no condition to drive and that the cut-off for itinerary changes had long passed. So in accordance with our previously scheduled program, Tracey proceeded to drive me to the beauty shop. There we met a good friend Kathryn who had flown in from New Orleans, and my flower girl, my niece, Amaya, who was happily eating a glazed donut the size of her head.

After my hair was shampooed and I was sitting under the blow dryer, Chad checked in with me to say good morning and see how everything was going. Having the luxury of being a man and not needing hair and make-up stops, Chad was heading out to IHOP with Shawn, Carl and my nephew, Eugene. Also while under the blow dryer, I received a text from a number that I did not recognize, saying "Good Morning, Bridezilla." To this day, I have no idea who sent the text but given the

Love is patient and kind. Love is not jealous, it does not brag, and is not proud. Love is not rude, it is not selfish, and does not become angry easily. Love does not remember wrongs done against it. Love takes no pleasure in evil, but rejoices over the truth. Love patiently accepts all things. It always trusts, always hopes, and always continues strong. Love never ends.
1 Corinthians 13:4-8 (partial) ICB

fact that I could not have been any more specific about every single detail of that day, the text was totally warranted and came across as comical to me.

Contrary to that joke, however, was the phone call that Tracey received while I was in the chair getting the final touches on my hair. This call was regarding the first sign of trouble for the day. It was our wedding day coordinator, my friend, Amber. She was calling to get a contact number for the event coordinator at the reception site, and had given Tracey the impossible task of obtaining this information from me without alarming me. After receiving the news that the vendors were beginning to arrive and the venue had not been set up as agreed to in the contract, I was very frustrated and began to tear up. However, by the time my lifetime beautician Janet, and one of her customers finished giving me a pep talk about the day, I was back on track in no time. Having done extensive (to the point of obsessive) research on weddings through a plethora of online bridal forums, one recurring theme was always to enjoy the day no matter what. I knew that this day would not be perfect, by the official definition at least, but it was at that moment, during the first major hiccup, that I decided to just relax for a change, cherish the moment and focus on the primary purpose for the day, to proclaim my love for Chad and marry my best friend.

The next stop was the MAC counter at the Fox Hills Mall. The makeup artist that I had previously done a trial run with was not working that day, but I had a list of all of the makeup to recreate the look that we had agreed on. While getting my makeup done, Jessica and Tiffany surprisingly stopped by the counter to snap a few pictures and mostly check up on my mood since the news had been leaked regarding the reception hall. Much to their surprise, I was fine; yet, they went out of their way to assure me that all was well with the reception hall. I had literally gone to the land of carefree, which was a totally foreign place

---

Love is patient and kind. Love is not jealous, it does not brag, and is not proud. Love is not rude, it is not selfish, and does not become angry easily. Love does not remember wrongs done against it. Love takes no pleasure in evil, but rejoices over the truth. Love patiently accepts all things. It always trusts, always hopes, and always continues strong. Love never ends.
1 Corinthians 13:4-8(partial) ICB

for me by the way. However, I was determined to not let anyone or anything (short of a tragic accident) ruin this momentous day.

With my hair and makeup done to perfection, Tracey and I headed back to the hotel where the other bridesmaids had begun to get dressed. Soon afterwards, the photographer arrived and began to take candid shots of me getting dressed with my mom and beautician, Janet, helping me. We also went to the hotel rooftop for posed pictures with my family and the bridesmaids. The day that had taken a year and a half to draft, was present and very much in motion.

From the roof-top of the hotel, we took the elevator down to the lobby and waited for our ride. In true go-big or go-home fashion, Chad I and had rented an ivory-colored stretch Escalade for our bridal party to ride in. The ladies were thrilled when they saw how they would get to the church. My dad and I hung back at the hotel for the more traditional limousine that we had rented for myself and Chad. The ride to the church with my dad was peaceful and possibly the last moment of clarity before it was show time. I remember arriving at the church and seeing a parking lot full of cars and thinking: *wow, this is really it.* The limo pulled around the back so that I could enter with minimal contact. The first person I saw was my godmother, Deborah. Her husband, my godfather, Daniel, had done all of the flowers for the day. She was apologizing for some minor mishap with one of the girl's bouquets, and I quickly told her that it was no big deal at all and that I was not worried about a thing. I then headed straight to a room that had been reserved for the bride. In the room, Chad had delivered a beautiful glass plague with a love statement on it, along with a card. I believe it was right around then that my out-of-body experience commenced for the day.

In addition to the absence of perfection, all of my bridal research had warned me that the actual wedding day would fly by in the blink of an eye, but somehow I did not want to believe it. Sure enough, it turned out that between the program, pictures, receiving line and simply blissful

Love is patient and kind. Love is not jealous, it does not brag, and is not proud. Love is not rude, it is not selfish, and does not become angry easily. Love does not remember wrongs done against it. Love takes no pleasure in evil, but rejoices over the truth. Love patiently accepts all things. It always trusts, always hopes, and always continues strong. Love never ends.
1 Corinthians 13:4-8(partial) ICB

state of mind, in many respects, I did not attend our wedding until we got the video months later. One thing I do remember very vividly though, is how extremely happy Chad and I were that day. Totally out of character for him, Chad was literally bouncing off of the walls. During our first dance to Maxwell singing "For Lover's Only," a rush of emotion came over me and I hugged Chad so tight that he asked if I was alright. Perhaps it was then that I had fully returned to the scene and realized that the man of my dreams had become my husband. A friendship that had flourished so beautifully had now morphed into a sacred union. Chad and I had stood before God, in the presence of about three hundred of our closest family and friends, looked into each other's eyes and solemnly vowed to be true to one other in sickness and in health. In years to come, these vows would serve as an irrefutable blueprint for our marriage.

Love is patient and kind. Love is not jealous, it does not brag, and is not proud. Love is not rude, it is not selfish, and does not become angry easily. Love does not remember wrongs done against it. Love takes no pleasure in evil, but rejoices over the truth. Love patiently accepts all things. It always trusts, always hopes, and always continues strong. Love never ends.
1 Corinthians 13:4-8(partial) ICB

AND THE TWO SHALL BECOME ONE

Kara

Honeymoon

Chad and I honeymooned in Maui for seven nights after our wedding. We stayed at the Fairmont Kea Lani, which was absolutely fit for a queen and king. We thoroughly enjoyed a daily breakfast at the resort, which Chad always concluded with a sticky bun. I remember the morning Chad received the tragic news that the sticky buns were out for the day and right there in the restaurant, he threw a pseudo tantrum, tucking his tiny bottom lip out and throwing the cloth napkin on the table. Outside of that minor (and very comical) mishap, we had a spectacular time in Hawaii. We drove around that island in our rented convertible Malibu, without a single care in the world besides our love for one another. We took canoe riding classes, attempted a "Snuba" lesson (where I failed miserably in the first few moments), completed a self-guided tour on the road to Hana, and went on evening swims where we extensively discussed our hopes and dreams for our life together. One day, it rained all day so we found ourselves in an arcade playing the Venus and Serena tennis game like two high schoolers on a ditch day.

We also went to the mall that day and ended up with matching tennis shoes (much to Chad's dismay), Homer Simpson house shoes for Chad and a few other items that resulted in us purchasing a piece of luggage to get everything home. One night, we went to a sunset dinner on the beach where I had a twice-baked pork chop that was absolutely delectable. And of course we could not visit Hawaii without attending a Luau, which we saved as the finale of our trip.

Chad and I had flown together many times prior to getting married, but we were accustomed to returning to our respective homes upon landing. This time, when the wheels were down and the plane was parked, I immediately began to rummage through my purse handing Chad his stuff. Then it instantly hit me that we were officially Mr. and Mrs. Charles Wesley Washington, III. We would finally get to reside under the same roof as both friends and lovers. This obvious fact yet sudden recollection was like starting our honeymoon all over again!

Bye-Bye Honeymoon

The first six months of our marriage fit the classic honeymoon phase to a tee. Every day, we would practically pinch ourselves because we couldn't believe how good our new life together was. However, exactly six months later, almost to the hour it seemed, we found ourselves in an entirely different phase and wanting to pinch each other instead (figuratively speaking that is). Our first major argument as a married couple was a continuation of the same disagreement that almost prevented us from setting a wedding date in the first place. Chad attended Dominguez Hills University at night while working at McBride Special Education Center during the day. He had somehow registered for a class at one point, but missed the starting date by a long shot. In fact, by the time this oversight was brought to light, it was too late to join the class. In addition to whatever the associated sunk costs of this mistake was, I had a hard time looking past the set-back this caused for our timeline.

Be completely humble and gentle; be patient, bearing with one another in love.
Ephesians 4:2 NIV

This first dose of reality and clear indication that the honeymoon was over felt a lot different than the theoretical conversations we had had in our premarital class. I, being the school nerd and chronic planner that I was, could not wrap my mind around how a mistake like this happened to us. The real problem was that I could not yet comprehend how Chad's way of doing things was so completely different than mine. Yes, we had been friends for a long time and spent ample time dating, so clearly our differences should have come as no surprise. I guess my young interpretation of "the two shall become one," really meant the two shall think and operate like Kara. Of course, I did not see Chad's mishap as simply an honest mistake. No, I took it very personally and spared no opportunity to let him know. I could not stop harping on the fact that his drive or lack of drive for school no longer just affected him, but was now encroaching on our hopes and dreams as a couple. At one point, during a heated discussion (probably more of an unfortunate monologue on my part), Chad actually broke down in tears and said that perhaps he was not the man that I needed him to be.

One thing about Chad that was an inherent benefit, given his heart condition, was that he was not easily frazzled. In fact, it was practically impossible to argue with him because if the discussion took a turn for the worse or went inappropriate in any way, he would immediately shut down and you would be talking to yourself. That is not to say that he ran from confrontation, he just did not do nonsense or allow for disrespect. He knew when to put a pin in things and come back later. Another thing about Chad was that he NEVER cried. I used to tease him and call him a Tin Man because he literally never cried. So to see him break down and doubt whether or not he was the man I needed him to be, simply broke my heart, definitely put a plug in my big mouth and immediately tapped into my compassionate side.

Although this unusual display of tearful emotion from Chad was difficult to stomach, it reiterated what I already knew but had chosen to forget prior to going down the dramatic path of self-righteousness. This rare emotional display immediately reminded me that Chad truly cared

Be completely humble and gentle; be patient, bearing with one another in love.
Ephesians 4:2 NIV

about our future as a couple and he was not intentionally trying to let me down. That night, I learned the obvious lesson that Chad was not me, and over time, I became increasingly grateful for his less intense mode of operation.

Once I had dismounted from my high horse and the playing field was even, Chad and I had a very civil and loving conversation. We discussed the previously overlooked fact but now glaring truth, that two primary benefits of marriage are to *lift each other up* and *play off of one another's strengths*. I quickly learned that it was my job as Chad's wife to help him get and stay organized so that he could achieve his academic endeavors. For after all, it was me in the first place who swore that getting married would help eliminate the distraction of courtship and allow for more focus on school. So that night, Chad and I agreed to work together as a team in all facets of our lives. He even allowed me to feed my nerdy fetish by taking his class syllabuses at the beginning of each semester, drafting a calendar for the entire span of the course, color coded for papers, tests, assignments, etc. It then turned out that "and the two shall become one," if interpreted correctly, is extremely powerful and beneficial. Thank God we learned this lesson in the infancy of our marriage, for it would reap us boundless benefits in the years to come.

Be completely humble and gentle; be patient, bearing with one another in love.
Ephesians 4:2 NIV

OUR FAVS

Kara

Like any new marriage, we had a ton to learn and the "tune-ups" would never cease. However, our love was definitely worth the temporary discomfort that each disagreement brought. After the six-month mark meltdown and our pivotal conversation, Chad and I resumed life as happy newlyweds. More importantly, we were friends again and not just roommates throwing verbal darts at any given opportunity. Now having established a mutually agreed-upon strategy to reach our short-term goals, we proceeded to enjoy our newly joined life together.

The year 2003 was a very popular year for weddings amongst our friends and family. We had tipped off the season with our wedding in July. In August, we traveled to Chicago to participate in my college friend Alicia's wedding. Next, was a Labor Day weekend wedding in San Francisco for Chad's cousin, Leah; followed by our BFF couple Tiffany (my sister) and Shawn, who tied the knot in Los Angeles in mid-November. Lastly, we abbreviated our Palm Desert Thanksgiving weekend that year and headed to the hills of Malibu to attend Chad's cousin Laya's wedding. We had five weddings in five months. Our world was full of young, positive, thriving love and it was a beautiful thing.

In addition to traveling for weddings, 2003 launched our travels as an officially married couple. This was definitely a hobby that Chad and I had in common. More often than not, we would find ourselves either planning a trip, fantasizing about places we'd like to visit at some point, or reminiscing on a trip we had already taken. Our first married couples' trip was in January 2004. Tiffany and Shawn, Desiree (whom Tiffany and I had grown up with in church) and her husband Eric, along with Chad and myself, all headed to the snowy mountains of Big Bear, California. It was the MLK holiday weekend, which also doubled as a birthday weekend for me, Desiree and Tiffany. The dynamic amongst our group was perfect. All young and having recently been joined in marriage, we were each madly in love with our spouses, but all the while still learning boundaries and overall respect. We rented a three-bedroom cabin home, and during our three-day stay, each couple was responsible for two meals for the group of six. The weekend was the perfect blend of time alone with our spouses, male and female bonding time, and couples camaraderie. Each couple cooked their assigned meal together, which brought about its own entertainment. While the gentlemen bonded over sports TV, we ladies chatted it up over a 5,000 piece jigsaw puzzle of New York's Time Square.

There were many highlights on this trip, but two far surpassed the others. The first is when we all played the board game Cash-flow. This game was created by Robert Kiyosaki, author of *Rich Dad, Poor Dad*. The game portrays a modern-day real-life monopoly scenario with occupations and salaries, ordinary bills and surprise emergencies such as flat tires and broken pipes in need of fixing. The six of us spent hours playing this game on Saturday night in Big Bear. The classic moment of our evening was when my brother-in-law Shawn had been given the option to buy something extravagant during one of his turns. Again, still learning our boundaries as new wives, my sister, Tiffany, strongly

So then, as Christians, do you have any encouragement? Do you have any comfort from love? Do you have any spiritual relationships? Do you have any sympathy and compassion? Then fill me with joy by having the same attitude and the same love, living in harmony, and keeping one purpose in mind. Philippians 2:1-2 GW

urged Shawn to think hard before spending the large sum of play money that this particular item called for. Yet, Shawn went ahead with the purchase anyways. Sure enough, on his next turn, Shawn rolled the dice, and before he could even realize where he was headed, Tiffany angrily announced, "SEE! You lost your job." There was an uproar of laughter amongst us—Desiree, Chad, Eric and me. In fact, Desiree and I laughed so hard that we fell out of our chairs and landed on the floor still hysterically laughing. Unfortunately, though, Shawn had recently been laid-off and had only just found new employment within the last month, so the loss of his job was not foreign territory in their real-life experience as a married couple. While four out of six of us laughed like crazy, the "game" had become all too real for the remaining two.

The second major highlight from Big Bear for me was when we all went inner-tubing. Just getting to the slopes alone was a wild ride. Apparently, the game of life had not ended on Saturday night, because when four of us went to get into Shawn and Tiffany's Range Rover, the suspension had given out and it would not rise up, making the truck virtually impossible to drive in the mountains. With it being a holiday weekend, getting the vehicle serviced was sure to be tricky. However, Shawn managed to make some phone calls and get something set up before we were scheduled to leave on Monday. But for Sunday, all six of us fully grown adults piled into Desiree and Eric's Honda Accord sedan and headed to the ski lodge. First up were the bobsleds which delivered equal amounts of joy and pain—joy, as we sped down the hill for the first time at top speed screaming, laughing and having fun; pain, as my bobsled was crashed into by a driver released to go, prior to me clearing the path. Next were the ski-lifts that were unavoidable if we wanted to ride the inner-tubes. Non-stop entertainment was provided as each couple attempted to get on and off this constantly moving death-trap. We got our tubes and rode down that mountain as many times as we possibly could. Finally, when our evening was approaching its end, we gathered up six tubes, interlocked arms, and rode down as one human

So then, as Christians, do you have any encouragement? Do you have any comfort from love? Do you have any spiritual relationships? Do you have any sympathy and compassion? Then fill me with joy by having the same attitude and the same love, living in harmony, and keeping one purpose in mind. Philippians 2:1-2 GW

avalanche. It was frightening and exhilarating all at the same time. The friendship and unity felt in that moment was magical! This was the ultimate highlight for that evening, a perfect culmination to our trip, and the reinforced beginning of our amazing support for one another as young, Christian, married couples and friends.

In addition to traveling, Chad and I also enjoyed entertaining guests at our home. We were so fortunate to rent the beautiful top unit of the duplex his parents owned. The location and layout of this place was not the average starter unit and it was perfect for entertaining our family and friends. For our first wedding anniversary (July 2004), we celebrated all month long including a family gathering with Tiffany and Shawn who had been married for six months at the time, Chad's parents for thirty years, my parents for thirty-five years, and Chad's grandparents approaching the fifty-year mark in their union. We had well over one hundred years of marriage under our roof that night. We were surrounded by a plethora of love and our own marriage was off to an incredible start!

So then, as Christians, do you have any encouragement? Do you have any comfort from love? Do you have any spiritual relationships? Do you have any sympathy and compassion? Then fill me with joy by having the same attitude and the same love, living in harmony, and keeping one purpose in mind. Philippians 2:1-2 GW

HOSPITAL BOOTCAMP

Kara

The Walls Came Tumbling Down

It took hardly anytime at all for us to exercise the "in sickness and in health" vow. Over the course of the next couple of years, Chad went through a series of episodes ranging in severity from a kidney stone, to diverticulitis, to a detached retina in his one good eye (twice!). I was gravely unprepared to enter this phase of our marriage so soon. But, yet, there we were, facing real life, real fast.

The first major hiccup came in November 2004. It was an ordinary Tuesday when Chad and I kissed good-bye, bid each other a good day and headed off to work. I would be home that evening long before Chad, since he had a Tuesday night class and I did not. My job at Farmer's Insurance was exactly one mile from where we lived so I was typically home before four fifteen in the afternoon. Just as I was getting comfortable after work that day, Chad pulled into the driveway. After an evening class and the thirty-five to forty-five minutes commute home, I was not expecting to see Chad until closer to 10PM, so my first natural thought was: *what's wrong?* Noticing that he stayed in the car longer than normal, I headed down the stairs to the driver's side window. "Are you okay?" I asked Chad who still had his hands on the steering wheel and was just sitting there looking out the window. A bit shaken up and definitely not himself, Chad nervously described a foreign object floating across his pupil. Again, having only one good eye, Chad explained how he almost couldn't drive home that day, but had somehow made it. So the prolonged driveway sitting session, and the extended grip on the stirring wheel, was Chad decompressing from a very scary journey home. Of course, my next response was, "Why didn't you call me?" But there was no time to ponder on that. For the first time that I could remember, Chad seemed genuinely afraid. Having no idea what to do next, we called his parents. They came over immediately and together, we headed to Kaiser Sunset Hospital.

We met with an ophthalmologist who informed us that Chad had a retinal detachment. This would be my first of many real-life science crash course studies. That evening, we learned that inflammation, vascular abnormalities or an injury can cause fluid buildup inside the eye and separate the retina from its underlying tissue.

Not exactly an all-star when it came to bedside manners, after explaining the issue at hand, the ophthalmologist proceeded to recite the statistics surrounding the successes and failures of retinal reattachment procedures, and ended his consult stating the sooner the operation, the better the odds. We had interpreted his last comment as, "The surgery will take place today." Yet, he proceeded to schedule Chad for surgery later that week. Totally overwhelmed with emotions (predominantly fear), as we stepped out of the room, my eyes began to fill with tears. Chad's mom, Charlotte quickly pulled me aside and firmly instructed that I hold it together for Chad. So for the first of infinite times to come, I found myself in the bathroom of the hospital privately sobbing, and

I can do all things [which He has called me to do] through Him who strengthens and empowers me [to fulfill His purpose — I am self-sufficient in Christ's sufficiency; I am ready for anything and equal to anything through Him who infuses me with inner strength and confident peace.] Philippians 4:13 AMP

quickly rejoining Chad and his parents with the appearance of a confident, supportive wife.

Needless to say, after being educated on the stats and the sensitive role of time in these scenarios, we were less than thrilled to take Chad home with his retina still detached. The next day, in an attempt to avoid the red tape that Kaiser had presented us, Chad's dad contacted an eye doctor at UCLA that had seen Chad as a young child. With Chad only holding Kaiser insurance at the time, his parents were willing to pay for the procedure outright, if that meant accelerating the process and increasing Chad's chances for full recovery of his already subpar vision. However, as Chad and I, together with his dad, were pulling out of the driveway, heading to Kaiser Bellflower Hospital to get cardiac clearance for Chad to have the eye surgery, we received news that the doctor at UCLA had respectfully declined and much to our dismay, elected not to participate. This was quite a blow to our already compromised frame of mind, but it was also the beginning of a much bolder faith building up in me, as I instantly remembered and stated to Chad and his dad, "When one door closes, God will open another one."

We proceeded on our journey to Kaiser Bellflower Hospital, for no matter where and when the surgery was to be performed, Chad would need medical clearance regarding his heart. The moment we entered the doctor's office at Kaiser, Chad was greeted by his pediatric cardiologist Dr. Angel, who at the time shared an office with Chad's current cardiologist. As God had so intricately designed it, Dr. Angel had long superseded the role of Chad's cardiologist. She was a neighbor to Chad's parents, a close friend of the family, and ultimately Chad's all-encompassing medical guardian angel. She immediately gave Chad a hug and offered words of encouragement. Dr. Angel also assured us that Chad would be taken care of. This was one of my most memorable, up-close and personal encounters with the phenomenon that when God closes one door, He will surely open another. Later that evening and

I can do all things [which He has called me to do] through Him who strengthens and empowers me [to fulfill His purpose — I am self-sufficient in Christ's sufficiency; I am ready for anything and equal to anything through Him who infuses me with inner strength and confident peace.] Philippians 4:13 AMP

well into the wee hours of the next morning, Chad's retina was reattached at Kaiser Sunset Hospital. Approximately ten hours after both me and Chad's immediate family had anxiously occupied the waiting room, we received a call from the surgeon stating that the operation had gone well and Chad was in recovery.

When Chad was released from the hospital, his dad temporarily moved in with us so that Chad would be accompanied during the day and my employment was not jeopardized. In order for Chad's eye to properly heal, he was required to spend the next six weeks lying face down for twenty-three hours a day. This was the first of endless roommate scenarios between Chad, myself and his parents, and also the point in time when they strongly recommended that I skip the formalities and call them by their first names, Michael and Charlotte, instead of Mr. and Mrs. Washington. This experience also resulted in the birth of the term "roomie," which my father-in-law still affectionately calls me to this day.

This was yet another hiccup in Chad's vastly extended college career. In an attempt to salvage the semester that was already well underway, I scrambled to contact Chad's professors and work out a plan of action for him to complete the courses. This included delivering a tape recorder and Starbucks gift card to the first willing classmate in Chad's all-day Sunday course. Later that month, operation salvage Chad's semester also included my sister Robyn reading a required novel to him as he laid face down in the Palm Springs timeshare that we had still managed to get to for Thanksgiving that year. Having not completely passed the six-week mark, Chad rode in the back of his CRV, head face down on a stack of pillows and I drove us out to the desert. That trip was a much needed break from our blessed yet highly challenged reality.

I can do all things [which He has called me to do] through Him who strengthens and empowers me [to fulfill His purpose — I am self-sufficient in Christ's sufficiency; I am ready for anything and equal to anything through Him who infuses me with inner strength and confident peace.] Philippians 4:13 AMP

Would Our Love Persevere?

Despite all of Chad's medical scares and roller coasters, from the outside looking in, you would never in a million years detect that he had any type of illness. He never complained and basically unless we were in the midst of an episode, Chad made it very easy for one to forget that he had any type of condition, let alone a major heart complication. For me being young and very new to the role of "caregiver," it was just easier to not think about the severity of his medical reality. However, I distinctly remember the epiphany episode in early spring 2005 that really opened my eyes to how sick Chad was. We had literally just survived and recovered the great scare of Chad's retinal detachment and repair surgery. Here we were, just a few months shy of Chad receiving his long sought-after degree, and yet again, we were facing a health condition that threatened an unfortunate alteration in Chad's educational timeline.

It was March 2005 when Chad had gone into arrhythmia (an irregular heartbeat), which was not uncommon for his condition. While a foreign object floating across his eye may have previously been unchartered territory for Chad, he recognized heart palpitations and the typical meaning behind his, like a mother identifies their child's cry in a crowd. Chad knew immediately that his cardiologist was going to perform a routine procedure to shock him out of arrhythmia. As I headed off to work for the day, Chad's dad took him to Kaiser Bellflower. The procedure was not considered major by any stretch of the imagination, and the thought was that Chad would be home when I got off from work that day.

Around 3PM, as the workday was winding down and I was looking forward to getting home to see Chad, my desk phone rang and it was my father-in-law on the other end. Michael asked me about my day and went on to casually say that there had been a slight change in plans and the doctors were going to keep Chad overnight to do some further

I can do all things [which He has called me to do] through Him who strengthens and empowers me [to fulfill His purpose — I am self-sufficient in Christ's sufficiency; I am ready for anything and equal to anything through Him who infuses me with inner strength and confident peace.] Philippians 4:13 AMP

observations. No matter how calm and assuring Michael tried to be, I knew in my gut that something was not right. So first, I went to the bathroom to cry privately as I often did during Chad's episodes. As long as I didn't have to verbally speak about Chad's condition, I was able to maintain a great poker face at work. Next, I completed the last hour of work and headed to my parents' house where Michael and I had agreed to meet and carpool to the hospital.

Somewhere between my parents' house and the hospital, I learned that Chad was in intensive care and on a breathing tube. This was a far cry from going in for a routine procedure. When we got to the hospital, my mother-in-law was in the waiting room, and from the look on her face, it did not appear good. I went to see Chad immediately and from the moment I walked in the room, it took every ounce of my effort to not break down crying. I believe this was the first time that I had seen anyone on a breathing tube in person, let alone the love of my life. Chad's arms were strapped down like he was a prisoner and the heavy breathing sounds coming from the contraption would later send me into mild hysterics anytime I saw or heard a darth vador impression. I inquired about the restraints on Chad's wrists and learned that this was not unusual protocol in order to prevent patients from ripping the tube out. Unable to absorb this disturbing scene for more than a few moments, I numbly walked back to the waiting room. I was speechless as I sat down next to my father-in-law. He put his arm around my shoulder and I immediately burst into tears. What in the world was going on? I had married the man of my dreams and was God now going to take him from me? My entire family came out to the hospital that night so I was surrounded with love, but I had little words for anyone because every fiber of my mind, heart and soul was with Chad.

In the days to come, we learned that Chad had congestive heart failure, and so it was highly recommended that he get a defibrillator implanted, and that he would eventually need a heart transplant. Being

I can do all things [which He has called me to do] through Him who strengthens and empowers me [to fulfill His purpose — I am self-sufficient in Christ's sufficiency; I am ready for anything and equal to anything through Him who infuses me with inner strength and confident peace.] Philippians 4:13 AMP

naïve and incredibly new to the game, after the doctor delivered this news, I asked my sister-in-law Elena, "Will Chad still love me?" I was wondering if the new heart would turn him into a completely different person. Boy, was I a tiny shrimp in a ginormous sea.

I can do all things [which He has called me to do] through Him who strengthens and empowers me [to fulfill His purpose — I am self-sufficient in Christ's sufficiency; I am ready for anything and equal to anything through Him who infuses me with inner strength and confident peace.] Philippians 4:13 AMP

GRADS, BAGS & DADS

Kara

Grads at Last

Despite the trepidation regarding our wedding date and school, regardless of the frustrating timeline modifications and notwithstanding numerous medical adversities, in May 2005, Chad received his Bachelor Degree of Interdisciplinary Studies from California State University, Dominguez Hills. That same week, I received my Masters in Business Administration from California State University, Long Beach. At last, we had closed a chapter in the book titled *Our Marriage* that had instigated our first major fight. A chapter that once closed, we felt would open the door for us to start a family.

Accompanied by our parents, we celebrated our accomplishments over lunch at The Reef in Long Beach after my graduation, and we partook in delectable Kobe Beef burgers in Marina Del Rey after Chad's graduation. Over the Memorial Day holiday weekend, we culminated our celebration with a gigantic family barbecue in the park. Both of our families turned out in massive numbers. Chad and I left Pan Pacific Park that day showered with gifts, and unequivocally reminded of the tremendous love that existed on our behalf. We were grads at last!

Bon Voyage

As the doctor had recommended after the spring episode, in September 2005, Chad had his first defibrillator implanted at Kaiser Sunset Hospital in Los Angeles, California. He had lived with a pacemaker his entire life, but this was the Ferrari of pacemakers and had been presented to us as a much needed upgrade, which at this point would be risky for Chad to live without. This small but powerful device would prevent Chad from going into a severe and potentially fatal heart rhythm.

After the defibrillator implantation and recovery, we proceeded to enjoy life. For the first time in our marriage, we were both done with school and had gladly waved good-bye to the task of holding down full-time jobs, juggling classes, studying and nurturing a new marriage all at the same time. We were very content with Chad's latest and greatest Band-Aid for his slow but steady health deterioration. In fact, we were so happy to get back to some normalcy that we booked a seven-day Eastern Caribbean Cruise and invited Chad's parents to join us as we sailed away from our recent loop of medical sorrows, into the sunrise of our future.

We set sail in April 2006 and had a great time bonding on the cruise. Many of Chad and his dad's similarities were highlighted on our vacation; particularly the rate in which they both moved remarkably slower than Charlotte and I when preparing for a day in port, as well as their highly predicable restroom sabbaticals immediately following every meal. Charlotte and I would call each other from our respective rooms, laughing as we confirmed that the men were on their genetically synchronized schedule. Hands down, my favorite port on the cruise was

I have told you these things, so that in Me you may have [perfect] peace. In the world you have tribulation and distress and suffering, but be courageous; [be confident, be undaunted, be filled with joy]; I have overcome the world." [My conquest is accomplished, My victory abiding.] John 16:33 AMP

St. Thomas (USVI). Having been at sea for a full day straight, I had big plans for this island and intended to not let one second go to waste. As the ship lined up with land to dock, I was standing right at the door anxiously waiting for clearance. Charlotte and I were hitting the jewelry district and I was so excited. The guys were still piddling around on the ship so we agreed on a time and meeting place to connect with them later. For the next four or five hours, Charlotte and I leisurely (without the guys on our heels) perused the jewelry shops. Charlotte taught me the art of negotiating in these types of scenarios, and also the patience to view all of my options before deciding on a piece to purchase. Thanks to this newfound strategy, I was more than happy with my selections at the end of day and I always think of St. Thomas when I wear the unique heart necklace or square-shaped ring purchased on that trip.

In addition to St. Thomas, we also visited Puerto Rico, the Dominican Republic, and Nassau Bahamas on this cruise. In Puerto Rico, Chad and I rode ATVs through a rainforest, and in Nassau, we relaxed on the beautiful beach of Paradise Island. While out to sea, we played cards around the ship with my in-laws, attended some of the evening shows, and had dinner at The Olympic, which was the Celebrity Cruise line's specialty restaurant offering a five-star dining experience. I remember feeling very privileged that evening; as to my recollection, I had never experienced dining on that level before. Having jointly endured the various dips and cliffhangers on Chad's medical roller-coaster, our Eastern Caribbean Cruise was a perfect way to simultaneously pay tribute to the recent struggle, while gleefully welcoming the highly anticipated future.

Gone Too Soon

We returned from our cruise feeling refreshed and energetic about our new chapter in life. With school finally behind us, starting a family

---

I have told you these things, so that in Me you may have [perfect] peace. In the world you have tribulation and distress and suffering, but be courageous; [be confident, be undaunted, be filled with joy]; I have overcome the world." [My conquest is accomplished, My victory abiding.] John 16:33 AMP

had become our number one goal. Shortly after the ship was docked and the waves had settled, we discovered that we had boarded the vessel as a party of four, yet disembarked as a party of five. Chad and I were going to have a baby! We could not believe it! We had been trying to conceive since our graduations the prior year. Our dream was finally coming true! We could not tell our family and friends fast enough.

Already in the process of scrapbooking the pictures from our cruise, I printed a picture of the positive pregnancy test and included it in the back of the album. Before the glue on the last page of the scrapbook had dried, we were in the car headed to spread the good news. Stop one was Chad's parents' house. Having accompanied us on the cruise, we figured Charlotte and Michael would enjoy being the first to relive the picturesque moments with us. As they slowly looked through the album and we reminisced about the trip, the anticipation grew with each flip of the page. The entire time Chad was beaming inside and out and I began to doubt if he would make it to the end of the album before the news erupted out of him. Finally though, as Charlotte turned to the last page, Chad and I practically held our breath as to not miss a single detail from their reaction. It took no time for them to translate that the photographed positive pregnancy test meant their first grandchild was on the way. They were ecstatic! Delivering the news of our eagerly anticipated bundle of joy was intoxicating. Two miles down the road at my parents' house, was our next news-telling fix. Despite this being their sixth grandchild, my parents were definitely thrilled that we were adding to the family. With each stop that Chad and I made that evening, our excitement organically increased. The crumb snatchers were expanding their scope!

In the weeks ahead, Chad and I went to sleep and woke up with a jubilant feeling that we could not shake even if we wanted to. With Memorial Day Weekend coming up, we decided to have a backyard barbecue. We invited some of our family, friends and co-workers and

I have told you these things, so that in Me you may have [perfect] peace. In the world you have tribulation and distress and suffering, but be courageous; [be confident, be undaunted, be filled with joy]; I have overcome the world." [My conquest is accomplished, My victory abiding.] John 16:33 AMP

basically could have called it the earliest baby shower ever. Outside of Chad's delicious barbecue feast, the primary buzz amongst our guests was regarding our tremendous blessing on the way. The photo album from our trip/baby announcement book was in play the entire day. Our baby, only a few weeks into development, was already taking over and would be welcomed with endless love.

Our first ultrasound was scheduled for the Wednesday following Memorial Day and it could not come fast enough. Of course, with Chad being a triplet, we received some speculation and teasing from our loved ones regarding the potential number of bundles we would be bringing home. I remember finding it difficult to see the humor in that particular possibility. Nevertheless, whatever God had in store for us would be well received. During our first ultrasound, we were speechless when the screen came to life and revealed our miracle. The heart beat overtook the room as if it were surround sound from heaven. This was our baby, a miraculous extension of the love that Chad and I had for each other. This was our future and it was amazing.

Chad and I returned to work and floated through the rest of the week on cloud nine. Hearing our baby's heartbeat was like an affirmation of our dreams. And of course, we reported back right away to our relatives the news that we heard a single heartbeat, not multiple. By that weekend, Chad and I were planning to take a deep breath and relax. We had been on a high from life for quite some time now.

On Friday, simply exhausted from the week, I fell asleep earlier than usual. Sometime in the middle of the night, I was suddenly jolted out of my sleep by a sharp cramp. Totally afraid of what I would find, I raced to the bathroom without waking Chad. There was some discharge but no blood. Next I did what I would never do again, I began to surf the web for answers. It took all of five minutes for me to be convinced that I had lost our baby and our dreams were definitely shattered. At the crack of dawn, with Chad still asleep, I got my sisters Robyn and Tiffany

I have told you these things, so that in Me you may have [perfect] peace. In the world you have tribulation and distress and suffering, but be courageous; [be confident, be undaunted, be filled with joy]; I have overcome the world." [My conquest is accomplished, My victory abiding.] John 16:33 AMP

on the phone. I described the symptoms and they told me not to worry but to put a call in to the doctor. I hung up with them and did just that. Shortly after, the doctor on call from Cedars Sinai Medical Group (who just so happened to have performed fibroid surgery on my mom years earlier) returned my call. After informing him of the current events, he was careful not to share any conclusions but said that a nurse would call me back shortly with an appointment time to see my doctor the following week. When Chad woke up, I failed miserably at playing it cool. Instead, I brought him up to speed and then burst into tears. The rest of the weekend passed in a gloomy blur.

Monday morning, we set off to see the doctor. We had spent the weekend rationalizing every possible scenario and landed on the conclusion that if there had been a major red flag or concern, the doctor would have sent me to the ER over the weekend. As Chad and I entered the ultrasound room, I was convinced that it had just been a typical early pregnancy scare. There had been no recurring symptoms over the weekend so everything was evidently okay. I climbed on the table and the technician slathered my belly with cold jelly. The room was silent as she repeatedly ran the wand across my belly from left to right, up then down, not a single sound emerged. With little poise or consolation, the technician announced that there was no heartbeat. Chad and I sat speechless, assuming she would continue to seek the miraculous sound that we so desperately wanted to hear. However, she excused herself from the room and her presence was replaced by a nurse. After taking my blood pressure, the nurse commented on the fact that it was elevated. I coldly responded, "Not surprising seeing as how we JUST FOUND OUT OUR BABY HAD NO HEARTBEAT." She had no further remarks and sent in the doctor.

The doctor entered the room, had her spin with the wand and confirmed the dreadful news. She offered her consolation and described our options to further complete the process. Option one was to schedule

I have told you these things, so that in Me you may have [perfect] peace. In the world you have tribulation and distress and suffering, but be courageous; [be confident, be undaunted, be filled with joy]; I have overcome the world." [My conquest is accomplished, My victory abiding.] John 16:33 AMP

a Dilation and Curettage procedure (D&C), which is where the cervix is dilated and a special instrument is used to scrape the uterine lining. The process typically took fifteen to twenty minutes and patients were advised to wait six months before trying to conceive again. Option two, where the miscarriage was confirmed but major bleeding had not commenced, was to take a drug called Misoprostol. It was an ulcer medication that had also been found helpful in the management of miscarriages. Approximately two days after administration of the drug, it would cause the cervix to dilate and the uterine lining to shed. Chad and I were both still numb and waiting to hear option three: rewind in time and hear our baby's heart beat again. Not even remotely close to being able to make a decision regarding anything, we opted to go home and think about it.

Once we got home, I retreated to the bedroom to drown myself in tears, while Chad called our jobs to report the loss. I eventually called my parents and Chad called his. I had very little words for anyone but after an hour had passed, I suddenly felt the walls caving in on me so abruptly, I decided that we should go to my parents' house. Once at my parents' house, I felt not one ounce better. We sat for a while and attempted to visit, only realizing that the pain was going nowhere. We said our goodbyes and headed back home. About a block from our place, Chad stopped to get gas. I called my best friend, Jessica, to inform her of the news. She insisted that she, along with another friend who had suffered multiple miscarriages, come over to visit. I assured her that I was useless in terms of company and she reiterated the importance of her coming by. The ladies came by and offered their encouragement and though there was nothing they could humanly do to reduce the emotional pain, their gesture was well received. In the days ahead, we were showered with love spanning from beautiful flowers from my friend Tara, food from my job, and cards from others.

I have told you these things, so that in Me you may have [perfect] peace. In the world you have tribulation and distress and suffering, but be courageous; [be confident, be undaunted, be filled with joy]; I have overcome the world." [My conquest is accomplished, My victory abiding.] John 16:33 AMP

Not knowing when I would return, I started with a week off from work. While I stayed home alone, I assured Chad that it was okay for him to go to work. He and his coworkers called to check on me often. The tears were endless and I was floored by the amount of love that I had already developed for this person that I would now never meet here on earth. Looking back, we learned a hard lesson that quickly became all too obvious. The major downside of telling the world about your conception was having to go back and tell the world of your misfortune. We would never put ourselves in this position again.

When we felt up to it, Chad and I discussed at length the cons versus cons of the two options the doctor had given us to complete the miscarriage. There were no pros in our eyes, as neither option would bring our dear baby back to life. In the end, although Chad had just as much vested in our tremendous loss as I did, he graciously left the ultimate decision up to me. His logic was that he unfortunately could not physically bare the loss for me, so he would respect and support my wishes on the matter. Unable to picture myself as mentally capable of walking into a room for a D&C, I elected for option two, the self-administered drugs to be taken in the comfort and privacy of our home.

Having made the decision and received the prescription from my doctor, I remained devastated and emotionally tapped out. Still naively hoping a sign of life would emerge from inside me, I could not bring myself to visit the pharmacy. Chad patiently gave me my space and did not press the issue. Much later in the week, after having an early dinner at The Grove with Jessica, she accompanied me to the pharmacy and we obtained the dreadful pills. That evening, I followed the instructions, completed the insertion and waited for our dream to be officially killed. A few days passed without a single sign of change. I called my doctor early the following week and she instructed that I repeat the process. Great, my precious baby was clinging to my body just as I clenched to the hope that he or she still had life.

I have told you these things, so that in Me you may have [perfect] peace. In the world you have tribulation and distress and suffering, but be courageous; [be confident, be undaunted, be filled with joy]; I have overcome the world." [My conquest is accomplished, My victory abiding.] John 16:33 AMP

I reluctantly repeated the process and this time, the symptoms were almost immediate. The next day, there was cramping and bleeding and the miscarriage was undoubtedly underway. The physical and emotional pains were in fierce competition for my attention. Suddenly, option one seemed to have been the better choice, but it was too late. A few days passed and the symptoms subsided. In an effort to start the process of moving on, I would return to work the following week.

Desperately needing a change in scenery, Chad and I found ourselves in Arizona early Saturday morning. It was Father's Day weekend and my parents, along with my sister, Robyn, and her family, were visiting my brother and his family. It felt good to be out of the confinement of the four walls at home. With no agenda in mind other than escaping, Chad and I accompanied my sister-in-law Nichole and kids on a few Saturday morning errands. In between errands, we stopped for our traditional Arizona visit to Sonic. As we sat outside eating tater tots and drinking limeades, I noticed my stomach began to hurt a little. I tried to downplay the pain, not wanting to make a big deal out of it. Our last stop was the grocery store in the same parking lot as Sonic. As we parked and got out of the car, my stomach began to hurt even more. No longer able to mask the issue, I told the group to go ahead and Chad and I waited outside. As the cramps quickly escalated, it dawned on me that the miscarriage had not concluded.

When Nichole and kids reemerged from the grocery store, I slowly made my way to the car and we headed straight to their house. During the ride home, there were foreign occurrences in my body that I had never felt before. Once parked, I apprehensively began to stand up and sure enough the pants of my beige jogging suit were soiled with blood, along with the passenger seat of their jeep. I was mortified and too embarrassed to enter their home. Nichole was very compassionate and assured me not to worry about the jeep. She retrieved a pair of pants for me to change into and I asked her to trash the others. I headed

I have told you these things, so that in Me you may have [perfect] peace. In the world you have tribulation and distress and suffering, but be courageous; [be confident, be undaunted, be filled with joy]; I have overcome the world." [My conquest is accomplished, My victory abiding.] John 16:33 AMP

straight to the bathroom to shower and Chad followed right behind me. He gave me privacy to use the restroom and I will never forget the visual of crimson mass that passed through my body. I must have showered for at least an hour, until both the blood and tears subsided. This was the most traumatic thing that I had ever experienced. As I exited the bathroom, I found Chad sitting silently outside the door. Although I had lied and said I was okay, he had never left my presence. I instantly felt protected as his wife, and though the clock had been somberly reset, I knew then that someday he would make an extraordinary dad.

I have told you these things, so that in Me you may have [perfect] peace. In the world you have tribulation and distress and suffering, but be courageous; [be confident, be undaunted, be filled with joy]; I have overcome the world." [My conquest is accomplished, My victory abiding.] John 16:33 AMP

FROM CITY TO DESERT

Kara

Although I greatly admired the patience, strength and confidence that Chad displayed as he faced one medical challenge after another, I quickly discovered that I did not embody these same characteristics. After the miscarriage, I slipped into a mild yet steady depression, holding frequent pity parties for myself. I developed a grossly increased awareness and ultra-heightened sensitivity to women everywhere who got "unexpectedly" pregnant. I detested women that I saw in the streets impatiently yelling uncontrollably at very small children, and I had zero sympathy for women who complained nonstop about being pregnant. I was the epitome of bitterness because I wanted so badly for Chad and I to have a baby of our own. I really struggled with why God had seen it fit for us to experience yet another medical disappointment.

Prior to the pregnancy and unfortunate loss, discussions amongst my family regarding moving to Arizona had begun to moderately arise in mid-2005. My brother, Kevin, and sister-in-law Nichole had recently purchased a home and done very well for themselves in Arizona. Chad and I were frustrated and discouraged by the fact that our home ownership dreams and standards did not align with our income in Los Angeles. In June 2005, we took an Arizona-bound caravan with a representative of each family unit on board. Both of my parents went; Kevin and his family, and my sister Tiffany sent her husband Shawn, as she was not exactly interested. Chad was sold on the concept sight-unseen, so he sent me. My oldest sister, Robyn, had recently purchased a fabulous house with her husband Carl, in Anaheim Hills, California so naturally she had no part of our Arizona venture.

After one open house, it was abundantly clear that Arizona was definitely a place to be considered. Chad was very excited when I returned from the trip no longer dead set against at least entertaining the idea. We took a few more trips and even entered the crazy lottery system that had become the new norm in Phoenix's suddenly booming housing industry. Over the next year, we casually looked and further weighed our options.

In late June 2006, having just visited Arizona for Father's Day and still recovering from the devastation of our recent loss, Chad and I were sitting at home on the Friday night that kicked off the Fourth of July weekend and spontaneously decided to drive to Arizona again. About an hour into the drive, we realized that we had bitten off more than we could chew for that night and we stayed at my Aunt Evelyn's place in Palm Desert, California, only two hours outside of Los Angeles. The next morning, we got up and completed the remaining four hours of our drive. Tiffany and Shawn were also in Arizona at the time, as they were starting their family road trip to Dallas, Texas.

As if he were a realtor, my brother Kevin immediately capitalized on his present audience and mapped out a weekend house hunting tour for us. By Sunday, July 2, 2006, we were all signing papers to live in the same neighborhood. My sister and I were going to live right next door to each other; just what our husbands had dreamed of. Although there was no need for a nursery just yet in our new home, I was finally able to smile again and had something to look forward to. Young, educated and

---

Brothers, I do not consider that I have made it my own. But one thing I do: forgetting what lies behind and straining forward to what lies ahead, I press on toward the goal for the prize of the upward call of God in Christ Jesus. Philippians 3:13-14 ESV

relatively carefree, we weren't worried about finding jobs in Arizona, as we knew it would all work out. Sure enough, by August 2006, I had been interviewed and offered two jobs, and Chad had landed a teaching job with just one phone interview. Everything was working in our favor and we were confident that our steps had been ordered by God.

Chad

We moved to Phoenix because we were looking to purchase a home, and didn't want to have to move into a half-a-million-dollar-plus shoebox, on the wrong side of the tracks to get it done. My brother-in-law Kevin was already in Arizona, and was campaigning to get the rest of his siblings there. After a couple of trips to Arizona, I was sold on the home values, cleanliness, and peacefulness that we could have there. Kara took a bit more convincing, but once her two-year older "twin" sister, Tiffany, was on board, it was no problem getting her to move. Looking back, it is clear that the entire situation was orchestrated by God. The entire process was fairly easy, and everything worked out for the best. In line with everything else, our new jobs came about almost seamlessly. I actually secured my position via phone interviews. Before we left Los Angeles, we were employed, insured and on track to complete the escrow process one week after our scheduled arrival to Phoenix.

The week before we left, while having a routine physical for my new job in Phoenix, I was diagnosed with Type 2 diabetes. This caused Kara to question whether or not this new factor was a sign that we should not move. However, we pressed forward fully believing that Arizona was an all-around better fit for us.

Brothers, I do not consider that I have made it my own. But one thing I do: forgetting what lies behind and straining forward to what lies ahead, I press on toward the goal for the prize of the upward call of God in Christ Jesus. Philippians 3:13-14 ESV

Kara

Heading East on the I-10

On Sunday, August 6, 2006, Chad and I drove to Arizona to begin a new chapter in our lives. We both started work the next day. We stayed in a timeshare in Scottsdale for two weeks until our house was ready. A large factor in our move was healthcare and whether or not Arizona had adequate and appropriate facilities to care for Chad's condition. Banner Good Samaritan Hospital rated very well in my extensive Internet research. Given that this was pre-iPhone days for us, I printed MapQuest directions from every possible location in the area, just in case...

Well, "just in case" manifested itself on Chad's fourth day of the new job. We failed to mention earlier that the new job role was a teacher of emotionally disturbed high school students, in a less than desirable area of Phoenix. It was the Thursday evening of our first week in Phoenix and Chad and I were hanging out at the timeshare. He was filling out paperwork for his job and I was reviewing paint color plans, as we were set to begin decorating our new home that weekend. Out of nowhere, I heard him yell and I immediately knew what had happened. Chad was never one to yell, nor did he really ever verbally complain about pain. I knew that this foreign noise from my husband could only mean one thing, and sure enough, Chad had received his first shock and his uncharacteristic scream was a direct result of the foreign object that had been planted in his chest. After a year of living incident-free in Los Angeles with the defibrillator, the emotionally disturbed high school students were able to trigger a shock to Chad's heart in just four days. Was this perhaps a second sign that the journey from city to desert was not meant for us?

Brothers, I do not consider that I have made it my own. But one thing I do: forgetting what lies behind and straining forward to what lies ahead, I press on toward the goal for the prize of the upward call of God in Christ Jesus. Philippians 3:13-14 ESV

MEET THE TEAM

Kara

At the first sign of trouble with Chad's health, I definitely had gut-wrenching doubts about our move. In Los Angeles, we always had the luxury of having his parents just a ten minute ride away. Now in Phoenix, I suddenly found myself experiencing the whole gamut of emotions: anxiety, fear, and panic as result of being fully responsible for my husband and his health condition. At twenty-seven years of age, was I really equipped to handle this level of responsibility? Unfortunately for me, the vows that we had taken on our wedding day had not been grouped into age brackets. So I had no choice but to step totally out of my comfort zone and be the wife that I had vowed before God to be.

I quickly learned that Chad's first shock to the heart was definitely a part of God's master plan. Little did we know that our first trip to the Banner Good Samaritan Hospital Emergency Room, would result in us meeting Chad's new team of doctors. Truth is, we had not yet identified a new doctor for Chad in Arizona and had just barely begun the process of asking around for personal referrals. I guess God saw the need to expedite our networking process and made sure that we were connected with a great cardiologist and a magnificent electrophysiologist, just five days after our move. In the end, this turned out to be a huge relief to us, but the process to get there was rather unnerving. That weekend in the emergency room was also the first of many medically supportive trips that Chad's parents would make to Phoenix. Good thing we had not moved too far from California because unbeknownst to us, we were all destined to have seemingly permanent seats on Southwest Airlines at any given time during Chad's medical roller-coaster.

On Saturday, August 12, 2006, in the Emergency Room at Banner Good Samaritan, we met Dr. William Cole, who immediately became Chad's new Arizona Electrophysiologist. He would be the doctor to monitor Chad's defibrillator and all related activity. It was then that we also met Dr. Thomas Bennett, Chad's newly found Arizona Cardiologist. At the end of the day, the consensus to address Chad's defibrillator shocks, was to prescribe a medication called Sotalol, which would help regulate Chad's heartbeat in an effort to prevent (or at least minimize) future shocks.

And we know that in all things God works for the good of those who love him, who have been called according to his purpose. Romans 8:28 NIV

DELIVERANCE IN THE DESERT

Kara

All things considered, our family migration from Los Angeles to Arizona was working out quite nicely. The summer of 2006 had been occupied by our move. So by the summer of 2007, Chad and I were ripe for vacation. In August, we found ourselves in Cabo San Lucas for the first time. We stayed at the Pueblo Bonito Sunset Beach. This resort was one of three related properties in Cabo. Positioned on a hill, giving each unit unobstructed views of the Pacific Ocean, I quickly deemed this newfound treasure our own Mexican apartment. Chad and I thoroughly enjoyed our time in Cabo, hanging poolside most days with the occasional venture off property for Mexican food where the locals ate. We also visited the sister properties, Pueblo Bonito Rose and Pueblo Bonito Pacifica. These two resorts were like night and day. The Rose had more of a Spring Break feel to it, while the Pacifica was literally heaven on earth. Our resort, Sunset Beach, was the perfect blend of liveliness, yet ample time and space to chill as well. Our first tropical vacation away from our new desert home base was truly a success, and Chad and I returned to Phoenix relaxed and rejuvenated.

The move to Phoenix and Chad's immediate health scare had kind of decelerated our intense focus on having a baby. It was still our earnest desire to start a family and we had certainly not given up, but we had learned to cope with the concept that the timing was ultimately in God's hands.

As with every year, after the summer passes, the holidays seem to arrive in the blink of an eye. This was no different in 2007. After Cabo in August, Thanksgiving was already on the brain. We made our annual trip to Palm Desert, California for our formal family Thanksgiving dinner at my Aunt Evelyn's Country Club, followed by our down-home family Thanksgiving dinner the next day at my parents' timeshare. At the end of the day, neither the location nor food really mattered; it was the games played, movies watched, and quality time spent making memories that made Thanksgiving priceless.

Naturally after Thanksgiving, Christmas was in full effect. About halfway through December, one morning, as I was getting ready for work, I realized that my cycle was late. Definitely not looking to make a big deal or raise false hopes, I did not say a word to Chad. I carried on with the day as usual, determined not to set Chad or myself up for disappointment. By now ovulation kits and pregnancy test were permanently stocked in our home, so my plan was to simply take the test in the middle of the night when I got up for my normal bathroom run.

Around 3AM, I initiated the plan. Totally bracing myself for another let-down, I peed on the stick and waited. After 120 seconds, I just knew that my eyes were deceiving me. *Could I really be seeing positive results?* I asked myself as I read the instructions for probably the 100th time on our journey to conception. I honestly did not believe it! As I witnessed the two lines become clearer and clearer, I felt myself gradually slipping out of astonishment into the realm of ecstasy. Before leaving our master bathroom, I convinced myself to let Chad sleep, and I would find a fun and creative way to tell him in the morning. Yet somehow on the very short walk from the bathroom to the bed, that plan went out the window as I shook Chad awake to deliver the news. "Chad, Chad wake up" I half

Then they cried out to the Lord in their trouble, and he delivered them from their distress.
Psalm107:6 NIV

whispered. "Hmmmmm, what is it?" Chad groggily said. "We are pregnant!" I proudly announced. "What?" Chad said as he sat straight up in our bed. It was not until I showed him the pregnancy test that he really believed me. We happily kissed and next just sat there in our own subconscious worlds for a minute. After the horrific loss of our first baby, it was inevitable that this pregnancy would carry extra baggage. Neither one of us wanting to ruin the moment for the other, we did not verbalize our fear at that point. Instead we remained cautiously optimistic as we laid back down to sleep. At last, we had found deliverance in the desert from our barren season.

Then they cried out to the Lord in their trouble, and he delivered them from their distress.
Psalm107:6 NIV

UNEXPECTED BLESSINGS IN AUGUST

Kara

Christmas 2007 came and went, and Chad and I did not utter one word to our family about our second bun in the oven. We had vowed that a repeat of our last premature announcement was not an option. I even joked that if there was a way to hide our pregnancy until it was time to deliver, I would. As far as I could tell, Chad did a great job of staying positive. However, excitement, fear and paranoia were in constant battle for my attention. No matter how common miscarriages are, they are rarely escaped without some level of self-imposed blame. I saw this pregnancy as our second chance and there was no way that I would screw it up.

During our first appointment with the OB-GYN, we heard our baby's heartbeat. Even after the treacherous road from our previous loss, this magical sound swept us off our feet all over again and suddenly, we could no longer hide the news. We made plans to have dinner with Tiffany and Shawn the following Saturday night. As the four of us sat down in the restaurant that evening, Chad and I spared no time in sharing the news. Tiffany and Shawn were so excited for us and it felt great to finally tell someone. Never in a million years though could Chad and I have guessed what was coming next. With a big grin on his face, Shawn said, "We have news also." They proceeded to announce that they were pregnant too. "No way!" Chad and I both reacted. This was unbelievable. Naturally, the next question was, "When are you due?" we both asked each other. Tiffany and Shawn were due to have their baby exactly two weeks before us. We all sat there in shock, overjoyed that we would get to share this experience.

We immediately put our four brains together to plan how we would tell my parents that they had TWO grandbabies on the way. After dinner, we stopped by CVS to get a pocket calendar for the New Year. We filled out family birthdays and other events throughout the calendar. On August 11, we wrote "grandbaby #6 due" and on August 25, we wrote "grandbaby #7 due." Beyond excited to deliver the news, we rushed over to see my parents. We presented the pocket calendar to my mom and she said thanks. When she saw the four of us standing there with grins plastered across our faces, she knew something was up but had no idea what. We strongly suggested that she flip through the calendar and she cooperated. She read each event listed as if to say "Okay, yes, the family birthdays and anniversaries have been filled in." We encouraged her to keep going until she finally reached the month of August. My dad's birthday and their wedding anniversary were penciled in. But my mom got a confused look on her face when she saw the two new family August occasions. When the light bulb in her head went off, she said "You all are both pregnant?" She immediately told my dad to look at the calendar. They were just as shocked as we had been a few hours earlier at dinner. Our family was growing by leaps and bounds!

For out of His fullness [the superabundance of His grace and truth] we have all received grace upon grace [spiritual blessing upon spiritual blessing, favor upon favor, and gift heaped upon gift]. John 1:16 AMP

YOU HAVE GOT TO BE KIDDING ME

Kara

In February 2008, during a routine electrophysiologist visit, Dr. Cole recommended that Chad undergo surgery to secure one of the leads to his existing defibrillator. During this procedure, they would also replace the actual defibrillator unit, due to its diminished battery life. The surgery took place on Monday, February 11, which just so happened to be the first day of my second trimester. In line with all of Chad's surgeries and procedures, it took longer than the average time. When Dr. Cole came out to let myself and Chad's parents know how everything had gone, it was then that he recommended we start thinking seriously about a heart transplant.

Despite the shocking news of Chad's heart transplant candidacy being sooner than later, the February defibrillator tune-up had been an overall success and my pregnancy was rolling along smoothly. Our excitement about the addition to our family grew exponentially with each week that passed. Life was good!

In April 2008, it was finally time for the appointment that every expecting couple looks forward to. It was time to find out if we would be decorating a room pink or blue. I remember Chad and I pulling up to the doctor's office in Paradise Valley as if it were yesterday. Due to scheduling, we were in separate cars.

After the usual wait, I was finally on the table and the ultrasound had begun. The technician took a few measurements and explained a few things about the anatomy of our baby, and then there was a pause. With zero effort of being discreet or trying to keep us calm, the technician said that it looked like something was wrong with the heart and that she was going to get the doctor. The doctor came in and did his own evaluation and confirmed that there was in fact something wrong with our baby boy's heart. From there, we were referred to a specialist that could not get us in for two weeks. So congratulations, you're having a boy, and you get to wait two whole weeks to find out what's wrong with his heart. 1 Corinthians 10:13 says that God will not give you more than you can bear, but at this point, we had to be pretty close to our limits, or so we thought.

On the way home from the appointment, I called Tiffany to share the dreadful news. She could barely decipher my words through my hysterical crying. All I could say was that there was something wrong with our baby's heart. Finally, unable to utter another word about it, I managed to whisper between gasps that I would call her later. Pulling up to the garage at the same time, Chad and I entered the house together. We embraced and he tried to convince me that everything would be okay. Still having minimum words to spare, I just shook my head in defeat. In one last endearing effort to calm my nerves for the evening, Chad drew me a bubble bath. As I attempted to soak my sorrows away, he stayed near in case I wanted to chat, but the pain was just too deep for me to speak.

The next day, I did what I rarely ever did, I called in sick. I just wasn't ready to face the world again with this new weight on my shoulders. At the time, due to health reasons, Chad had stepped down from full-time

But He said to me, "My grace is sufficient for you [My lovingkindness and My mercy are more than enough - - always available - - regardless of the situation]; for [My] power is being perfected [and is completed and shows itself most effectively] in [your] weakness." Therefore, I will all the more gladly boast in my weaknesses, so that the power of Christ (may completely enfold me and] may dwell in me. 2 Corinthians 12:9 AMP

teaching and was a substitute teacher instead. I remember laying in the bed that next morning and the phone ringing. Thinking that it was Substitutes Unlimited, I answered prepared to tell them that Chad was unavailable that day. Instead, I was greeted by the heart transplant coordinator at the Mayo Clinic who wanted to speak with Chad regarding being evaluated as a transplant candidate. Really? This was all happening in the same week? Less than twenty-four hours after a bomb had been dropped on us regarding our son's health? It was truly a classic *you have got to be kidding* moment. But unfortunately, there was nothing even remotely funny about either situation and life was far from good at this point in time.

Two weeks later, after many tears and sleepless nights, we met with the Perinatologist. The doctor had a calm and reassuring nature to him, which we were so grateful for. He and his team ran a series of tests, some of which we would have to wait until the following week to get the results. At the conclusion of the appointment that day however, the doctor was able to explain to us that our baby boy had a partial AV Canal Defect that would need to be repaired at some point during the first two years of his life. In layman terms, of the four chambers that a heart consists of, the wall to separate the top two chambers of our son's heart had not grown. We also learned that day, that this particular heart defeat was typically coupled with Down Syndrome. So Down Syndrome was also presented to us as a potential condition that we would have to contend with. I pretty much went numb at this point.

Based on the findings by the end of our appointment, it was inevitable that our son would have open heart surgery where an artificial wall would be implanted. Despite all that Chad had already endured with his health challenges, it was not until the split second after receiving this earth shattering news, that I became keenly cognizant of the fact that "normal," in terms of our family's medical status, had permanently exited

But He said to me, "My grace is sufficient for you [My lovingkindness and My mercy are more than enough - - always available - - regardless of the situation]; for [My] power is being perfected [and is completed and shows itself most effectively] in [your] weakness." Therefore, I will all the more gladly boast in my weaknesses, so that the power of Christ (may completely enfold me and] may dwell in me. 2 Corinthians 12:9 AMP

the realm of possibility. Nothing about our lives would ever be normal again.

But He said to me, "My grace is sufficient for you [My lovingkindness and My mercy are more than enough - - always available - - regardless of the situation]; for [My] power is being perfected [and is completed and shows itself most effectively] in [your] weakness." Therefore, I will all the more gladly boast in my weaknesses, so that the power of Christ (may completely enfold me and) may dwell in me. 2 Corinthians 12:9 AMP

NEW BEGINNINGS

Kara

May 2008 brought with it Chad's first official appointment at the Mayo Clinic. We were both totally clueless in terms of what to expect. We even debated on whether or not Chad should wear a suit. Oh, how naive we were at the time to this entirely new world.

The evaluation process was a series of appointments and interrogations that ranged from your classic echocardiogram and stress test, to a psychological and financial review. There seemed to be four potential barriers that had to be eliminated before we could proceed. First, they had to determine if all other medical avenues had been explored and that a heart transplant was the only option left. Next, they needed to determine if Chad's body was in a position to realistically have a fair chance of successfully undergoing a transplant. Determining whether or not Chad had the moral support needed to endure the process was also an integral part of the inquisition. We were also asked if we had the financial means to sustain the gift. Meaning, could Chad afford to be off work and how would we pay for the operation, hospital time, and subsequent lifetime maintenance medications?

The initial process was rather intense and took place over the course of two weeks. I accompanied Chad on as many appointments as work would allow at the time, and his parents and sister took turns coming out from Los Angeles as well. We definitely showed a united front, which made it abundantly clear to the team of doctors, that Chad's support system ran deep and wide.

On Thursday of the second week of testing, we got a voicemail from the transplant coordinator saying that they needed to see Chad on Friday to discuss something. Unfortunately, by the time we got the message, it was after office hours and I ended up spending the entire night neurotically speculating on what the impromptu appointment could be about. Chad seemed unmoved by the message and strongly encouraged me to not worry about it. Fortunately, staying calm and not easily frazzled was one of Chad's biggest strengths and a tremendous asset given his condition. I did not share this with him at the time, but my biggest fear was that a conclusion had been reached, that for whatever reason, Chad was ineligible for a heart transplant.

The next morning from the parking lot at work, I proceeded to "blow up" the coordinator's phone prior to going in the office. I eventually got her on the phone, but much to my dismay, she said that she could not discuss the matter with me and that I would have to wait for Chad's appointment later. I pried a little more for clarity or at least a hint, but her responses led me to feel even more anxious. This conversation all but threw me into hysterics. I remember sitting at my desk, totally unable to focus and being about two seconds away from a breakdown. I asked my good friend and co-worker at the time Lillian, to step outside with me. She offered to pray for me, which thankfully provided the bridge that I desperately needed to carry me to the appointment time.

During the appointment later that day, Chad and I learned that a wildcard had been flagged in his testing. Unfortunately, having

Don't fret or worry. Instead of worrying, pray. Let petitions and praises shape your worries into prayers, letting God know your concerns. Before you know it, a sense of God's wholeness, everything coming together for good, will come and settle you down. It's wonderful what happens when Christ displaces worry at the center of your life. Philippians 4:6, 7 MSG

undergone multiple surgeries as a kid, Chad had also received numerous blood transfusions. Blood transfusions that had taken place before modern medicine had the capability to test and screen blood donors as they do today. Therefore, somewhere along the line, Chad had contracted Hepatitis C. This was not news to Chad or me. He had been warned by doctors long ago, but the disease had never been active in his body.

Well, thankfully, it was not active in 2008 either. Nevertheless, the Mayo Clinic team had to address this new red flag, so that it would remain inactive post-transplant as well. The rest of the meeting that day was to go over the treatment plan. Chad would undergo six months of Interferon (a protein that had the property of inhibiting virus replication), in the form of daily self-administered shots. After the treatments were complete, the team would evaluate Chad for six more months in order to be sure that the wildcard had successfully been put to rest. Although this unexpected twelve-month delay to being listed came as a huge surprise to us, it immediately extinguished the anxiety that we had regarding the timing of our son's birth. Our days of wondering if Chad would get a call for a heart right before, during or after the birth of our first child, were instantly behind us. Needless to say, God knew this was a non-issue all along; yet, we were grateful to have this piece of our very large puzzle settled.

In addition to the self-administered shots, the summer of 2008 was also filled with baby preparation, CPR class, a baby-moon/stay-cation to celebrate our fifth wedding anniversary, baby showers and birthing classes. In early August, my prenatal doctors began to discuss with us the birthing plan. Prior testing had confirmed that Down Syndrome was no longer a concern, but in light of our son's known heart condition, they wanted to make sure I delivered while specific doctors were on call. Although my official due-date was August 25, they gave us the option of inducing labor on Monday, August 18. Chad and I were very excited to

Don't fret or worry. Instead of worrying, pray. Let petitions and praises shape your worries into prayers, letting God know your concerns. Before you know it, a sense of God's wholeness, everything coming together for good, will come and settle you down. It's wonderful what happens when Christ displaces worry at the center of your life. Philippians 4:6, 7 MSG

finally meet our son, but we were still a little nervous and very unsure about the whole concept of labor inducement. The doctors understood our concerns and told us to take the weekend to think about it and give them a call that Sunday, should we choose to come in on Monday.

On the morning of Wednesday, August 13, Tiffany went into labor. By early afternoon, it was looking like my nephew would be born any minute. Having never witnessed the birth of a child, around 1:30pm, I asked my manager if I could be excused for the day. Chad and I drove out to the hospital in Surprise, Arizona and as we inquired about the location of the maternity ward, the staff naturally assumed that I was the one in labor. After assuring the nurses that I was fine, I finally reached my sister's room. With Tiffany silently crying and clearly in pain, I immediately began to wonder if I had made a mistake in coming. Was this scene just going to add fuel to my already brewing anxiety about delivery? Nonetheless, I decided to stay and tough it out. We had arrived around 2:30PM and by 3PM, my nephew Carlton was born. Thirty minutes and barely three pushes later, a real bonafide newborn had entered the world. From my very limited view, delivery was a piece of cake and Chad and I were totally ready.

The next day, I returned to work over the moon excited about what I had witnessed. Chad and I had decided to proceed with a scheduled inducement on Monday, and Friday the 15th would be my last day at work. However, the onset of pregnancy "weirdness" began that Thursday. For some reason, I had been unable to stay "dry" since that afternoon. By early evening, it became abundantly clear to us that my water had in fact broken. With everything already meticulously packed from the recommended lists in our one thousand and one pregnancy books, we headed for St. Joseph's Hospital in downtown Phoenix.

Although my sister and I are very close and had, through zero effort or even awareness of our own, managed to conceive around the same time, much to my disappointment, our deliveries carried no similarities.

Don't fret or worry. Instead of worrying, pray. Let petitions and praises shape your worries into prayers, letting God know your concerns. Before you know it, a sense of God's wholeness, everything coming together for good, will come and settle you down. It's wonderful what happens when Christ displaces worry at the center of your life. Philippians 4:6, 7 MSG

On that Thursday the fourteenth of August, I was admitted to the hospital. Although my water had broken, I was barely dilated and a long way from delivery. The following day was the longest day of the year. They began the process of inducing me, and by late afternoon, it seemed that the pain materially increased with each hour that passed by. Chad, being a professional patient by nature, was very uncomfortable and out of character in his suddenly newfound role. It was evident that seeing his wife in pain was highly unnerving to him. Yet, witnessing his concern for me and the well-being of our son was beyond endearing. As the time of delivery drew closer, the room began to fill with people. Again, the known condition of our son, factored with the potential unknowns, automatically called for tons of medical staff to be present. With the exception of Chad's mother and sister, the other twenty people present in the room ranged from the OB/GYN, cardiologists, respiratory nurses and neonatal intensive care nurses. It was not until 3:15 that Saturday morning, August 16 that Amare Charles Washington decided to crash the scene. This was the best day of our lives.

As we had been warned, very shortly after Amare was born, he was whisked away to the Neonatal Intensive Care Unit (NICU), with the whole medical team and of course Chad in tow. I was left behind in the delivery room alone with my nurse. Once presentable and able to leave the room, I was rolled over to the NICU to see Amare. Everything appeared to be going smoothly and Chad, the new dad, was off-the-charts ecstatic. While having lunch the next day in my hospital room, having not stopped beaming since 3:15 that morning, out of nowhere Chad blurted out, "I just love him so much!" That was merely the beginning of a father-son bond that would irrefutably stand the test of time.

After convincing the hospital staff to let us stay for one night longer than usual, I was discharged on Tuesday, August 19. Thankfully, Amare was free of unforeseen complications and the previously discovered

Don't fret or worry. Instead of worrying, pray. Let petitions and praises shape your worries into prayers, letting God know your concerns. Before you know it, a sense of God's wholeness, everything coming together for good, will come and settle you down. It's wonderful what happens when Christ displaces worry at the center of your life. Philippians 4:6, 7 MSG

heart defect was still the only issue. Yet, just to be certain, Amare had to remain in the NICU for further observation. In accordance with hospital protocol, on my discharge day, they rolled me to the car in a wheelchair. The split second the nurse closed my passenger door and Chad proceeded to drive off, a wave of motherly water works came crashing down on me. As I looked back at the empty car seat that Chad had so carefully installed, this was not at all how I had envisioned our first ride home from the hospital. Albeit delirious from the weekend's events and long overdue for sleep and a shower, were we crazy for leaving that hospital without our baby?

Over the course of that week, we spent every waking moment sitting at the side of Amare's incubator. The hospital staff ran test after test which they assured us was normal protocol, yet at times it felt as though they would not stop until they found something wrong. Nevertheless, as bad as we wanted Amare out of there and home with us, we did not want him to have to come back, so we went along with the seemingly endless examination. In true "God fashion," there was another young African-American couple with a baby in the incubator next to Amare. Their family had undergone major complications and trauma, so they had been there for quite a while and knew all of the staff and the ins and outs of the entire unit. They were able to give us some coping mechanisms and sound advice. To this day, we are still friends with this family and often refer to our children as NICU neighbors.

On Friday morning of that same week, Chad and I set out to the hospital in accordance to what had become our normal routine. Upon arrival to the unit, the nurse gave us the good news that as long as the doctor cleared him, Amare would be released that day to come home with us. This was magical music to our ears! We had to sit through a few videos and sign tons of papers, but by 2PM or so, Amare had received the doctor's clearance and we were packing our baby up. This time when we pulled out of the same hospital driveway, the tears from

---

Don't fret or worry. Instead of worrying, pray. Let petitions and praises shape your worries into prayers, letting God know your concerns. Before you know it, a sense of God's wholeness, everything coming together for good, will come and settle you down. It's wonderful what happens when Christ displaces worry at the center of your life. Philippians 4:6, 7 MSG

earlier in the week had been substituted for the world's brightest smiles. At last, our family of three was headed home together to sleep (or at least reside) under the same roof.

Don't fret or worry. Instead of worrying, pray. Let petitions and praises shape your worries into prayers, letting God know your concerns. Before you know it, a sense of God's wholeness, everything coming together for good, will come and settle you down. It's wonderful what happens when Christ displaces worry at the center of your life.   Philippians 4:6, 7 MSG

PARENTHOOD

Kara

The Initiation

It took no time at all for Amare to wear his new parents down. Throughout his entire first night home, Chad and I both jumped up to tend to his every move. The next day, we were complete zombies and knew from that point on that we would have to divide and conquer. Suddenly, we had found ourselves back in school taking a sink or swim course titled *Parenting 101*. Of course, being new parents, Chad and I were determined to do everything by the book. Amare had a sponge bath every other day as the hospital had instructed. Outside of his doctor's appointments, we did not take him to public places. Our most exciting field trips were to my sister Tiffany's house. No longer their neighbors in Surprise Arizona, Chad and I had eliminated my commute and moved to Phoenix the previous summer. But by the time we packed up everything that we thought Amare might need during our twenty-five mile venture away from home, we were exhausted.

I remember Amare's first doctor's appointment. I was so excited to get him dressed to go out of the house that I picked out one my favorite outfits for him and took a dozen pictures before we left. After parking the car, Chad and I had agreed to keep the blanket over his carrier until we reached the inside of the doctor's office. But somehow when we got in the elevator with a few other ladies, Chad could not contain himself and he removed the little blanket in a rather dramatic fashion, as he could not bypass the opportunity to show off his son. Chad's action drew the compliments that he was subconsciously seeking, and his excitement to reveal his son to the world was both endearing and hilarious at the same time. This excitement never changed as Chad was always thrilled at the opportunity for someone else to meet his son and witness his awesomeness.

I, on the other hand, love my son more than anything in the whole wide world and I genuinely cherished our daily cuddle time together, but by the end of my six-week maternity leave, I felt as though I were on house arrest. Clearly not cut out to be the stay-at-home type, we were tremendously blessed that Chad had the patience and calling for this role. When it was time for me to return to work, I was excited to resume a daily routine of waking up, getting dressed and leaving the house before 11AM to go somewhere that was not surrounded with stars, moons and rainbows. By supermom standards, I guess I came off as quite strange, but hey, we all have our strengths and thankfully, Chad and I made a phenomenal team. On my first day back to work, I was all smiles, practically skipping down the hall to the break room for coffee and adult chit-chat.

I know that the story would have been completely different if Amare were not staying home with the only other person on the planet that could even possibly love him more than me. But how blessed were we that he and Chad were able to extend their male-bonding time in a society where some fathers viewed time spent with their own kids as babysitting. Chad would take offense to the very thought, instead he saw the opportunity to stay home with Amare as a privilege. That is not to say that every day was perfect, or always easy, but then again, what job is? Chad took great pride in his most treasured career and he took Amare

Behold, children are a heritage from the Lord, the fruit of the womb a reward.
Psalm 127:3 AMP

everywhere that he could. Even if I was home and he needed to run to the store, he would forego convenience in a heartbeat and take his sidekick with him every time. They basically had another family at the local grocery stores. Chad would always tease me and refer to one cashier as Amare's Wal-Mart mom. Chad and Amare would also meet me for lunch sometimes and instantly turn even the worst days into great ones. Seeing the two of them together never ceased to delight me.

By October 2008, we had our little routine together. We had certainly lost some battles along the way and could predict a few things almost like clockwork. Amare did not sleep through the night, period. At one point, I was afraid that if one more person started a sentence with "All you have to do is (*fill in blank here with yet another technique that did not work for us)," Chad and I would totally lose it. Another consistent occurrence is what we began to affectionately call the "bewitching hour." Every night between 9 and 10PM, almost to the second, Amare would cry non-stop. Outside of the clock changing to 10:01PM, there was rarely anything that would console him. I can vividly recall one isolated occasion when the bewitching hour was abbreviated. I remember Amare crying and me pacing the floors trying to rock him to sleep. Because of the time lost when Amare spent his first week of life in the NICU, breastfeeding had not gone as planned so I just pumped instead. On this particular evening however, I decided to give it another try. With Amare screaming at the top of his lungs, I sat down on the ottoman in front of our bed and began another attempt at breastfeeding. Next, like something out of a movie or an incredible magic show, the very second that his lips came in contact with his source of milk, he was knocked out. I mean he was fast asleep as if it had been hours since his last crying spell. Although the bewitching hour returned to its regularly scheduled time and duration the next day, that one instance of magic was amazing.

The last highly predictable memory of Amare's early years was the fourth family member that we had not signed up for. This was the almighty pacifier. It was virtually impossible for us to go anywhere without Amare's rubber companion. And on those brave days when we

Behold, children are a heritage from the Lord, the fruit of the womb a reward.
Psalm 127:3 AMP

forgot it at home and thought we could seize the opportunity to break the habit, we would inevitably end up at the closest Target that we could find, to add to the collection. I remember being so upset one night when we tried to evict the pacifier from our family tree, that I posted the following Facebook status at 1AM, on a WORK NIGHT!

 Kara CW III
July 7, 2010 ·

The Pacifier: A human plug that they introduce in the hospital and then send you home with a baby that's ADDICTED and literally stomps up and down in the middle of the night yelling MINE like the exorcist and reaching for the unseen plastic piece of crap...

First Holidays

Amare's first Halloween was in Los Angeles. His grandmommie (Chad's mom) wanted to throw a shower to introduce him to all of her friends and family. It was a highly active yet special day. Although Chad and I were excited to introduce Amare to his relatives, the number of kisses and touches that our baby boy received that day was rather unnerving to the strictly-by-the-book new parents. The most precious moment of the day was when Amare met his great-grandparents and four generations of Washington men were captured in one photo.

Amare's first Thanksgiving feast took place in Orlando. Prior to Tiffany and I knowing we were pregnant, we had planned a big family trip to Disney World for the week. Chaperoned by Chad and I, my parents, Tiffany and Shawn and their seven-year-old daughter Amaya, Amare and Carlton took their first airplane flights together at four months old. This was just the beginning of many "firsts" that the boys would experience together. Given their unusually close proximity in age, they have been cleverly labeled "cousin-brothers."

Behold, children are a heritage from the Lord, the fruit of the womb a reward.
Psalm 127:3 AMP

When it came to Amare's first Christmas, I was over the moon excited to finally be able to wake up at home with presents under the tree for our very own baby. Having spent countless Christmas mornings enjoying the thrill of watching my nieces and nephews open their gifts, I couldn't believe that we finally had a little munchkin in our very own home to open presents. Now granted this said munchkin was only five months, but of course, that did not stop me. Against Chad's sound judgment, I purchased every tickle-me Sesame Street character that I could get my hands on, and wrapped them up in the most beautiful wrapping paper that I could find. And needless to say, on Christmas morning, the wrapping paper was the bigger hit.

In January 2009, I celebrated my thirtieth birthday. This particular birthday served as a subtle reminder that our plans are not always God's plans. In the vision of my life plan, Chad and I would have had a total of three kids, with the last one being born by the time I was thirty. Yet, here I was thirty years old having barely had our first child, and given the pace of the heart transplant process, there was no telling when we would even be able to try for another.

To celebrate my birthday, Chad and I flew to Las Vegas for the weekend. This was the first time that we were away from Amare overnight, and I learned the hard way that it was way too soon. On the morning that we were flying out, my mom came over to pick up Amare. He had no problems going with her, but it was not easy for me to say good-bye. It was then that I began to question our decision to go to Vegas, although once we arrived at the airport, excitement began to set in. Chad and I checked into the hotel and hit The Las Vegas Strip. We had a wonderful dinner overlooking the city and enjoyed each other's company as we strolled down the magically lit streets full of entertaining characters. The next morning, however, I woke up with a pit in my stomach and a longing to get back to our baby boy. I searched flights online but of course, the last minute rates were astronomical. I was in the middle of a one-way rental car search when Chad finally talked me off the ledge and convinced me to just enjoy our time together, so that

Behold, children are a heritage from the Lord, the fruit of the womb a reward.
Psalm 127:3 AMP

is exactly what we did. We spent the next two days going from casino to casino window shopping, people watching, eating and gambling as little as possible, yet dreaming of hitting it big. We did hit the jack-pot on that Monday afternoon (MLK weekend), when we flew home and were reunited with our pride and joy! It would be a long time before I made travel plans without our little wingman.

By spring 2009, Amare had definitely developed into quite the character already. He kept Chad and I entertained at all times and outside of the still sleepless nights, we thoroughly enjoyed his company. In April, Chad's sister, Elena, got married in Los Angeles so Amare had his first wedding appearance as the sleeping Ring Bearer who was carried down the aisle by his dad. For Amare's first Easter, Chad's good friend Aaron was in town to visit. For Chad's birthday that May, my good college friend Tracey and her daughter Hope were in town. Chad and I both loved company and any chance for a close friend or relative to bond with Amare. We cherished these opportunities and were so blessed to have such an extensive rooster of family and friends. We were simply thrilled to be in this new chapter of our lives called parenthood.

Behold, children are a heritage from the Lord, the fruit of the womb a reward.
Psalm 127:3 AMP

THE WAIT THAT NEVER ENDED

Kara

By the end of May 2009, Chad's Interferon treatments were complete and the post evaluation tests rendered successful results. Thank God, we were closer to being listed, or so we thought. Chad continued his routine check-ups and stress tests in hopes of becoming a transplant candidate soon. However, it was beginning to feel as though candidacy was a far-fetched dream that we had somehow concocted in our heads. With each appointment that got scheduled, we found ourselves fantasizing and talking through what it would be like once Chad was listed and we got "the call."

That summer, we went to a family reunion in Chicago. Tiffany and I sent Chad and Shawn on a Kansas City BBQ trip as a Father's Day gift. Chad and I celebrated our 6th Anniversary at a resort in Scottsdale, Arizona, and we threw a fabulous combined 1st Birthday Party for Amare and Carlton. Their Sesame Street extravaganza was big fun with family and friends. Childhood all-stars such as Elmo, Big Bird, Cookie Monster and Oscar were well represented with the cupcakes that my niece Amaya and I had feverishly worked on. Hosted at a community pool house, this one-year-old birthday party might have set a record, running ten plus hours long. The pictures from that day were vibrant and exploding with color. For Chad and I, the day served as a great party for the boys yes, but it also symbolized our survival of the first year of parenthood and gave us momentum going into the next inevitable activity on our itinerary.

Monday, August 31, 2009, was the date we had selected for Amare's heart repair surgery. We had been advised to select a time between birth and eighteen months so that he would not remember the experience. I will never forget the moment that we had to hand him over to a nurse who would carry him back to the operating room. Amare barely looked back and later we were told that the entire team was impressed with his fearlessness and extreme curiosity as he intently looked around the surgical unit until the medication put him to sleep.

The nurses on the other side of the picture, in the unit where he spent a week recovering, did not share this sentiment. By then, Amare was on to them and knew what the people in uniform were up to. In the recovering unit, he was known as the "nervous patient," as it was extremely difficult to calm him and get him to stay in the children's hospital bed that resembled a large cage. After a day or two of watching Chad and I take turns sitting in a chair beside the cage, trying to console Amare, the hospital staff ordered a normal size bed for the room so that one of us could lay with our "nervous patient."

The surgery was a great success and the outstanding surgeon Dr. Burgess, immediately informed us that our son would now have MORE energy. We did not think it was possible, as Chad had already nick-named him "mooter-scooter," given the lightning speed in which he crawled. As far as we were concerned, Amare was definitely off the charts in energy levels, so with this news, I imagined he would be jumping from the floor to the ceiling in no time. To this day, his energy has yet to subside. Amare even speaks of it in terms of battery percentages, starting the day at 100 and finally calling it a night around fifteen percent.

"My thoughts are nothing like your thoughts," says the LORD. "And my ways are far beyond anything you could imagine. For just as the heavens are higher than the earth, so my ways are higher than your ways and my thoughts higher than your thoughts. Isaiah 55:8, 9 NLT

This certainly went down as one of the top five longest, most agonizing weeks of our lives. Chad struggled a bit more than myself, having again been used to being a patient but finding great difficult in the foreign role of caregiver, and having to witness a piece of himself suffer in pain. Yet, we were both able to carry ourselves with confidence and in great unity, as we knew without one ounce of a shadow of a doubt, that God would see our baby boy through this. The following weekend, which was Labor Day 2009, Amare was released from the hospital and we were immensely relieved to finally extinguish the dreadful thoughts that we had tried to bury, yet subconsciously carried since my fifth month of pregnancy.

By Christmas of 2009, we were pretty bummed that Chad was still not listed. As insensitive as this may sound, we had this preconceived notion that matching and transplant rates around the holidays were higher than the rest of year. So for another New Year to be approaching without Chad on the list, seemed to be a huge opportunity lost in our eyes. Nonetheless, confident that it was only a matter of time before he was listed, we decided to take an impromptu family trip. We had a few airline points but not a ton of money. So we decided to try something different and go visit my aunt, uncle and cousins in Alabama and our friend Kathryn and family in Atlanta. This did not fare as easily in person as it did on paper. Even though he was only eighteen months, Amare was well into the terrible twos at this time and he drove us crazy from the moment we left our home. While it was nice to see our relatives and friends, Chad and I quickly came to the consensus that this was not the season for Amare to take these types of trips with us. By the time we boarded the plane to return to Phoenix, Chad declared that Amare would be banned from these trips until age seven. And by "these trips," he meant an airplane ride longer than one hour, staying at people's home versus a hotel, and basically any human contact with the outside world.

Despite our stress and frustration with toddler travel, Amare's ban was short lived. It turned out that February 11, 2010, was "the

"My thoughts are nothing like your thoughts," says the LORD. "And my ways are far beyond anything you could imagine. For just as the heavens are higher than the earth, so my ways are higher than your ways and my thoughts higher than your thoughts. Isaiah 55:8, 9 NLT

appointment." How ironic seeing as how February 11 (2008), had been the date of Chad's last defibrillator procedure where we learned that it was time he be considered for a transplant. After two years had passed, countless evaluations, treatments and meetings had occurred, we finally heard the words that we had been waiting for. "Congratulations, the team has decided to list you as a heart transplant candidate, welcome to the family!" It would take the next couple of days to get insurance approval, etc. Once listed, we would not be able to travel outside of a two-hour radius from the hospital. In light of this upcoming stipulation, we decided to lift Amare's moratorium and take a quick family trip to the Grand Canyon. We spent Valentine's Day weekend that year as a family of three, exploring the beautifully snow-capped (marshmallow-like) peaks and valleys of one of the world's seven natural wonders—a very clear and picturesque testament to God's existence and power. By Tuesday, February 16, 2010, Chad was listed as a heart transplant candidate through the Mayo Clinic of Arizona. Little did we know at the time, this was at best, equivalent to passing mile marker one, in a full (26-mile) marathon.

"My thoughts are nothing like your thoughts," says the LORD. "And my ways are far beyond anything you could imagine. For just as the heavens are higher than the earth, so my ways are higher than your ways and my thoughts higher than your thoughts. Isaiah 55:8, 9 NLT

Amare's Anecdotes #1

Medical Gloves

During the summer of 2011 Chad was required to wear an intravenous drip that supplied Milrinone to help increase his heart's contractibility. A nurse was scheduled to come to the house weekly and change the dressings and lines on the IV site. But every other day I was required to clean around the site. Needless to say, with this type of activity going on regularly, we had medical gloves and supplies all around the house.

One random weekday morning as Amare and I were getting ready for work and school, Chad was still dozing in the bed. Thank God, Chad's chronic heart failure had not reached an all-time low, because on this random weekday morning, he woke up to the youngest nurse he would ever have. Amare was standing over him bedside with a glove on and when Chad opened his eyes, he snapped the glove and said "So, are you ready, Mr. Washington?"

TALK ABOUT STEPS ORDERED BY GOD

Kara

It's amazing how many times as a Christian I have asked the Lord to order my steps, yet more often than not, it is not until I'm looking back on a particular set of circumstances that I realize just how precisely God had in fact been ordering my every move. This was certainly the case in my employment transition from Cox Communications to PetSmart back in November 2009.

I had been at Cox Communications for almost three years and the company had recently undergone a fairly sizable labor force reduction. Being the primary bread-winner for our family and having recently had our first child, the looming possibility of additional layoffs was a major source of stress. However, the thought of losing our main income stream was far less scary to me than the possibility of lost medical benefits.

The speculation of future layoffs left a constant pit in my stomach, and I'm convinced it was the reason for my nearly thirty-pound POST-baby weight gain. However, despite the uncertainty, I had convinced myself that changing jobs at this point was too risky. For after all, Chad was already under evaluation to be listed as a heart transplant candidate.

Surely, it would not be long before he received his new heart and we would be free to move on with our lives.

Well, God certainly knew that my measly thoughts and grossly inaccurate mental timeline was way off. In July 2009, a former colleague from Cox who had left to go to PetSmart contacted me to see if I had interest in a finance position that would be opening up there. Still fairly apprehensive about the timing of any change, I debated, talked it over with Chad and decided to give it a try. In late September, I had a phone interview with a recruiter from PetSmart, which led to a half day of interviews on October 9 and my first day as a PetSmart employee on November 9, 2009. After working closely with the PetSmart recruiter and my future director, we settled on a favorable solution to compensate for the insurance gap between when my Cox benefits would end and my PetSmart benefits would begin. After all, given Chad's condition, we could not risk a day, hour, nor minute, without coverage.

On Friday, November 6, my last day at Cox, I received a call from the benefits manager at the Mayo Clinic. She had got wind of my employment switch, which would move us from Aetna and a lifetime maximum of five million dollars, to United Healthcare and a lifetime maximum of two million dollars. Just my luck, it was this day, when my Cox desk was cleared and I had a desk waiting for me at PetSmart, that I was emphatically warned to think long and hard about going through with the switch. I remember calling my sister, Robyn, nearly in tears, and she assured me to suck it up, keep it moving and God would make a way.

Well, it turned out that God making a way was a huge understatement. God made a million ways. My first position with PetSmart was a financial analyst supporting store operations. This meant that my primary business partners were in the field running the stores, districts, and regions. I would travel periodically to regional meetings, but for the most part, I only had face time with my business partners twice a year. Meanwhile, back in Phoenix, my desk was right outside of the break room/kitchen on our floor. In the mornings and at lunch, I found

---

The steps of a good man are ordered by the Lord: and he delighteth in his way. Though he fall, he shall not be utterly cast down: for the Lord upholdeth him with his hand.
Psalms 37:23, 24 KJV

myself chatting with the people who worked in a different department one area over from where I sat. I didn't know a whole lot about what they each specifically did, but I knew the department was payroll and benefits. There were a few ladies with whom I found myself chatting with more than others. I knew some of their names but not all, and after so much time had passed, it was too late to ask their names again without being embarrassed, especially since they would call me by name. So instead, I just smiled and continued to enjoy the wonderful conversation and friendships in the making; I was hopeful that at some point, I would catch a glimpse of their badges and try to commit my new friends' names to memory.

In February 2010, four months into my time at PetSmart, Chad was officially cleared, approved, and listed as a heart transplant candidate through the Mayo Clinic of Arizona. After two years and what seemed like thousands of tests, Chad was finally on the list and accumulating time and seniority that would eventually lead to a transplant. Life was good, with just one caveat being our home and mobile phones quickly morphing into virtual leashes and very prominent focal points in our lives. For after all, we were waiting for the call of a lifetime. Undoubtedly, this was one game of phone tag that we did not want to lose. Although we had been warned on multiple occasions that Chad's heart transplant and recovery would be no easy feat, Chad and I never once entertained the notion that the mission would be anything other than successful. We were both anxious and excited to get the call, receive the precious gift and resume our lives as we had planned.

By fall of 2011, Chad and I had become very well acquainted with the Mayo Clinic Transplant Team. We actually looked forward to Chad's appointments, for the opportunity to say hi to our extended family and even more in hopes of getting a better idea of Chad's position on the Transplant List. Sometime in September, Chad stopped by my job on his way home from a Mayo appointment, just to check in and say hi. As usual, I asked if there had been any indication of his position on the list,

The steps of a good man are ordered by the Lord: and he delighteth in his way. Though he fall, he shall not be utterly cast down: for the Lord upholdeth him with his hand.
Psalms 37:23, 24 KJV

and as a usual, the answer was no. But Chad did inform me that it was casually mentioned that perhaps he would benefit from a larger program in a more dense population such as Los Angeles. Our reaction to this idea was unanimously, yeah right, we are a family and how would Chad just up and move from his wife and son for an indefinite amount of time?

By now, Chad had been on and off the list for twenty-one months. Nevertheless, each time the phone rang and the Caller ID read "Mayo Clinic," our hearts would skip a beat. From the beginning, while no one could predict with certainty the length of time that we would have to wait, we had been warned multiple times that it was not a process to be entered into lightly. Due to Chad's congenital condition and extensive history of open heart surgeries, the Mayo Clinic had declared that there were only two surgeons in town that would be most appropriate to perform Chad's surgery in the event of a match—Dr. Edwards who was the head of the Mayo Clinic Heart Transplant Program; and Dr. Pophal, a pediatric cardiac surgeon from Phoenix Children's Hospital who had expertise in children born with congenital heart disease. This in turn meant that every time either of the two very busy surgeons went out of town, Chad was listed as inactive and unable to participate in the matching program during that time.

On one particular day in October of that same year, I came home from work and after our usual greeting and family dinner, Chad very gently informed me that what had previously been a casual suggestion, had now been presented almost as an ultimatum. It was now strongly and highly recommended that Chad move to Los Angeles and be listed through UCLA's program. This could not be happening. Our little family of three had adapted to life on the waiting list and we were rocking and rolling, enjoying life despite the constant state of uncertainty which had become our norm. There was no way that I could simultaneously quit my job, forfeiting our medical insurance and expect UCLA to pick up Chad as a heart transplant candidate. At this point, I realized that Chad

The steps of a good man are ordered by the Lord: and he delighteth in his way. Though he fall, he shall not be utterly cast down: for the Lord upholdeth him with his hand.
Psalms 37:23, 24 KJV

and I were right back to where we had started. We were facing a long-distance relationship again, but this time, we weren't just teenagers missing out on regular dinner and movie dates. We had a three-year-old son who absolutely needed both of his parents.

I was really struggling to digest this information. I remember feeling the need to escape and have a moment to process my thoughts. I went on a jog around the neighborhood and came back with a refreshed resolve. From there, I turned to my supportive wife and mama-bear channel, and assured Chad that we could do this and that God would continue to take care of us—for surely, He had not brought us this far to leave us.

Chad

The Uniqueness of My Transplant Listing and its Stipulations

In many cases, when patients are placed on the transplant list, they are on the list continually until their transplant. Of course, transplant candidates that need to have procedures or recover from any sort of infectious disease are placed on a sort of administrative hold while they recuperate. Once healed, they are placed back in the queue. My case is nothing like either of the described. As a congenital patient that has had two previous open heart surgeries, there is more scar tissue and other physiological features to contend with. Given the extra scar tissue, the surgeon that will be performing my transplant, who happens to be the head of the transplant program also wants a Pediatric Cardiologist to be present at the time of my surgery. This in and of itself is not such a huge deal. The issue is that said surgeon works at Phoenix Children's hospital and has his own hospital schedule. Because the Mayo Clinic of Arizona does not have a Pediatric Congenital Department, they must look elsewhere for their Pediatric Surgeon. When either surgeon was out of town, I was moved to a status seven on the transplant list, where I no

The steps of a good man are ordered by the Lord: and he delighteth in his way. Though he fall, he shall not be utterly cast down: for the Lord upholdeth him with his hand.
Psalms 37:23, 24 KJV

longer accrued time. As of October 17, 2011, I had a total of 388 days active time on the list, and I had been listed since February 16, 2010. There is no need to be a mathematician to see that this did not add up too nicely.

Kara

Navigating the Seesaw

Monday, October 24, 2011, was our first meeting at UCLA Medical Center. I took Monday off from work as clearly this was one appointment that I could not bear to miss. We were scheduled to meet someone by the name of Dr. DuBois'. We had been in Los Angeles all weekend visiting and staying with Chad's parents. It was a rather low-key weekend that seemed as though with every moment that inched us closer to Monday, the proverbial elephant in the room got bigger and bigger. Always determined to stay strong and not stress Chad out with my emotions, I found myself in a silent panic on this particular morning. I could not believe that we were about to go discuss in great detail a plan that would leave our family separated for any length of time, let alone an indefinite amount of time. At this point, tears were inevitable and before I could make it to the bathroom, my mother-in-law caught wind of my distraught state of mind and quickly encouraged me before Chad entered the room. I gathered my composure in the bathroom as fast as I could, jumped in the car, and unbeknownst to us, we were off to meet our new family.

I remember when Dr. DuBois' walked in the room, we were silently taken aback by his apparent youth. Surely, after traveling from Arizona to discuss something of this magnitude, we automatically assumed we would be meeting with the department head. Nonetheless, we proceeded to fire off our list of questions and he answered every single one with great confidence and basically without blinking an eye. We left that

The steps of a good man are ordered by the Lord: and he delighteth in his way. Though he fall, he shall not be utterly cast down: for the Lord upholdeth him with his hand.
Psalms 37:23, 24 KJV

meeting and drove back to Arizona highly encouraged and cautiously optimistic that this program would be a great fit for Chad's situation. Our fear and resistance to the change had almost instantaneously turned into excitement and a question of, how soon they could get Chad on their list.

By mid-November, Chad had had a few follow-up appointments at UCLA, including a meeting with the surgeon who had started UCLA's transplant program—his name is Dr. Allen (later secretly named "the Fonze" by us because of his laid-back demeanor, super cool tennis shoes and two-man posse usually in tow). While we were still less than thrilled about the separation, we had finally come to the conclusion that yes, the time apart would suck, but it sure beat the alternative which at that point was looking like never being matched. This conclusion was not reached of course until after we had explored and inquired about a dual-listing in both Phoenix and Los Angeles, and how much it would cost to have a private plane on call in the event that Chad lived in Arizona but was matched for a heart in California. Yes, we were that serious about staying together; however, reality and simple math quickly laid that idea to rest.

Once we had wrapped our minds around the concept of Chad moving, as much as we possibly could, we began to get anxious about when the actual move would take place. With the holidays right around the corner, what could we expect logistically? Just when we thought we had crossed all our "Ts" and dotted every "I", I received a call from Chad at work. He informed me that a financial representative from UCLA had just contacted him to let him know that they would be unable to list him, because his insurance limits were not enough to cover him for the operation or the post-transplant maintenance medications. To say I hit the roof would be putting it nicely. First, why in the world would this not have been checked prior to Chad making multiple visits to Los Angeles for medical evaluation? Second, and in my mind really first, why would you call someone who was being recommended for a HEART TRANSPLANT to give them this news? So, of course, I called the

The steps of a good man are ordered by the Lord: and he delighteth in his way. Though he fall, he shall not be utterly cast down: for the Lord upholdeth him with his hand.
Psalms 37:23, 24 KJV

person back immediately to inquire about more details and specifics. With the end of the work day quickly approaching, I must have called this guy no less than ten times within a forty-minute window. But unfortunately, I got a voicemail each time.

Naturally, the last thing that I wanted to do was to swallow my pride and contact the very person who had issued me the first warning about the potential impact on our insurance with my change in jobs. Yet, I could not let the business day end without some type of answers and logic. So with Chad on three-way, I made the dreadful call. We were just trying to get an understanding of why our insurance plan was good enough for the Mayo Clinic but not UCLA. The end result was something to the effect of UCLA being a certified Center of Excellence, which by definition required more coverage. So to recap, in a matter of one month, we had gone from almost debilitating resistance to the idea of Chad moving, followed by sheer excitement and rejuvenation of confidence in the concept of being listed through a different program, swiftly followed by pure anger and fear at the idea of Chad not being able to move and be listed through UCLA. That evening, we were so crushed in spirit and at a loss for words, so we simply went out to eat as a family to decompress.

By now, I'm sure you already know the first number that I dialed the very next day: none other than the financial wizard from UCLA. I was finally able to get an explanation regarding what their program required in terms of insurance limits and where our insurance was lacking. The representative recommended that I speak to my benefits department and assured me that nothing further could be done for us until our limits were raised to meet their standards. Immediately, I looked up our benefits department to see with whom I should speak. The name I found was Janet Price so I took a stroll in the neighboring department looking for her. I walked into a cube with her name posted on it, and when she looked up, I was like, "Oh my gosh! I know you."

The steps of a good man are ordered by the Lord: and he delighteth in his way. Though he fall, he shall not be utterly cast down: for the Lord upholdeth him with his hand.
Psalms 37:23, 24 KJV

Of course, it was one of my new friends that I had been chatting with in the break room for at least a year now. Only God could have had the wherewithal to set up this type of "fate." As I began to explain the dilemma to Janet, she pulled up a chair for me to have a seat. She, like most of my co-workers who weren't in my immediate department, had no idea that I had an ill husband, let alone one in need of a heart transplant. So far, I had protected my work space from this compartment of my life and basically used work as an escape from the heavy burden of Chad's major health challenges. Plus, the last thing I wanted to do was to be identified as the employee with the mountain of personal baggage.

On this particular day however, there was no cube, cabinet or office big enough to secretly store all of this baggage. Little did I know, there would be a countless number of angels that we would encounter on our journey, but on Thursday, December 8 2011, Janet Price was by far leading the pack. Janet was so patient and kind as she calmly pulled up the benefits website and began to comb through the endless details. In the end, she did confirm that what we needed was a raised limit that would typically only be requested through a PetSmart application process, in which a committee met and discussed once a month. Before I could even register what that meant for our timeline, Janet interjected and said, "But you do not have time to wait for the committee's next meeting so this will need to be escalated right away."

Next, she regretfully informed me that all of the senior team was at an offsite meeting for the rest of the week, and that she would do the best she could, but wasn't sure how far she could get before the following week. In my mind, this minor delay was far from a problem. My spirit was leaping at the sheer fact that we had already seemed to push beyond the recent "no" from UCLA, and had landed back into the realm of possibilities. This was more than enough for me to go into the weekend smiling.

The very next day, Friday, December 9, Janet stopped by my desk that morning with tears in her eyes to let me know that she had received

The steps of a good man are ordered by the Lord: and he delighteth in his way. Though he fall, he shall not be utterly cast down: for the Lord upholdeth him with his hand.
Psalms 37:23, 24 KJV

a text from her boss, the Director of Benefits letting her know that she had spoken with her boss, the Vice President of Benefits, who had in turn spoken with the CEO. All parties had agreed that they could make the proper adjustments so that we could be serviced by UCLA. I remember Janet saying something to the effect that she had worked in benefits for many years and to see a company so compassionate about their employees and their families, just really struck a special cord in her heart. She assured me that my case had remained anonymous, as to avoid any accusations of bias or things of that nature. Of course, this made it difficult in the short run, as I literally wanted to just hug and thank the senior team every time I saw them in the hallways. But instead, I tried to express my gratitude by being the best employee/team member that I possibly could, even under the stressful circumstances.

Bright and early the following Monday morning, December 12, 2011, another friendly and familiar face stopped by my desk. This person, without a doubt, quickly landed very high on our top ten list of bonafide angels. It was Irene Smith, the Director of Benefits. She was stopping by to let me know that everything should be squared away in terms of the dollar amount that UCLA was requiring. She said it was an easy sell to the VPs and CEO on Friday because they all felt like it was the right thing to do. Next, she and her team were just working on the prescription part of the plan and looking to get something in writing for Chad's post-surgery medications. By the following day, our insurance plan had been officially changed and there was nothing stopping Chad from being listed. Wow, how was that for quick turnaround!

Unfortunately, the financial wizard at UCLA could not quite keep up with PetSmart's fast and very efficient response. After multiple voicemails and re-dials, it was not until I got home from work that I got the financial representative on the phone. Sadly, he was clueless as to who he was working with—a psycho wife who would do anything within her means (and often beyond her means) to get her extraordinary husband listed and on the road to better health. I was very clear on my

The steps of a good man are ordered by the Lord: and he delighteth in his way. Though he fall, he shall not be utterly cast down: for the Lord upholdeth him with his hand.
Psalms 37:23, 24 KJV

role. He, unfortunately, had a temporary lapse in sanity regarding his role. After explaining to him the urgency of our matter and my lack of appreciation for having spent an entire day trying to reach him, he proceeded to tell me that he had multiple cases in front of Chad that were far more severe than ours. Needless to say, I was blown away as I had no idea that the UCLA financial representatives were also trained and certified doctors, able to determine the level of urgency between heart transplant candidates simply by reviewing their insurance records. At this point, I do not recall exactly what I said because my anger and rage had hit a record high. Apparently, I had reached that emergency pitch in my voice where Chad knew it was time for him to step in. That was the last day that I ever spoke to that particular representative. The next day, Chad's profile was buttoned up and passed on to the next department for final review. By Friday, December 16, Chad was all set to be officially listed through UCLA.

God had no doubt ordered each and every one of my steps, not only from a switch in employment, but right down to the positioning of my desk and its proximity to the break room that just so happened to be shared with some of our top ten angels. What a mighty God we serve! Little did we know, this was only a prelude to countless blessings that PetSmart would bestow upon our family in the months and years to come.

The steps of a good man are ordered by the Lord: and he delighteth in his way. Though he fall, he shall not be utterly cast down: for the Lord upholdeth him with his hand.
Psalms 37:23, 24 KJV

WELCOME TO WESTWOOD VILLAGE

Kara

On Saturday, December 17, 2011, Chad and I packed his car from top to bottom and initiated his temporary relocation. We had spent the better part of the week tangled in red-tape and battling with our financial friend at UCLA to clear Chad for listing, stat. Yet, by Friday evening, Chad had not packed one single bag. Clearly, this was one trip that no one was prepared for. The plan was for us to drive both of our cars to my sister Tiffany's house in Surprise, Arizona, where we would drop off my car and Amare for the weekend. Chad and I would then drive his car and the things he had packed, to his parents' house in California. I was scheduled to work remotely that Monday and return to Phoenix Monday night. Then the following weekend, Amare and I would fly to Los Angeles to be with Chad until New Year's Day.

So the move that we had fought for, yet dreaded just the same, had inevitably arrived. I was an emotional wreck that Saturday morning. As we prepared to leave, Chad walked abnormally slow throughout the entire house. He took in every area of our home, saying a temporary goodbye in his own way. Due to the lack of space in his car (packed from floor to ceiling), and wanting to spend every moment possible with

Amare, Chad drove my car to Surprise while I drove solo in his car. I cried from the moment we pulled out of the garage to the time that we entered my sister's neighborhood thirty-five minutes later. Before exiting the car, I forced myself to pull it together.

After visiting for a few minutes with my sister and her family and Chad stealing Amare away to say a special good-bye, my brother-in-law Shawn asked us to all join in circle for prayer. He prayed an amazing prayer asking God to provide a heart and return Chad to us in ninety days or less. Needless to say, by the time we said Amen, my face was covered in tears all over again. I quickly excused myself to the bathroom in order to regain my composure. Next, we said our goodbyes and started a journey destined to be full of surprises, frustration, triumph, defeat, victory, sadness, and extreme growth.

The Lord bless you and keep you; the Lord make his face to shine upon you and be gracious to you; the Lord lift up his countenance upon you and give you peace. Numbers 6:24-26 ESV

AND SO IT BEGINS

Chad

On January 4, 2012, I checked into UCLA for what was to be a Cardiac Catheterization (a medical procedure used to do diagnostic tests and treatments on the heart). At least that was what everyone thought—except me. I was told on a prior clinic visit in November that the team would more than likely admit me to the hospital for the duration of my wait. There was a slight chance that they would let me wait at home depending on how good my test results were—though highly unlikely.

I migrated to Los Angeles on December 17. Kara and I picked this date so that we could have a nice Christmas holiday in Los Angeles as a family before separating for the first time, long term, since before we were married. In retrospect, the separations, fast hellos, and long goodbyes were the toughest part for me.

In light of the already major logistical change in our family, I could not bring myself to share this additional layer of news that was sure to damper the holiday mood even more. So I kept the information regarding my impending hospitalization to myself. I hoped that the numbers or data they used to make that determination came back as good as possible. Nevertheless, hope was not the winning strategy.

It was decided that the best plan of action would be to keep me in the hospital where I could be continuously monitored using a Swan-Ganz Catheter, which helps detect heart failure or fatal inflammation. Also, the doctors have added another intravenous drip called Dopamine, which is a chemical messenger that helps with the transmission of signals in the brain and other vital areas. Lastly, they have increased my Milrinone, a medication given to patients with heart failure, to help increase my heart's contractibility. As a result of the newly increased Milrinone dose, and the addition of Dopamine, I am now a status 1A. I will be in the hospital until I receive my transplant.

Wait on The Lord: be of good courage, and he shall strengthen thine heart: wait, I say, on the Lord. Psalms 27:14 KJV

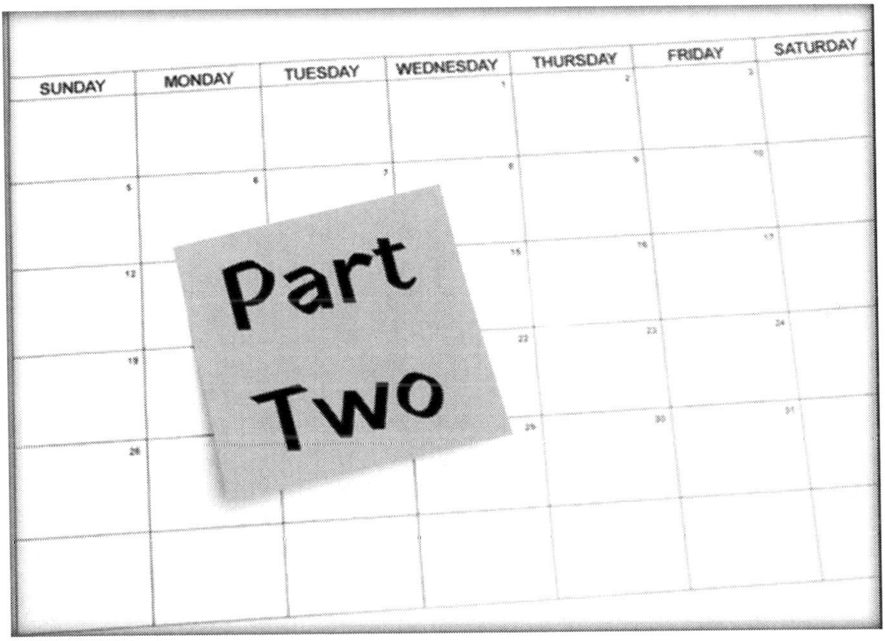
SUNDAY
MONDAY
TUESDAY
WEDNESDAY
THURSDAY
FRIDAY
SATURDAY
Part Two

DRY RUNS

Chad

I had three offers or "dry runs" before getting my heart. The first was perhaps the most emotionally taxing. It was also the most helpful. It was the first run through and a good look at the processes that would take place on Transplant Day. As hard and emotional as it was, it was an invaluable experience. The first offer came on January 18, 2012. I was told at 7:15PM that I was being made NPO (Latin abbreviation for *nothing by mouth*). A potential heart had come up and a nurse practitioner (NP) would be stopping by to have me sign consent forms. The NP came by around 9PM with the forms and explained the possible complications and risks. While we were in the middle of signing consent forms, her pager went off, and she went to answer the page. At 11:30PM we completed signing the forms. I called my wife and she started her drive from Phoenix to Los Angeles. I was told that my surgery was scheduled around 8AM the following morning. The caregivers came in to prep and bathe me around 5AM. My wife arrived around 7AM. We were told that things had been pushed back until 10AM or so. At some point, I fell asleep and woke up a little after 11AM, at which point I recall thinking that the transplant was not going to happen. I was right.

Kara

On the night of Wednesday, January 18, 2012, around 11PM, I was fast asleep at our home in Phoenix when I received a call from Chad stating "this is that call." Having fantasized, agonized and pondered over "the call" since our listing journey began in February 2010, it was absolutely surreal that it was actually happening. When Chad admitted to the hospital in early January to wait it out, we began to discuss various plans of how Amare and I would get to Los Angeles in the event that Chad was matched for an organ while we were in Phoenix. Plan A was of course to just hop on a plane, assuming the call was received before the last plane for the night had taken off. Plan B was that Amare would stay with Tiffany or my parents, and Shawn and I would hit the road if a call came in the middle of the night. Either way, I kept a bag packed.

After hanging up with Chad on the evening of the call, I jumped out of bed in a bit of panic. My parents were already in California to celebrate our nephew Morris's 5th birthday. Tiffany was very pregnant and due to deliver in a just a few short weeks. Nevertheless, I called Tiffany and Shawn and Plan B was in full effect. After pacing the floor a bit and finding myself going in circles to just put a few last minute items in my pre-packed bag, I finally snapped out of it. I put the luggage in the car, retrieved Amare from his bed, strapped him in his car seat and we were headed to Surprise. When we reached Tiffany and Shawn's, Amare woke up and after I informed him that I needed to go to California, he immediately began to cry, saying that he wanted to go with me. With emotions already running high, I began to question if I should just take him with us, but Tiffany assured me that he would be fine and Shawn and I should just go. Sure enough, Amare fell asleep very shortly after we left.

The ride to Los Angeles was fast. Shawn drove the entire way and I made phone calls, sent text messages and quietly shed many tears. I was equally excited, scared and nervous all at the same time. Chad's parents were on a cruise in Australia, but his sister Elena was there with him.

"You will only need to remain calm. The Lord will fight for you." Exodus 14:14 ICB

When Shawn and I reached the hospital around seven the next morning, I had somehow worked up in my head that we would catch Chad just as he was being rolled off to the Operating Room (OR). Instead, we walked into a dark quiet room with Chad asleep in the bed and Elena asleep on the couch. This was quite contrary to the scene that I had imagined. They both woke up and updated Shawn and I on the status and plan for the day. Basically, Chad had been bathed and prepped for the OR, but they were waiting for the arrival of the organ. Of all the stories and different scenarios that we had heard about through support groups, I did not recall ever receiving warning that it was a game of hurry up and wait.

By now, having spent three weeks in the current unit, we had developed relationships and became familiar with many of the nurses. I was happy to see one of our favorites assigned to Chad that Thursday morning. She was very careful to give us just the right mix of information to keep us informed, yet steer us away from panic. Over the course of the morning, family and friends began to filter into the hospital to check on Chad and anxiously await the beginning of his operation. Meanwhile, Elena stayed in contact with her parents who were experiencing some difficulty being released from the cruise ship in order to catch a flight home. Around noon, Chad's nurse Claire came in to draw blood from Chad. Shortly after, she returned to the room to inform us that due to antibodies, the organ was deemed as an unviable match for Chad.

WHAT?!? Devastation and shock were my immediate feelings. In true Chad fashion, he remained calm, and though undoubtedly disappointed, he somehow managed to see the bright side. He'd come this close to a donor, so he'd come closer the next time.

But I didn't feel that way. In that moment, I felt devastated, angry and offended. We had heard first-hand accounts of other heart transplant candidate's trial runs, but for some reason, I did not think that would be our story. Again, I had not built that chapter into our timeline. So in that moment, I was offended that God had allowed this to happen. What lesson could possibly be learned from this?

"You will only need to remain calm. The Lord will fight for you." Exodus 14:14 ICB

With the shocking news and nonstop chatter in the room, the walls seemed to quickly close in and though looking back, it seemed selfish to have left Chad, I desperately needed to escape. I quietly excused myself, stopped by the waiting room to deliver the unfortunate news to the overflow of family and headed outside as quickly as I possibly could. I found a quiet sitting area about two blocks from the hospital and I called my oldest sister, Robyn, to inform her. I was so upset that I could hardly speak. She got the message though and agreed to pass it on. After sitting outside for a while and gathering my composure, I called our Mayo Clinic family to inform them and also get a quick education on exactly what antibodies were, as I could not recall hearing about them before now. Antibodies are primary immune defenses that, as we learned on that disappointing Thursday, have a tendency to develop in one's body after major surgeries. With Chad being no stranger to operations, antibodies had instantly become a very present and prominent factor in our journey.

After speaking with the Mayo Clinic transplant coordinator who had been our very first point of contact at the start of this entire journey, I felt a bit more at peace with the unexpected turn of events. Still incredibly disappointed, I walked slowly back to the hospital and asked God for the strength to return to Chad's bedside with my supportive wife hat strapped on tight. The last thing I wanted was for Chad to spend any energy trying to lift my spirits. I needed all of his energy directed at keeping himself motivated for the journey ahead. For on this day, it was abundantly clearer than ever, that the itinerary I had envisioned, was not the one in play.

Later, once all of the visitors cleared out, it was explained to us in more detail that the blood work taken earlier in the day, had revealed antibodies in Chad's system that would have more likely than not, rejected the foreign object known as the transplanted organ. With this more in-depth explanation and reiteration of my earlier conversation with the Mayo Clinic, Chad and I were able to find peace and encouragement in the fact that his illness had not reached a point where he had to take the first organ presented. Thank God, he was still in good enough condition that the doctors had the luxury to be very cautious and

"You will only need to remain calm. The Lord will fight for you." Exodus 14:14 ICB

selective in regards to the best match for Chad. Onward and upward, back to the waiting game we went.

The next morning, Chad's parents made it home and Shawn and I drove back to Phoenix. Amare and I were reunited in time to catch our regularly scheduled Friday evening flight so back to LA we went. Although we had recovered from the week's devastation, our family needed to be together. We spent the night at Chad's parents' house and headed to the hospital first thing Saturday morning to spend time with Chad. He seemed to be in good spirits and seeing Amare was always the best medication. Still on the IV drips that had rendered Chad's original inpatient status, and having already received one offer, everyone kept telling us that more offers would shortly follow since Chad had reached the top of the list. Later that afternoon, Amare and I attended Morris's birthday party out at my sister's house in Anaheim.

We returned to LA that evening with a plan to bathe and head to the hospital to spend the night with Chad. My cell phone rang while I was in the shower, and by the time I got out of the shower it was ringing again. Both calls were from Chad so I instantly knew that the second offer had come in. Having left Amare in Phoenix after receiving the first call, there was something gratifying and special about the three of us being together to wait out the results of this second call. Seeing as how only a mere seventy-two hours had passed since the first false alarm, our spectrum of nerves and expectations were kept to a minimum as we now had intimate insight on how the process could potentially go. This time, instead of blasting off a hundred text messages to everyone we knew, I simply called my sister, Robyn, and let her know that we would keep them posted. Chad, Amare and I hung out for a while and then we all went to sleep as if it were a normal evening. Sure enough, around two that morning, we received the news that the operation had been called off. At this point, we did not even inquire as to the reasons for the cancellation. Chad and I, again, counted our blessings for the gift of time to be selective and we both went back to sleep. Amare and I spent the rest of the weekend with Chad and headed back to Phoenix on our regularly scheduled 6AM Monday morning flight.

"You will only need to remain calm. The Lord will fight for you." Exodus 14:14 ICB

The following Thursday, January 24, Chad informed me early that afternoon that there was potentially another match in the works. After the second false alarm, we had already succumbed to the fact that perhaps it was not the wisest idea for me to rush to town every time an offer was presented. We decided that we would wait until a little more information was received regarding the likelihood of the operation occurring. It turned out that our discernment had paid off in this scenario because early that evening, that offer was rejected as well. By now, Chad and I were numb to the rejections and made little to no inquiry regarding the reasons behind them. We remained very encouraged and felt that as long as the offers kept coming, we had to be headed in the right direction. With each "no," surely there had to be a "yes" at least approaching the horizon.

The "yes" came when we least suspected it. It was Friday, February 3. My mom, Robyn and I had planned a baby shower for Tiffany to be held at my parents' house. Robyn was flying in from California on Saturday morning and the shower was scheduled for Saturday afternoon. My best friend, Jessica, was scheduled to fly in Friday evening. My plan for Friday after work was to come home, wash, blow dry and flat iron my hair, finish the final shower preparations and pick Jessica up from the airport. Excited about her visit, I'd communicated a few times that day with Jessica and last we spoke, she was headed to the airport. Just as I was about to get into the shower to wash my hair, Chad called and calmly, almost nonchalantly, let me know that he had received another offer. This presented a bit of a dilemma with Jessica headed to town, Tiffany's shower the next day and the fact that every other offer had not materialized. Surely, no social visit or event was more important than Chad's heart transplant, but would this one really be "the one" or would I be missing the festivities in vain for another false alarm? It was about seven that evening and Chad would not have a more clear answer regarding the likelihood of an operation for quite some time. We both agreed that Amare and I would forego the mad dash to the airport and instead catch the first flight out the following morning, should the match be deemed viable. Grateful that Chad had caught me just before I had

"You will only need to remain calm. The Lord will fight for you." Exodus 14:14 ICB

wet my hair and started that project, I hung up from him and immediately called Jessica. She had already checked her bag and was sitting at the gate waiting for her flight to board. I explained the situation to her and let her know that she was more than welcome to come, but of course, there was a 50/50 chance that I would have to fly out in the morning. In the end, she decided to cancel her trip and just save the credit and visit when my life and schedule was a little less crazy.

Later that evening, Chad received additional news that the match was looking extremely good and he had been scheduled for an OR time the following morning. I went ahead and booked Amare and I on the first flight out Saturday morning. I also called my mom and Robyn to inform them, sparing Tiffany from any potential stress given her very pregnant state. Sensing that this was "the one," I packed a few extra items for Amare and me, completed the baby shower preparations and attempted to get some sleep. My mom picked us up around five the next morning and Amare and I were off to the airport. I spoke to Chad that morning and neither his parents nor sister were at the hospital yet. One of my biggest fears had been the vision of Chad being rolled off to surgery with no one there to support him. This vision left me just shy of hysteria so after hanging up with Chad, I immediately called his sister, Elena. Thankfully, she was already on her way. She had been debating with her parents who had sensed that Chad wanted and needed time and space to just process and relax.

By the time my mom dropped Amare and I at the airport, I was a nervous wreck. Chad and I had talked through at length how it was not feasible for Amare and me to hop on a plane every time an offer came up. I thought I was at peace with the concept, but as I sat there with our busy toddler, it suddenly hit me like a ton of bricks that this was likely the biggest surgery of Chad's life, and I was sitting in an airport terminal instead of by his side.

In the end, Elena and Chad's dad were there to see Chad off to surgery, even documenting the moment with video footage. The live footage was the perfect cure for my rapidly growing anxiety. Chad's demeanor on the video was as if he were going to have minor knee

"You will only need to remain calm. The Lord will fight for you." Exodus 14:14 ICB

surgery or a noninvasive procedure. He was calm as always and even cracking jokes as his hospital bed was rolled into the elevator and the doors slowly shut. This was the moment that in some way, shape or form had dictated our lives since February 2008 when we first learned of his need to pursue a transplant. No more dress rehearsals, this was the real McCoy.

"You will only need to remain calm. The Lord will fight for you." Exodus 14:14 ICB

February 4, 2012

Chad

I received my new heart on the morning of Saturday, February 4. I was told the night before, that there was a match for me and that the donor was actually at the hospital. The harvesting of the organs was to begin sometime between 1AM and 7AM on Feb 4. After my surgery, the surgeon said that I needed that heart on that day and that my heart was extremely enlarged. He illustrated how large by holding his hands up about 1.5 feet apart. My heart was actually stuck to the back of my sternum and adhered to one of my lungs.

Kara

Amare and I landed in Los Angeles around eight on Saturday morning. Charlotte (Chad's mom) picked us up from the airport and we dropped her back at the house. Chad had been taken to the OR around 7:30 that morning, but Amare and I still headed to the waiting room to join the family. Once at UCLA, we settled into Maggie's Room. This was the main waiting room for families with loved ones in surgery. On this day and in the days ahead, we would become very familiar with this space. After a couple of hours of waiting, Elena's husband, Justin, came to rescue Amare to hang with him and his cousin Jayson for the day. Not really needing much convincing to go play with his cousin, when inquiring about seeing Chad, I let Amare know that it was a big day for Daddy and that he would need rest later when he got out of surgery.

Throughout the course of the day, we received sporadic updates from the operating room. Every time the waiting room phone rang, it was like time stood still until the patient's last name was called and a family member rushed to the phone to anxiously receive an update. At some point, I ventured upstairs to visit our nurse friends in the unit where Chad had spent the last thirty days. The charge nurse was able to check the system and let me know that the actual surgery had begun around 9:30am. Around noon, we received a call from the OR to let us know that Chad was on the bypass machine. The next update was hours later when Chad was off of the bypass machine and the new heart was pumping. This was one of many surreal moments to come.

Later that afternoon when the surgeon Dr. Allen came out to the waiting room to speak to us, he informed us that Chad needed that heart, that day. His heart was so dramatically enlarged that it was stuck to his sternum. Dr. Allen compassionately explained that just the first step of opening him up for the surgery had presented a great challenge, which later the OR nurse explained as the reason for the far and few updates. They had their hands full and we were ultimately grateful that they had stayed focused on Chad's immediate needs. I was beginning to see a theme in Chad's surgeries. From the pacemaker battery dying on the operating table just moments after being replaced, to the enlarged heart holding on long enough for Chad to be matched for a transplant, it was impossible to doubt that God was working on our behalf.

It was not until around nine or ten that evening that we were able to peek in and see Chad after he returned from the recovery room. The site of all the machines was pretty overwhelming and the nurses and doctors were working overtime to get him situated. They repeatedly assured us that Chad was in good hands and that we should all go home

Faith means being sure of the things we hope for. And faith means knowing that something is real even if we do not see it. Hebrews 11:1 ICB and get some rest. I left the hospital that evening with my heart overflowing with thankfulness. God had provided just what we needed right when we needed it. Our lives, and perspective on it, would never be the same. After reuniting with Amare and getting ready for bed that evening, as we said our prayers, he just kind of verbally thought back over the day and recalled that we had been to the hospital but he had not seen Daddy. Thankfully, he was not really looking for a response from me, so I took the rare break and we said our goodnights.

The next morning when I woke up and called the hospital to check on Chad, the nurse said that he was already awake, off of the breathing machine and asking for his glasses. I couldn't believe it. How was that even possible? I rushed to get dressed and immediately headed to the hospital to see my love and deliver his glasses. After all that he had endured, he should not have to want for anything. At that point, I didn't know who was showing out the most, God or Chad, but I was totally enamored with both of them and full of hope for the future.

Faith means being sure of the things we hope for. And faith means knowing that something is real even if we do not see it. Hebrews 11:1 ICB

A MEDICINAL COCKTAIL GONE BAD

Kara

On Sunday, February 5, less than twenty-four hours after receiving his new heart, Chad was sitting up in a hospital chair eating and watching the Super Bowl. We were all on cloud nine and it was almost like you would not believe it unless you saw it with your own two eyes. How in the world could a man have a heart so enlarged that it was stuck to his chest one day, and the very next day have a completely different heart and be feeling better than ever? Only one explanation: God.

That evening, I returned to my in-laws home feeling even happier than the day before. Our four-year dream and fantasy was unfolding right before our eyes. I got home in time to hang out with Amare and get him ready for bed. Just as we said our prayers and our heads hit the pillow, my cell phone rang and it was a call from UCLA. I cautiously answered and immediately heard an angry man say, "I need you and my dad to get up here right now!" Not even recognizing the voice through the rage and convinced that it was the wrong number, my reply was "Who is this?"

"This is your husband!" the man cried.

I couldn't believe it. The voice did not even sound remotely close to that of the calm, gentle man whom I had known since I was thirteen. He reiterated that he needed us to get to the hospital stat (immediately). When I hung up the phone, I was shaking and totally at a loss. Amare started crying when I began to get dressed and he sensed that I was leaving again. Here I was once again, tasked with choosing between being there for my son or being there for my husband. Man, was I tired of playing this agonizing game!

Chad's dad was not home at the time so I informed Charlotte of the phone call, and seeing how upset I was, she strongly suggested that I not drive and let Chad's dad, Michael, go instead. A few minutes later, the phone rang again and this time, it was a nurse explaining to me that everything was okay and Chad seemed to be hallucinating as a result of the mixture of pain medication that they had given him. While this was a bit of a relief to hear, I was still pretty concerned and wondering if this new "angry Chad" would become the product of his new heart. Michael came home right away, packed his bag and headed for the hospital. In the meantime, Chad called again inquiring as to our whereabouts. I told him that his dad was on the way and Chad snapped back his original request which was that we both come. I then explained that it was best if I stayed with Amare that night. Not having asked for much, ever, Chad was not happy that I had not followed through on this request, but his dad walked in the hospital room while we were on the phone so I was off the hook for the moment.

Michael later explained that he had never seen Chad so upset and snappy. He finally extended his hand and was able to convince Chad to just squeeze it as hard as necessary and try to calm down. It was not an instant process, but the fuse was eventually dissolved. Chad described the scene as the nurse had come in the room, shut the sliding glass door, and had a plastic knife that he would periodically flash. Chad was 100% convinced that this nurse had unquestionable intent to harm him. When Chad demanded to see the charge nurse, he was highly insulted when the

Though the mountains be shaken and the hills be removed, yet my unfailing love for you will not be shaken nor my covenant of peace be removed," says the Lord, who has compassion on you. Isaiah 54:10 NIV

nurse questioned how he knew the term "charge nurse." It was like adding fuel to a fire and the scene just escalated from there.

We later laughed uncontrollably about it, but for a very long time, Chad stood by the theory that the nurse was out to get him. We would see the nurse in the hallway long after that night, and Chad would give him the cold shoulder even when he tried to speak. I almost felt sorry for the guy. Although we felt safe in believing that Chad was hallucinating, it was best for all parties that that particular nurse was never assigned to him again. In fact, it was then that we deemed that particular unit as the Twilight Zone and we could not get out of there fast enough. It was also then that Chad set a hard-fast rule that whenever he had surgery, a family member was to stay at the hospital with him until he was awake, alert and able to think and speak for himself again. It seemed like the least that we could do at the time of his request, so we all agreed to adhere to it.

The following morning, Monday, February 6, Chad's dad called just beaming and elated to report the notes from the doctor's morning rounds. He described the presentation that the day nurse, Sheldon, had given to the doctors, as extremely impressive. He also described the doctors as absolutely beaming with pride regarding both Chad's status and recovery thus far, as well as the viability of the newly gifted organ. Having agreed to work remote that morning, I instantly felt extremely bummed out to have missed what sounded like a very magical moment. It was then that I realized I was insane for thinking that I could work remote that week. I immediately contacted my manager who assured me that, despite the fact that it was our fiscal year-end, everything would be fine at work. I shut down my laptop and made my way to where I belonged: in the presence of my husband, cheering him on in his quest to recover and rebuild his strength. Later that afternoon, Chad was up walking with the assistance of a walker, and we were filming and celebrating. The moment was absolutely surreal and I remember

Though the mountains be shaken and the hills be removed, yet my unfailing love for you will not be shaken nor my covenant of peace be removed," says the Lord, who has compassion on you. Isaiah 54:10 NIV

thinking nonstop about how great was our God and that surely if we could survive this test, we could survive anything.

Though the mountains be shaken and the hills be removed, yet my unfailing love for you will not be shaken nor my covenant of peace be removed," says the Lord, who has compassion on you. Isaiah 54:10 NIV

BOOMERANG

Kara

Once the forbidden medicine mix was identified, the rest of the week went relatively smoothly. There were already talks of Chad being released from the hospital the following week. On Thursday morning of the first post-surgery week, we received family training in Chad's hospital room. The primary trainers were the pharmacist to go over Chad's plethora of medicine, a nurse from the Endocrinology Team to cover Chad's Insulin Management Plan (in light of all of the post-transplant medication that would challenge his levels), and lastly the sociologist to discuss Chad's life post-transplant. She stressed the importance of him not living in a bubble and being afraid to enjoy life. Yes, there were a list of precautions to be taken but ultimately the goal of a transplant was to provide the recipient the opportunity to enjoy life.

With six successful post-transplant days under our belt, my plan was to spend my second week off from work with Chad at his parents' house once released from the hospital. Then, after a week with Chad home from the hospital, I would work remote for my last week in Los Angeles. Once I returned to Phoenix after the third week, Amare and I would resume our Los Angeles visiting schedule. Friday, February 10 was the first time that we met our now good friend Heather. I remember a young, pint-sized, African-American woman walking into the room with her chart and equipment. There were a lot of things going on that morning, including the "Bicycle Man" who was relentless about Chad participating in his study, which was designed to measure the level at which a transplant recipient could perform on a stationary pedaling device. Also, in the middle of Heather's assessment, Amare arrived at the hospital having hitched a ride with his grandmommie, Charlotte. He was coming to deliver his dynamic dose of love to his daddy before he headed back to Phoenix. Heather stepped out to give us some family time and afterwards, Amare and I left the hospital. Later Chad filled me in on how the pint-size therapist was packed solid with power and definitely a force to be reckoned with.

That afternoon, Amare and I flew to Phoenix and my parents met us at the airport. They would take care of Amare until I returned. He needed to resume his preschool schedule, returning to structure and interaction with his peers. I hung out at the airport and caught our regular (pre-scheduled) Friday night flight back to Los Angeles. Although Chad was making great progress, this monumental week had still taken its toll on everyone. As I sat in the airport waiting for my flight, it felt great to just take a pause and reflect.

Meanwhile, in the midst of my "pause," I heard Tiffany was in labor and baby Joy was on her way. As a devoted wife, relatively new mom, loving sister, aunt, and caring daughter, it seemed that these days often called for me to choose one role over the other. No matter where I was physically, I was always fully cognizant of where I wasn't. During this brief and rare intermission from all of my roles, I contemplated for a split second whether or not I should deviate from the plan and go meet my new niece instead. But in the end, I decided that Joy would understand and it was best I get back to Chad. Joy was born at 6PM that evening on Friday, February 10. Once reunited with Chad in his hospital

I consider that our present sufferings are not worth comparing with the glory that will be revealed in us. For the creation waits in eager expectation for the children of God to be revealed. Romans 8:18-19 NIV

room, we celebrated the news of our new niece and congratulated the proud parents.

We also celebrated Chad being downgraded from the ICU to the COU (Cardiac Observation Unit), which we affectionately called "the apartments." This unit consisted of a row of rooms outside of the ICU for patients who were basically just awaiting release papers to go home. On Monday, February 13, Chad received his glorious papers. When I arrived at the hospital that morning, Chad was up and dressed, sporting his Kango hat and a smile that instantly lit up my world. This was yet another day, moment and milestone that we had dreamed of for what seemed like eons. Here it was just twelve days post-transplant and Chad had a magnificent pep in his step and overwhelming joy in his new heart.

Like all hospital releases, the process was drawn out and it was well into the afternoon before we actually fled from Westwood. When we arrived at Chad's parents' house, they welcomed him with open arms and smiles that exuded gratefulness. Their son had survived his most major surgery to date and he was doing great. In line with the transplant program's protocol, Chad was required to remain in Los Angeles for at least the next three months. As he settled back into his temporary home, we all just kind of watched. We were in total awe at what God had done. Chad took an extra, extra, extra long shower that afternoon. Previously not wanting to risk infection in his swan site, for the first time in six weeks, Chad was totally free of tubes and licensed to shave. He stepped out of the bathroom with his new heart, and a young fresh shaven face to accompany it. He literally looked at least ten years younger and seemed baffled by the youth that had suddenly been returned to him.

The next day was Valentine's Day and needless to say, there was no store, restaurant or otherwise, that could provide us with anything remotely close to the gift that had been bestowed upon us just ten days prior. Chad and I rented movies and just hung out enjoying each other's company. We went on a walk around the block which was further than Chad could have comfortably walked in the last year. I remember Chad

I consider that our present sufferings are not worth comparing with the glory that will be revealed in us. For the creation waits in eager expectation for the children of God to be revealed. Romans 8:18-19 NIV

shaking his head and raising his fist in utter amazement. Having tried desperately to plan perfect Valentine's Day celebrations in prior years, this particular Valentine's Day effortlessly went on permanent record as one of the best ever!

The rest of the week followed suit and life was shaping up quite nicely. The countdown had been on all week for a very special guest that weekend. On Saturday, February 19, my parents drove Amare to town for a visit. This would be the first time that he saw his daddy outside of the hospital since New Year's Day. Witnessing Amare's reaction to Chad turning the hallway corner to greet him was pure utopia. It was enough to make a grown man cry, but not Chad off course. Thankfully, we captured the moment on video and it still melts my heart to this day.

Although it was just for the weekend, our family of three being reunited under one non-hospital roof was purely delightful. For the past few months, there had been a bowl of square Godiva Chocolate in a candy dish in our room at Chad's parents' house. When we first "moved" to Los Angeles, Amare would ask for the chocolate all the time. After a while, we made a pact that it was very special chocolate and that we would save it for our celebration when Daddy came home. So after his exhilarating reunion with Chad, Amare immediately escorted us to the bedroom for the special Chocolate Ceremony. He made sure that we each had one in hand, and the three of us chocolate toasted to Daddy being home, and then of course, Amare relieved us from our chocolates and ate it all.

We spent the rest of the weekend hanging out at the house, simply thrilled to be together. Watching Chad and Amare kick the soccer ball around the backyard was an amazing dream come true. The three of us walked around the neighborhood together. The excitement of our reunion never wore off. We all felt exceedingly blessed and the atmosphere radiated thankfulness. The hardest part of the weekend, of course, was when Amare had to head back to Phoenix with my parents. Again, my plan was to work remotely during my last week in Los Angeles

I consider that our present sufferings are not worth comparing with the glory that will be revealed in us. For the creation waits in eager expectation for the children of God to be revealed. Romans 8:18-19 NIV

and then fly home Saturday afternoon to spend some time with Amare before we hit the play button on our "normal" routine of school/work Monday through Friday and bi-weekly Los Angeles visits.

My third week in Los Angeles seemed to fly by with work for me during the day and a few doctors' appointments for Chad throughout the week. We were thoroughly enjoying being in each other's presence. Pillow talk had never been so special and had taken on a whole new value. Chad's weekly clinic visits had so far gone very well, until Friday the 24th of February.

Chad

On February 24, I was called by a transplant coordinator and told that I was showing signs of cellular rejection based on the last biopsy. Also they were concerned because my ejection fraction had decreased from 55 to 35. The coordinator said that normally they wouldn't even treat this level of rejection, but given the rejection coupled with the drop of my ejection fraction, they wanted to treat this as quickly and as aggressively as possible. That meant me being admitted to the hospital for high dose steroids.

UCLA is a large institution serving an exponentially larger populace, and often times, the hospital is filled to capacity. This was the case on Friday, February 24. I was told that there were no hospital beds at that time, and to report to the ER as soon as possible. They would start the steroids, and I would wait there until a bed became available in the hospital. I reported to the ER around a quarter to one, and was admitted to the hospital around 9PM. They administered three doses of Solumedrol over a period of three days. I was released on Sunday, February 26.

I consider that our present sufferings are not worth comparing with the glory that will be revealed in us. For the creation waits in eager expectation for the children of God to be revealed.
Romans 8:18-19 NIV

Kara

Chad being readmitted to the hospital had totally caught us off-guard. Having been in Los Angeles for three weeks, I was scheduled to go home on Saturday and return to the office on Monday. Now I questioned what I should be doing. After work and a bubble bath to calm my nerves, I visited Chad that evening and Dr. Hill, a Cardiologist on the Transplant Team explained to us the weekend treatment plan that Chad would receive. She made everything sound very routine and non-alarming and I believed her. Also, I really missed Amare and had already promised to return to work where I now had a new manager. Because I was convinced it was a small hiccup in Chad's recovery, I decided to fly home to Phoenix that Saturday.

My reunion with Amare was great and we enjoyed spending time together the rest of the weekend. While I was excited to return to the office Monday morning and get caught up with my PetSmart family, I was disappointed in the fact that I was a bit preoccupied with how I had left Chad. I could not believe how well the three weeks post-transplant had gone, then just when it was time for me to leave, we had hit a bump in the road. They'd told me it was routine, still I felt worried.

Somehow, I powered through the workday checking in with Chad periodically, who had been released on Sunday and was back at his parents' house. That evening, Amare and I had completed our all too familiar meal from Panda Express, had our baths and were tucked nicely in our respective rooms. I was sound asleep when the house phone startled me awake. It was a call from a medical operator seeking to connect me with Dr. Hill. She was returning a message from Chad who had reporting feeling sick. I explained that they had called our home in Phoenix and that Chad was at his parents' house in Los Angeles. Of course, I immediately called Chad to see what was going on and he was beyond displeased that they had called me. Apparently, he was thinking that I could sit this one out for a change, but UCLA had missed the

I consider that our present sufferings are not worth comparing with the glory that will be revealed in us. For the creation waits in eager expectation for the children of God to be revealed.
Romans 8:18-19 NIV

memo. In my frustrated fatigue, I began to wonder if Chad was a boomerang destined to be tossed between Westwood and his place of residence forever.

Chad

Late Monday night, February 27, I went back to the ER with severe vomiting, diarrhea, and nausea. I was given an injection for the nausea and it subsided. That was when the diarrhea began. At this point, I was also given Flagil and Cipro, intravenously. There were no beds in the hospital at that time so I spent two days in the ER. I was eventually moved to a room in an observation unit where I spent another night, and then I was moved to the Cardiac Observation Unit. I was released on Thursday, March 1. My earnest prayer was to uneventfully fulfill the duration of my three-month mandatory visit and return to my loves in Phoenix.

I consider that our present sufferings are not worth comparing with the glory that will be revealed in us. For the creation waits in eager expectation for the children of God to be revealed. Romans 8:18-19 NIV

Amare's Anecdotes #2

Admittedly, this is far from my proudest moment as a mom. But in the spirit of sharing our journey, I could not omit this episode.

DAMMIT!

Upon realizing that Chad would permanently reside in Los Angeles until he received his new heart, we were devastated. The thought of our little family being split up by state borders was just something that I never imagined we would have to face. One thing that brought some consolation was the fact that my job agreed to let me work remote from California on Mondays. This way Amare and I could fly out on Fridays after work and stay in LA until Tuesday morning. On Tuesday mornings, we would catch the 6AM flight from LAX and head straight to work and school, thankfully on the same campus.

In theory this sounded like a wonderful plan, but I definitely had some anxiety as the time to execute drew nearer. All I could imagine was a flight full of serious businessmen, joined by the Kara and Amare circus.

On the morning of our first flight, Justin, my sister-in-law's husband picked us up from Chad's parent's house at 4:30AM sharp. Charlotte and Michael were out of town at the time. Just as we were locking up the house and turning off all of the lights, the driveway sprinklers came on. So right off the back, Amare and I were headed to the airport soaking wet. Not a good start by any stretch of the imagination. We get to the airport and security was a breeze. It turned out that you get VIP treatment when you have a kid in tow. So I'm already making a mental note that next time we can sleep a little longer and get to the airport a little later. The boarding process and flight go as smooth as a whistle. As we approach Phoenix, I begin to gather all of our belongings and prepare to do a mad dash off the plane, to the shuttle bus, to our car, and off to work. Because of Daylight Savings time, Phoenix was one hour ahead of Los Angeles at the time. So although we would leave LA at 6AM, and the flight was less than an hour, we would not land until just after 8. My weekly goal was to get to work between 8:30 and 9. After all, it was Tuesday, and my manager had already been kind enough to let me work remote on Mondays.

The plane lands, taxis, parks, and the seat belt signs are turned off. Everyone jumps up and prepares for the mad dash. Amare decides that this was the exact moment in which he would begin his entertainment segment.

Gentleman seated behind us: "Hey, big guy, how are you?"

Amare: "Stop that man, YOU HAVE GOT TO BE KIDDING ME!"

Me: Just shake my head and turn away, hoping the other passenger would not proceed to converse with him.

At last, there was movement ahead and we were off the plane. As we began to walk up the tunnel, Amare decides to play the stop and go game. Not a good idea when you have a plane full of business people anxious to get to their destinations. I ask him to keep walking, but he proceeds to play. I go into the momma-stretched-lips mode and ask again in a threatening tone. Again, no improvement. By now, I am just outdone with the entire scenario so before thinking I say, in a rather low tone, "Go, dammit go." Of course at this moment his hearing becomes crystal clear, as he proceeds to say, "DAMMIT, DAMMIT, Mommy you said DAMMIT." And that was the opening act of our traveling spectacles.

MY FAMILY

Kara

In March and April 2012, the UCLA ER hit a magnificent milestone, having had two months straight without a visit from Chad. This was huge progress in our eyes. Amare and I had returned to our two-week cadence of California visits. When doing my usual calendar analysis and traveling "forecasts," I discovered that Easter was on April 8 this particular year. This unfortunately meant that if we wanted to spend the holiday with Chad (which was a no brainer), there would be a three-week stint between one of our visits. Having done this length of separation before, it had already proved itself way too long and basically detrimental to our already weary mind-frames. We all needed to see each other and encourage one another. Skype and FaceTime were great interim tools, but nothing could replace the physical embrace of a son and a father or a husband and wife.

To supplement our un-ticketed weekend, Tiffany, Amare and I simply hit the road after work on Friday, March 30. We decided to surprise Chad, who thought he would not see us again until Easter weekend. I was careful not to talk to him too much that day, in order to avoid spilling the beans about our trip. He called one time while we were on the road and my response was a text message that we were in the movies and would call him later. That brought us a good deal of time, plus, given Chad's extraordinary patience, he was not the type to anxiously call again and again, unless of course there was a heart to be transplanted.

When we reached Chad's parents' home in Los Angeles, Chad's dad, Michael, answered the door and invited us in. Chad was at the kitchen table when he turned and saw his son walk in saying, "Hi, Daddy!" The look on Chad's face instantly made every mile driven beyond worth it. Once again, our family was reunited and this trip dispensed thirty-six hours of therapy that no doctor could prescribe or pharmacy could fill.

On Saturday, we walked to the LaDera Center, which is about one mile from Chad's parents' house and includes one intermediate hill. When we reached the top of the hill, Chad pumped his fist in the air celebrating the ability to accomplish something he hadn't been able to do for years. This was a beautiful moment that will never be forgotten and certainly drove home our massive appreciation for things that otherwise are easy to take for granted.

Saturday evening, we had a family dinner to celebrate Elena's birthday. We had a Washington favorite meal which was lamb, potatoes, pita bread and taziki sauce—good food, great company, awesome weekend, until the dreadful goodbye of course on Sunday. Nevertheless, the sting on this particular good-bye was much milder than the rest, for in five short days, Amare and I would be back for Easter weekend.

Easter weekend 2012 was beautiful. After work and school on Good Friday, Amare and I flew to Los Angeles. On Saturday, we packed picnic lunches and rescued Chad from cabin-fever. We drove up the coast and ended up at Zuma Beach. Despite the inherent Los Angeles challenges of traffic and beach parking, we were determined that nothing would spoil our day. We found a spot on the beach, enjoyed our picnic lunch and we were thoroughly entertained by Amare's fascination with the ocean. He instantly turned into Karate Kid, substituting wood for waves. We took family selfies on the beach with smiles bright enough to light

Every good and perfect gift is from above, coming down from the Father of the heavenly lights, who does not change like shifting shadows. James 1:17 NIV

up the world. The day was simple yet exhilarating. Could this possibly be the beginning of our new normal? It was one of those days that you never wanted to end.

Like all good things, our family beach day came to an end too. Despite the numerous times we read the signs and the fact that we had followed the other driver's que in the parking selection, we still had a "love note" from the Malibu City Police waiting for us on our windshield when we returned. At first, I was slightly offended, for how could they not know that Chad had received a heart transplant and we were simply trying to enjoy some quality time together? Obviously they did not know, but it's amazing how when you are going through life challenges, you expect the world to know and respect it. This and many other moments along our journey had raised my awareness and sensitivity to the fact that you never ever know what people are going through. So when the person on the road cuts you off for no apparent reason, do your best to simply laugh it off and say a quick prayer for them. For the truth is, no matter what faux-polished exterior that others may see, at different points in our lives, many of us are simply one incident (big or small) away from a major breakdown. So we took the "city love letter" in stride and still cherished and thanked God for such a refreshing and "normal" family day.

On Sunday, we opted out of Easter Service, shying away from a closed-in setting on arguably one of the most crowded Sundays of the year; not to mention a church setting where there was a perpetual tendency to greet and high-five your neighbor. However, in typical "Charlotte" fashion, an Easter spread was well underway at the house. She had ordered a feast from a local new favorite spot, PIPS. My aunt, uncle and cousins stopped by on the way to their own brunch. It was nice to visit with them for a while. Later, we had dinner with the family and the next morning, Amare and I returned to Phoenix.

Following Easter, we were practically on cruise control for the duration of April. Sadly, Chad missed the annual family event/carnival at PetSmart. My parents, along with Tiffany and crew, were more than

Every good and perfect gift is from above, coming down from the Father of the heavenly lights, who does not change like shifting shadows. James 1:17 NIV

happy to attend and keep Amare and me company. Realistically, this was probably for the best given the endless culinary temptations presented at this annual extravaganza. All of this was simply background noise to the countdown well underway. With each day that inched us closer to May fourth, the three-month mark since Chad's transplant, our excitement grew exponentially.

Chad

During this highly dynamic process, my entire family has been extremely supportive and helpful. My in-laws, who reside in Phoenix, visited me several times, both inside and outside of the hospital. They have prepared meals that fit into my specific dietary restrictions, as well as meals for my wife and son. They provided them with a home cooked meal at least once a week, since I do all the cooking and grocery shopping in the house. This really means a lot to me to not have to worry about if my family is eating well.

My parents have been immensely helpful during this process as well. I'm actually staying with them as I write this. They have been chauffeuring me to and from all my doctors' appointments, and unexpected ER visits. My mother has been making dietary-acceptable meals for me. My father encourages me daily, to stretch, bend, and breathe. He also attempts to keep me entertained. They may not be aware of it, but both of my parents keep me feeling optimistic and hopeful. With the joy that they feel about my recovery and current status, and the constant hugs and kisses, it has a way of permeating one's spirit. For this, and the countless other things, I thank you.

While I am forever grateful to my parents for opening their home to my family and me, and providing a comfortable, inviting, warm atmosphere, I have the utmost desire and need to return to my own home. It is my hope that my desire to go home does not come off as ungratefulness, or a foul attitude. In the event that it may, blame it on my head, and the Prednisone, not my heart.

Every good and perfect gift is from above, coming down from the Father of the heavenly lights, who does not change like shifting shadows. James 1:17 NIV

THE BEST SUMMER EVER

Chad

Home Sweet Home

After some back and forth with UCLA, I finally returned home on Saturday May 5, 2012. My biopsy from that Monday came back clean. I picked Kara up from the airport that Friday. We left Los Angeles on Saturday around 8AM and made excellent time back to Phoenix. The scenery was never so splendid and vivid. Kara and I were overjoyed at the chance to resume our normal lives together and Amare was beyond thrilled to have me back with the family. I have been getting the biggest, tightest, most spontaneous hugs from Amare, and I love it. I know that I was blessed to have been able to visit with him as much as I did, and I am grateful for that. Yet, as much as I did see him, I can't help but notice how much he has matured. Praise and thanks to God for making my wife who she is that she has been able to hold EVERYTHING down. I haven't stopped smiling since I've been home. I drive around the neighborhood frequently, just to look at it. In short, I am overjoyed to be back home. The reunion has exceeded all the expectations that I had in my head.

Real Talk

I had had some trouble with maintaining an erection for some time prior to the transplant; most likely due to my heart failure and diabetes, not to mention the great deal of stress that I was under at the time. I was prescribed a pill to help, but used it very little because even when I could get it up, I was always too tired to do anything about it. Post-transplant, there was at least a six-week moratorium on lifting, weight bearing, and strenuous exercise (i.e., sex). I think my wife and I made it four weeks, and we only made it that long because we were not in the same city. Revatio is a drug used to control hypertension in transplant patients, and it is also used to negate erectile dysfunction. I was taking 30-40 milligrams a day. This drug was coursing through my veins and I was waking up with erections. Needless to say, I wondered if it was my new and improved heart and circulatory system or the drug. I feared it was the latter, but sincerely thought it was both. It soon turned out, it was my new pump. I'm chasing my wife around the house now. Things are better than they've been in a long time.

Kara

The Best Summer Ever

Summer 2012 was by far the best summer that we had had in a long time. Every summer together had been good, but this one was extra special. The four-month post-transplant countdown was finally over and Chad returned home on Saturday, May 5. After work that Friday, I took Amare to my parents' house and then I flew to Los Angeles. Chad and I were so excited for him to be coming home that we probably could have

By entering through faith into what God has always wanted to do for us—set us right with him, make us fit for him—we have it all together with God because of our Master Jesus. And that's not all: We throw open our doors to God and discover at the same moment that he has already thrown open his door to us. We find ourselves standing where we always hoped we might stand—out in the wide open spaces of God's grace and glory, standing tall and shouting our praise.   Romans 5:1-2 MSG

driven back to Phoenix that same night. Instead, we got a few hours of sleep and loaded the car up from top to bottom the minute the sun was up. By 8AM, we had prayed with the Los Angeles Washingtons, said our good-byes and we were on the road headed back to Phoenix to reunite with our kid, our home, and our life.

We had kept Chad's return a surprise for Amare and for the first time in his life since he learned to speak, the kid was actually at a loss for words when Chad rang the doorbell. He was so overjoyed for Daddy to be home. That night, there was a fight party (Mayweather vs. Pacquiao) at my sister's house, and everyone was excited to see Chad. However, Amare was adamant about staying home with just the three of us and watching a movie together. This was such a special time for our family. I remember the next morning at church, I could not stop the tears of joy from falling because it felt so surreal for Chad to be back. We went out to eat afterwards with my sister Tiffany and her family. It was like old times and it was beyond amazing.

Next up was Mother's Day. This year, we all agreed to a low-key holiday so we did our own thing. Chad, Amare and I skipped church, again for fear of the massive crowd. We went to lunch and a movie and just relaxed at home for the day—another great day just spending time together under one roof, our roof.

Two weeks later was Memorial Day. This was always a special weekend because it was Chad's birthday weekend. I like to celebrate all birthdays, but I always made sure that we went out of our way to celebrate Chad's birthday. Although we never verbalized it, I think our close family and friends just naturally understood that Chad's birthday was a big deal. Anyone who had survived everything that he had been through and lived another year to tell it, had a million and one reasons to celebrate. So celebrate is what we did. Chad's 35th birthday festivities consisted of Friday night dinner and bowling at Dave & Buster's with

By entering through faith into what God has always wanted to do for us—set us right with him, make us fit for him—we have it all together with God because of our Master Jesus. And that's not all: We throw open our doors to God and discover at the same moment that he has already thrown open his door to us. We find ourselves standing where we always hoped we might stand—out in the wide open spaces of God's grace and glory, standing tall and shouting our praise. Romans 5:1-2 MSG

just the three of us, a Saturday afternoon gathering/game night at our house with close friends and family, a couples' dinner at Fleming's Steakhouse that Sunday with my two sisters and their husbands, and a relaxing Memorial Day with a traditional birthday visit to Baskin & Robbins. After ice cream, Chad had to hit the road again, hitching a ride to Los Angeles with my sister Robyn and family for a routine check-up at UCLA that week.

Chad

Dream Interrupted

The week of May 27 brought with it a minor unsuspected setback. On May 31, I went to UCLA for both an ICD (Implantable Cardioverter Defibrillator) removal consultation and my monthly clinic visit. Around 5PM, I got a call from my transplant coordinator asking me to report to the emergency room. My tests results had revealed a low white blood cell count, along with leukocytes and nutrafills that were off kilter. In short, I was neutropenic, which in essence meant that I had an infection, or at least signs of one. Once in the ER, I was given an injection of Neupogen, an intravenous broad spectrum antibiotic used to boost white blood cells. I was also given additional antibiotics to fight the infection. The ICD extraction that was scheduled to take place on June first was cancelled. The number one priority now was to identify the type of infection and fight to stop it. I was really looking forward to bidding a farewell to the excess piece of equipment still lodged in my abdomen. However, with the presence of infection, it was decided not to proceed with the surgery until my white blood cell count had been stabilized for several weeks. I remained hopeful that the surgery would take place during my next scheduled clinic visit in Los Angeles.

By entering through faith into what God has always wanted to do for us—set us right with him, make us fit for him—we have it all together with God because of our Master Jesus. And that's not all: We throw open our doors to God and discover at the same moment that he has already thrown open his door to us. We find ourselves standing where we always hoped we might stand—out in the wide open spaces of God's grace and glory, standing tall and shouting our praise. Romans 5:1-2 MSG

Kara

Dream Continued

Despite Chad's brief medical hiccup that extended his post Memorial Day clinic visit to UCLA, the man of mine and Amare's dreams made it home for Father's Day! On the actual holiday, the ladies in our family cooked for the men. Along with their plates, we served up complimentary toasts to our spouses, acknowledging them as awesome fathers, husbands and men of God.

Next up was the Fourth of July, which was another fabulous weekend for us because we got married on July 5, 2003. We celebrated the fourth at Tiffany and Shawn's house. My Aunt Adrienne and Uncle Brandon were in town and we had a great time talking and laughing with everyone that day, and watching the fireworks that evening. Things were really starting to feel normal again. The 4th fell in the middle of the week that year so the following day was a work day. That weekend, Chad and I went to Fleming's Steakhouse to celebrate our 9th wedding anniversary. I was so excited about how awesome he looked that I could not resist telling our waitress, "I bet you would never guess that he just had a heart transplant."

Later that July, we went to San Diego to celebrate my Aunt Kathryn's 90th birthday. She looked absolutely amazing, and again, it was just so great to be away from the hospital scene, done with the waiting game, and able to participate in family events again. We were back to living and had a whole newfound appreciation for the simple days. In August, we did our annual staycation at the Cibola Vista Resort to celebrate Amare's birthday. This year's festivities consisted of Dave & Buster's, a Cerreta Candy Company Factory Tour, the Play Factory (a children's jump

By entering through faith into what God has always wanted to do for us—set us right with him, make us fit for him—we have it all together with God because of our Master Jesus. And that's not all: We throw open our doors to God and discover at the same moment that he has already thrown open his door to us. We find ourselves standing where we always hoped we might stand—out in the wide open spaces of God's grace and glory, standing tall and shouting our praise. Romans 5:1-2 MSG

center), *Brave* (the movie), and of course a family birthday/pool party at the local resort that Saturday.

Two weeks later, we were headed to Hawaii for the trip of a lifetime. Chad, Amare and I would embark upon our first, and unbeknownst to us, last tropical vacation as a family. We left for Hawaii on Tuesday, August 28 and we were scheduled to spend four nights in Oahu and six nights in Kauai. Over the last eight months, we had boarded countless flights to Los Angeles and each time, we had been excited to see Chad of course, but less than thrilled about the overall journey. This trip to the airport however, was quite different. Not only were the three of us flying together, but instead of a medically purposed trip, we were headed to paradise! Excitement does not even begin to describe our emotions surrounding this vacation.

My mom picked us up at the crack of dawn that Tuesday morning and before we knew it, we were boarding a Hawaiian Airlines aircraft and heading towards the land of beautiful beaches, luxurious palm trees and delectable pineapples. Between the LeapPad, iPad and general toys, Amare who was a frequent flyer by now, was a total rockstar throughout our six-hour flight. Upon landing in Oahu and retrieving our luggage, we were greeted with leis by our shuttle driver. Once on the shuttle and headed to our hotel, we had a brief interruption that almost brought our paradise experience to a screeching halt. Chad received a phone call from UCLA regarding his labs. My heart immediately sank and our entire trip flashed right before our eyes. We hadn't even left the Honolulu Airport yet, and were we about to find ourselves heading back to Phoenix already? Thankfully, no, they had not received Chad's last lab report and just wanted to be sure that he had completed them before leaving. Chad assured the nurse that he had and the call ended with her telling him to enjoy his trip. Whew, close call, but paradise was still on our horizon!

By entering through faith into what God has always wanted to do for us—set us right with him, make us fit for him—we have it all together with God because of our Master Jesus. And that's not all: We throw open our doors to God and discover at the same moment that he has already thrown open his door to us. We find ourselves standing where we always hoped we might stand—out in the wide open spaces of God's grace and glory, standing tall and shouting our praise.   Romans 5:1-2 MSG

While in Oahu, we visited the Pearl Harbor and Punchbowl Cemetery. We spent one entire day on a city bus adventure to a North Shore beach that had been ranked high for its kid-friendly atmosphere and really cool tide pools. The atmosphere was in fact family-oriented and inviting, and we even ran into a lady that recognized Amare from the Phoenix flight over and commended us on his flying behavior. We couldn't believe how small a world that we would cross paths again with someone clear across town from where we were staying. After a long and rather tiring trek along the shoreline in hunt of the tide pool, Chad eventually had had enough and called the search off. Definitely for the best, since our wait for the city bus was about five times longer than we anticipated, and long outlived the shaved ice that we had gotten to pacify us in the interim.

The next day, we stayed local in Waikiki and visited the many shops along the main drag. We had no idea that Waikiki was like the Rodeo Drive of Honolulu. One of the shops had a live Teddy Bear outside that tourist could take pictures with. Somehow, our darling four-year-old quickly discovered that it was a costume and each time the bear leaned in for a picture, Amare would twist the headpiece around on the Teddy Bear's neck. After multiple attempts, we gave up on the picture and I'm positive the bear was happy to see us go. Although we tried to keep a poker face with Amare, Chad and I laughed about this scene for days.

One evening, we had reservations at the Oceanarium Restaurant inside the Pacific Beach Hotel. The restaurant is built around a towering aquarium with almost 400 fish, representing 70 different species on display. Thankfully, our table was right against the glass display, which enhanced our dining experience even more. Amare was mesmerized and really got a kick out of the mermaid feeding the live stingrays. This was definitely a unique dining experience that we would look back on fondly for years to come.

By entering through faith into what God has always wanted to do for us—set us right with him, make us fit for him—we have it all together with God because of our Master Jesus. And that's not all: We throw open our doors to God and discover at the same moment that he has already thrown open his door to us. We find ourselves standing where we always hoped we might stand—out in the wide open spaces of God's grace and glory, standing tall and shouting our praise. Romans 5:1-2 MSG

For our last full day in Oahu, we decided to rent a car and visit the Dole Pineapple Plantation, and also headed back to the North Shore for a shaved ice spot that we were instructed to not miss. Both destinations were a huge hit. Pineapple is absolutely my favorite fruit, so I was like a kid in a candy shop from the moment we parked the car. Chad just shook his head as I practically skipped from the parking lot to the entrance. We had arrived just as they opened for the day, and were amongst some of the first guests to enter. We took a train ride tour through the pineapple fields, shopped in the gift-shop and indulged in a fresh Dole Pineapple Whipped Ice Cream Sundae, topped with fresh pineapple chunks. I was in pineapple heaven and experienced mild separation anxiety as our plantation visit came to an end.

We spent the next couple of hours at another highly recommended North Shore beach, watching Amare ride the baby waves along the kid-friendly shore. We also snorkeled as a family around a beautiful lagoon. Before leaving the North Shore, we stopped for Matsumoto's Shaved Ice. Our friend, Tara, had strongly recommended that we not leave the island without tasting this stuff and it certainly did not disappoint. Between that delightful creation and my unforgettable pineapple delicacy, I was ready to establish residency on the island. But instead, we headed to Kauai the next afternoon for the second leg of our trip. The attendant at our Waikiki hotel was sad to see Amare go, so she showered him with gifts including a cute beach backpack, sand toys, a Lorax water bottle, and chocolate candy. Chad and I suddenly felt like we were guests just tagging along on Amare's vacation.

After a quick thirty-minute flight, we found ourselves on the rustic yet beautiful island of Kauai. Although Oahu had brought great adventures, we were anxious to start the more relaxing leg of our trip. After we claimed our luggage and picked up the rental car, we headed to our beach vacation rental in Poipu on Kauai's South Shore. Amare was

By entering through faith into what God has always wanted to do for us—set us right with him, make us fit for him—we have it all together with God because of our Master Jesus. And that's not all: We throw open our doors to God and discover at the same moment that he has already thrown open his door to us. We find ourselves standing where we always hoped we might stand—out in the wide open spaces of God's grace and glory, standing tall and shouting our praise. Romans 5:1-2 MSG

elated to learn that he would have his very own room in the two bedroom condo that we had rented. Having shared a quaint hotel room for four nights in Oahu, Chad and I were also thrilled to get some privacy of our own.

In addition to the "cozy" accommodations in Waikiki, we'd also had our share of eating out and were long overdue for a home-cooked meal. Thankfully, we had invited the perfect person along to cook it, Chef Chad himself! Our first mission in Kauai would be Costco, but for that evening, we settled on take-out from a local pizza parlor. While waiting for our food, we witnessed our first Hawaiian rainbow and it was gorgeous.

The next morning, we lounged around for a bit and then set out on our quest for groceries. Since we seemed to have such a good rapport (via email) with the landlord of the condo that we were renting, we had pre-arranged a lunch meeting with him at Costco just to say hi and formally meet. He was a Hawaiian native and we enjoyed chatting with him for a while, but then it was time to get down to business and get our groceries. While I was busy securing Hawaiian Rum and POG (Passion Orange Guava) Juice, Chad had planned and shopped for our entire week of meals.

For the rest of the day, we just relaxed around the condo. We were steps away from the ocean, but it was not a safe area to actually swim in. It was a rocky shoreline where the waves were constantly crashing. We saw countless sea turtles that appeared larger than life. We had a blast hanging by the pool that afternoon, and after a while, Chef Chad took his post. When Amare and I came in for dinner, Chad had prepared an absolutely delicious mango chicken dish with accompanying vegetables. The three of us toasted to our Hawaiian Vacation and the rest of the evening was history.

By entering through faith into what God has always wanted to do for us—set us right with him, make us fit for him—we have it all together with God because of our Master Jesus. And that's not all: We throw open our doors to God and discover at the same moment that he has already thrown open his door to us. We find ourselves standing where we always hoped we might stand—out in the wide open spaces of God's grace and glory, standing tall and shouting our praise. Romans 5:1-2 MSG

While in Kauai, we enjoyed a Luau, although opting out of the dinner portion as to not risk Chad's health. Amare had seen a video of the dancers in the hotel lobby back in Oahu, so we thought it would be cool to take him to a live show. Although the show was a bit lengthy for all of us, it was nice to experience it together. We also went on a Sunset Dinner Cruise, where we discovered that Amare suffers from mild motion-sickness, but again, it was an overall pleasant experience together. We found a few waterfalls, which never cease to amaze me. One day, Chad gave me the pleasure of an afternoon at the beach by myself. I snorkeled, read a book, and just allowed myself to bask in pure paradise. We, of course, had family beach time as well where we built sand castles, played in the water, and marveled at the sea-life.

On our last day in Kauai, we had to check out of the condo that morning, but were scheduled for a red-eye flight home. We had breakfast in the condo prior to checking out, and then sought after what we had heard to be the best shaved ice on the island. JoJo's Shaved Ice was indeed the best. The Mac Nut Ice Cream buried at the bottom of their shaved ice creations, was out of this world! I went back to Phoenix on a serious hunt for that stuff.

After enjoying our delicious treats on the side of JoJo's hut, we headed to Waimea Canyon, which was also known as the Grand Canyon of the Pacific. This place provided striking beauty from every angle. I almost lost my mind when we discovered a stream of water amongst an orangish clay-like area, on top of a mountain overlooking the ocean in the far distance. It was one of those moments where you would have had to be blind in order to deny God's existence. Needless to say, we took quite a few pictures in this State Park, and each time I got in the car to drive away, another view would catch my eye and beckon me to park again. Thank God, patience was one of Chad's greatest virtues, as he simply shook his head each time I jumped out of the car.

By entering through faith into what God has always wanted to do for us—set us right with him, make us fit for him—we have it all together with God because of our Master Jesus. And that's not all: We throw open our doors to God and discover at the same moment that he has already thrown open his door to us. We find ourselves standing where we always hoped we might stand—out in the wide open spaces of God's grace and glory, standing tall and shouting our praise. Romans 5:1-2 MSG

When we left Waimea Canyon, we still had ample time before our flight so we stopped at the Kauai Coffee Company, which we were randomly passing by. We took a tour through the grounds learning about the different types of coffee beans, we sampled multiple flavors of coffee and then we spent a small fortune in their gift shop securing souvenirs and treats for ourselves and our loved ones back at home. From the Kauai Coffee Company, our 360-degree tour around the island sadly inched us closer to the airport and the conclusion of our trip. We stopped for dinner at a burger place just outside of the airport and from there, we returned the rental car and kissed paradise good-bye.

Our Hawaiian family vacation was absolutely amazing and Amare still talks about the trip to this day. Although there was debate about whether or not we should travel yet, the staff at UCLA did not have a problem with Chad traveling and were very supportive of him not living in a bubble. In hindsight, I thank God that we took the trip and had that incredible time together as a family. Certainly, only God had the wisdom and foresight to know that we would need those happy memories to reflect on during the turbulent days that were just around the corner.

The instant we touched down in Phoenix, our days of aloha and mahalo were over. We returned on a red-eye flight early Saturday morning and while Amare and Chad slept that afternoon, I began my preparations for a new opportunity at PetSmart. I was scheduled to interview with the Marketing Finance Department that week. I was also traveling for work the following Tuesday, returning on Thursday, the same day that Chad and Shawn were headed to a Men's Church Retreat in Tucson. Our Hawaiian pace of life was a distant memory. Two weeks after our Hawaiian vacation, Chad flew to California for his routine check-up at UCLA. It was then that the best summer ever, quickly spiraled into the worst nightmare imaginable...

By entering through faith into what God has always wanted to do for us—set us right with him, make us fit for him—we have it all together with God because of our Master Jesus. And that's not all: We throw open our doors to God and discover at the same moment that he has already thrown open his door to us. We find ourselves standing where we always hoped we might stand—out in the wide open spaces of God's grace and glory, standing tall and shouting our praise. Romans 5:1-2 MSG

FREE FALL

Kara

Back in 2008 when the entire heart transplant journey was initiated, we were warned that it would be the ride of our lives. Between 2008 and mid-2012, we were strapped in tight and for the most part always on the lookout for the next sharp turn. When Chad returned to Phoenix on May 5, 2012, we were overjoyed and consumed with excitement. We felt as if we were on top of the world and there was no stopping us. In our minds, we had survived the worst of the worst and there was nothing that we couldn't handle, or so we thought. I remember Robyn asking me, "So, you all made it through, how does it feel?" I didn't even have the words to convey the pure triumph that we experienced. It felt as though we were living in a fairytale and life simply could not have been better at the time. However, what happened next was far from a Disney ending.

Chad

On Monday, September 24, I went to Los Angeles for a clinic visit. Due to the results from my routine tests, it was decided that I should be admitted to the hospital for rejection. I was admitted via the ER because there were no beds available in the hospital. I was subjected to a rather rough right heart catheterization and biopsy. I went up to recovery following the procedure. While in the hospital I was given three large doses of Solumedrol to help manipulate my immune system. Next, I underwent three days of plasmapheresis.

Kara

Plasmapheresis unfortunately became an integral part of Chad's routine treatments. It is the process where the liquid in one's blood (also known as plasma), is separated from the cells. Chad was considered in rejection status because his plasma contained antibodies that were attacking his immune system. The goal of the plasmapheresis treatments was to substitute the infected plasma with good plasma. The treatments typically left Chad feeling nauseous and weak, but we remained hopeful that it would solve our problems and morph our nightmare back into the fairytale that we were still growing accustomed to.

Chad was released later that week with two follow-up appointments scheduled over the next two weeks. After his check-up appointment on Wednesday, October 3, Chad was clear until his next appointment the following Wednesday. Much to our excitement, Chad flew home to Phoenix on Thursday, October 4 and surprised the rest of our family at my mom's birthday celebration on Saturday, October 6. It was an enjoyable day and it felt amazing for Chad to be there with us, but something did not feel quite right. Chad's recent bout with rejection and his looming return trip to Los Angeles just seemed to taunt the two of us all weekend like an elephant rain cloud hovering over an otherwise sunny day.

The evening before Chad was to return to Los Angeles (Tuesday, October 9, 2012), was probably the eeriest night of our entire marriage. Chad was pretty low on energy and did not feel well overall. After putting Amare to bed, I remember him sitting in Amare's room on his

A healthy spirit conquers adversity, but what can you do when the spirit is crushed?
Proverbs 18:14 MSG

basketball bean bag for what seemed like hours. Chad would always hang out with Amare until he was fast asleep. But on that particular night, Chad seemed to linger longer than usual. Looking back now, it was almost as if Chad knew that it would be the last time he tucked his son in at home. The following afternoon, I took Chad to the airport and the same eerie feeling from the prior evening, still lurked throughout our curbside good-bye. Once back on the freeway, my subconscious fears turned into unstoppable tears. Where in the world were we headed next on this roller-coaster called life?

Chad was admitted back into UCLA Medical Center the very next day. My father-in-law called me at work with the news. My stomach was in knots and I found it extremely difficult not to panic. Meanwhile, I had been fortunate to get the Marketing Finance Analyst position that I had recently interviewed for. I was very excited about the new opportunity and had purposely not gone out for positions earlier, trying to give time for Chad to receive his new heart and my personal life to be more stable. Just when I thought the coast was clear, the thick fog was rolling in and my visibility for hope was less than optimal. I had a training meeting in exactly thirty minutes and the knots in my stomach had upgraded themselves to almost debilitating. I let my co-worker Kristen know that I needed to head across the street to Target and secure some type of remedy for my stomach. The second that my car was parked in the Target parking lot, I began to cry hysterically. I could not for the life of me grasp the notion that we had endured years of uncertainty and finally reached our mountain-top joyous position, only to be knocked back down to what felt like lower than square one. We had literally no idea what the step after rejection looked like. Before I could go into Target, I called my friend, Tracey, and she gave me the tough love encouragement that I needed at that moment. After hanging up with her, I knew what I had to do. I had to maintain face for Amare, continue to be a strong encouraging wife for Chad and try not to lose my mind or my job in the meantime. These were consistently my marching orders throughout our entire journey, but somehow I had

A healthy spirit conquers adversity, but what can you do when the spirit is crushed?
Proverbs 18:14 MSG

allowed myself to falsely believe that their intensity had been decreased with our recent triumph.

At this point, I had missed the scheduled training meeting but my co-worker understood. Before heading back into work, I called my college girlfriend's mom, Ms. Stephens. She was a serious prayer warrior and I was so grateful when she answered on the first ring. I immediately blurted out what was going on and she prayed for Chad and all of us. She too offered reassuring words and encouragement and I was able to return to work in peace. Yes, our world was no doubt falling apart once again, but God was still on the throne and more than capable of putting our lives back together again.

A healthy spirit conquers adversity, but what can you do when the spirit is crushed?
Proverbs 18:14 MSG

Amare's Anecdotes #3

Flight Etiquette

Just as we were beginning our second season of separation and flying back and forth to visit Chad, Amare and I had achieved A-List status with Southwest Airlines. This came with a number of benefits which included being automatically checked into our flights three days ahead of time. Gone were the days of setting a reminder to log in a few minutes early and click check-in the second the 24 hour period began. This also meant that we were always in the first group of people to get on the plane, granting us first dibs on any seats.

By now we had our program down to a tee. While boarding the plane, we would inquire if it was a full flight or not. If it was, then I sat in the aisle seat and Amare sat in the middle. If it wasn't, this meant Amare could sit by the window, I still sat in the aisle seat, and we would leave stuff in the middle seat until everyone was onboard.

Well on one Friday evening, for whatever reason I think I knew the flight was full but Amare had somehow missed the memo. A lady walked up and asked if the third seat was occupied? At that exact moment, it was like an imaginary bullhorn had appeared and Amare immediately began asking, "IS IT A FULL FLIGHT? IS IT A FULL FLIGHT?" He may as well have told the lady, go find another seat. And of course I was left to pick up the awkward pieces.

LIVING IN A FISHBOWL

Kara

It had been five short months since Chad had relocated back to Phoenix from Los Angeles. Within those five months, we had celebrated Chad's 35th birthday, our 9th Wedding anniversary, Amare's 4th birthday, and the overall magnificent privilege of being reunited as a family of three in our own home. After a whirlwind of festivities, our hopes and dreams for establishing our "new normal," were instantly shattered. Chad was back in LA, back in the hospital and the plasmapheresis treatments were not yielding the immediate results that the doctors were hoping for. We began to receive reports like, "Worst-case scenario, we'll have to just get you another heart."

Clearly, things were not going well and we all seemed to be struggling with this huge disappointment and set-back. I personally was having a very hard time finding positive motivation to stand strong at the starting line AGAIN. Tensions were on the rise and unfortunately, relationships were in jeopardy. We were all in need of major prayer. Chad and I continued to do what we seemed to do best, which was protect each other and encourage one another. We discussed our faith in God and elevated our resolve to trust Him even more. There was no doubt that we had had the wind knocked out of us, but we still believed that with God, nothing was impossible and together, we could conquer anything.

Chad's parents had a previously scheduled trip and left town on Wednesday, October 17, planning to return on Monday, October 29. Chad remained in the hospital and had received a series of treatments to address his declining heart function. On Friday, October 19, Amare and I flew to Los Angeles and Chad was released from the hospital the following day. With all of the back and forth between Phoenix, Los Angeles, and the hospital ER, Chad understandably expressed concerns about even leaving the hospital and giving up his secured room. The staff reassured him that he seemed to be on the mend and if not, he would be welcomed back. At this point, the hospital discharges were inherently becoming less and less celebratory and more and more stressful. It was almost as if we had begun to subconsciously hold our breath and hope like crazy that "this time," everything would be okay. Nevertheless, by late Saturday afternoon, Chad was discharged and we were headed to his parents' house with an agenda for the rest of the weekend that exclusively consisted of relaxing, regrouping and spending quality time together as a family.

At some point during the night on Sunday, Chad woke up short of breath, and for the first time during this entire journey, he openly expressed his anger and frustration. As he struggled to get comfortable and find a viable position, he threw his pillow across the room and sat up completely. Our return trip to the hospital was imminent and it felt as though our fate was spiraling out of control. Early Monday morning (October 22), we called the hospital and subsequently made arrangements for Amare to spend the day with Elena. Chad and I headed back to the ER for a series of tests, evaluations and inevitable readmission. By Monday afternoon, Chad was settled back into the same hospital room that he had been reluctant to leave in the first place. Amare was dropped off to spend some time with his daddy before we headed

---

We have troubles all around us, but we are not defeated. We do not know what to do, but we do not give up. We are persecuted, but God does not leave us. We are hurt sometimes, but we are not destroyed. 2 Corinthians 4:8-9 ICB

back to Phoenix later that evening. Chad was in good hands, amongst some of his favorite nurses, and with his parents out of town, Elena would check in on him until Amare and I returned the following weekend.

On Tuesday, October 23, I returned to work and allowed myself to be totally consumed by my new position. I desperately needed to escape my personal life, if only for eight hours at a time. Naturally, I checked in with Chad throughout the day and for the duration of the week, the consensus amongst the doctors was that his case was up for discussion and we would be informed once the experts in the field had determined the next best course of action.

On Friday, October 26, Amare and I drove to Los Angeles after a half day at work and school. It had become abundantly clear to me that Chad would be in Los Angeles for much longer than we planned, so having our own car in town would be useful. We made great timing on the road and we were even spared from the dreadful LA traffic. Chad seemed to be in good spirits when we spoke on the phone and I couldn't wait to see him. Upon arriving at the hospital and settling in for our evening visit, there did not seem to be any major developments that Chad had to share with me. Around 6PM, I saw Dr. DuBois' at the nurses' station as I was heading down for dinner. I asked him if he would be around long enough for me to grab a bite to eat from the cafeteria and come back up. He responded in his consistently polite manner, "Yes by all means, please get some food before I talk to you." Hmmm, I thought that was a rather odd statement but tried not to read too much into it. However, by the time I reached the cafeteria my stomach had launched the knots that had become all too familiar so I just grabbed some soup for myself and pasta for Amare and headed back up.

Shortly after I finished eating, Dr. DuBois', accompanied by a medical assistant that we had not met, entered Chad's room. Amare immediately jumped up and went into interview mode. "What is your name?" he asked the doctor. Dr. DuBois' introduced himself to Amare

We have troubles all around us, but we are not defeated. We do not know what to do, but we do not give up. We are persecuted, but God does not leave us. We are hurt sometimes, but we are not destroyed. 2 Corinthians 4:8-9 ICB

as Winston (his first name), and from that moment on, their friendship flourished. Unfortunately, though, the conversation took a turn for the worst after that. Dr. DuBois' went on to recap to me what had apparently been explained to Chad earlier in the day, but Chad had not wanted to stress me out on the road. In short, the rejection treatments for his current heart were not working and the doctors had explored all options. Because of Chad's elevated level of antibodies, he was not eligible to be listed for another heart transplant at this time. The next step for Chad was looking like a totally artificial heart.

I was speechless. Through the Mayo Clinic support group, we had heard of patients who had used the artificial heart (also known as "Big Blue"), as a bridge to their heart transplant. Chad had even met and spoke with some of these patients. But, when Chad received his first transplanted heart, I was actually super-relieved that we had been able to skip this step in the process. Nevertheless, here we were just nine short months later. Chad seemed unmoved by this news and instead focused on how grateful he was to have participated in the Mayo Clinic support group. His angle was that, at least he was familiar with the entire concept of the artificial heart and this wasn't the first of him hearing about it period.

At this point my brain was unable to further process the words coming out of Dr. DuBois' mouth so I simply wrote down everything he said so that I could review and report back to the family later. Dr. DuBois' went on to explain all that needed to happen both with examinations and insurance clearance before the surgery would be a definite go. Two things that did resonate in my brain were the fact that they were looking to do this operation as early as Monday, October 29, three days away, and this would be the first artificial heart ever implanted at UCLA. Was he (Dr. DuBois') serious? Was God serious? Was this really happening?

Dr. DuBois' ended the conversation by saying that he had been with us from day one of our UCLA journey and he reassured us that he would

---

We have troubles all around us, but we are not defeated. We do not know what to do, but we do not give up. We are persecuted, but God does not leave us. We are hurt sometimes, but we are not destroyed. 2 Corinthians 4:8-9 ICB

continue to be there with us. He gave us his cell phone number and insisted that we not hesitate to call at any time should we think of questions or have concerns that we would like to discuss with him. After speaking further with Chad and very slowly beginning to process the latest development, Amare and I called it a night and headed to the Washingtons' for what would likely be a sleepless night. I called Robyn and delivered the news in an almost trancelike state. She immediately drove down from Orange County and spent the night with Amare and me. At this point, I was numb to everything.

Throughout the weekend, I kept my strong face on for Chad but in his absence, my questions were: How in the world could this be happening? Why did God see fit for us to go through this? Was this some type of sick joke? What had we done to deserve this? Of course, Chad's position was ever positive and encouraging. I would likely be naive to think that Chad was void of his own concerns, but even as he faced this frightful predicament, he in his warrior frame of mind presented a polished and confident persona that no one could fathom. As we sat around the hospital room on Saturday evening with family, he even joked about a punch card and how he should be entitled to at least one free operation by now. The truth of the matter was that Chad ultimately saw himself as a medical pioneer whose case could be used to help others in the future. He had already proclaimed to me his aspirations to become an ambassador in this arena and use his story to encourage and motivate others struggling with medical challenges.

Saturday had come and gone and now Sunday was the only thing standing between Chad and an artificial heart. For the entire day, Chad, Amare and I hung out at the hospital playing games, watching movies, and fielding phone calls and visits from well-wishers and prayer warriors. Late Sunday afternoon, I needed to step away from the hospital to get some fresh air, gather my thoughts and calm my nerves. While Robyn was at the hospital with Chad and Amare, I went to Chad's parents' house for a quick shower, Ross for a new waiting room toy for Amare,

We have troubles all around us, but we are not defeated. We do not know what to do, but we do not give up. We are persecuted, but God does not leave us. We are hurt sometimes, but we are not destroyed. 2 Corinthians 4:8-9 ICB

and last but certainly not least, the infamous pre-surgery meal for Chad. A surgery of this magnitude called for an equally epic meal. After an extremely tedious and thorough online analysis, Chad landed on a pasta dish from Compari's Pizza & Italian. As we settled in for the "night before surgery" hospital sleepover, Pastor Rogers from First Church of God where I grew up, stopped by to pray for Chad. Always amazed by Chad's demeanor, Pastor Rogers proceeded to pray a prayer of healing and peace over all of us and we were grateful for his visit.

As the clock ticked closer and closer to the next day, my anxiety levels began to play the elevation game. At one point, around 10PM, the nurses retrieved the measurement that was being gathered from the Swan Getz Catheter in Chad's neck and they indicated that the numbers were improving. The tool was basically a right-heart catheterization used to monitor the heart function and blood flow. A light-bulb in my head immediately went off and I couldn't help but think that if the numbers were improving, perhaps Chad did not need this artificial heart in the first place. There was no way that I could not pose the question, so naturally we decided to give Dr. DuBois' a ring. After all, he had assured us that we could call anytime so that is exactly what we did. He answered right away and I explained the nurses' report and raised our questions. Dr. DuBois' very politely and thoroughly explained to me that those numbers were only a fraction of everything being monitored and that Chad was in fact very ill and limited in his options regarding next steps. I hung up disappointed that there had not been a miraculous healing, yet relieved that we had at least asked and would not have to wonder. I also felt reassured that this was the right next step for Chad.

The next morning, as the sun broke through the darkness of the night, I woke up with a constant prayer on my heart. "Lord, please let Chad survive yet another surgery. Please do not let this be the one that takes him from us." My nerves were like a bag of popcorn with kernels exploding left and right. On the inside, I was a catastrophe waiting to happen, but on the outside, I tried to keep a calm and confident

---

We have troubles all around us, but we are not defeated. We do not know what to do, but we do not give up. We are persecuted, but God does not leave us. We are hurt sometimes, but we are not destroyed. 2 Corinthians 4:8-9 ICB

demeanor for both Chad and Amare. Thank God that my parents, Robyn and Chad's Aunt Karen arrived bright and early to support us. I do not know how long I would have been able to hold it together alone.

The morning started like most pre-op mornings start, with a wash down for Chad at the crack of dawn, followed by multiple visits from various nurses and doctors. However, this particular operation came with a whole new wave of visits. Given that this was the first artificial heart to be implanted at UCLA, the research team was all over it. There was question after question and survey after survey being thrown at Chad, and he of course was being a very good sport about the entire process. However, for me, the walls seemed to be closing in more and more with each moment that passed. Thankfully, Clair, one of our favorite CTU (Cardiac Thoracic Unit) nurses was assigned to us for yet another pivotal day. We were very grateful to have a familiar face in our corner. As they were switching out the monitors in preparation to transport Chad to the OR, he was still being asked questions by one of the VAD (Ventricular Assist Device) coordinators. Something clicked inside of me and I had had enough. There was no way that Chad was heading to the operating room before we prayed so I finally asked the device representative if we could have a moment as a family and he immediately excused himself. My mom prayed a powerful prayer asking that God cover Chad and guide every person and tool that came near him, and she also informed Satan that he might as well go back to hell where he belonged because he would have no victory that day.

Thankfully, they allowed us to escort Chad down to the operating room. There, we met Dr. Hart, who would be performing the surgery, as well as the instructing surgeon Dr. Walsh, who is known worldwide as the total artificial heart pioneer. Amare looked them both in the eye and introduced himself. "I am Amare and this is my dad!" he proudly said. We all expressed our gratitude and felt confident that Chad was in great hands. Yet, needless to say, we were still in for a very long, extremely anxious, highly stressful day of waiting.

We have troubles all around us, but we are not defeated. We do not know what to do, but we do not give up. We are persecuted, but God does not leave us. We are hurt sometimes, but we are not destroyed. 2 Corinthians 4:8-9 ICB

As we settled into the waiting room and claimed our family oasis for the day, as present as I tried to be amongst the family and friends that had joined us in waiting, my mind constantly reverted back to Chad and the overwhelming magnitude of this situation. My constant prayer remained, "Lord, please let Chad survive yet another surgery. Please do not let this be the one that takes him from us." At some point, I finally realized the primary source of my anxiety on this particular day. The first heart transplant had been a tremendous gift and what we thought was a victorious culmination of a very long journey. With this operation however, the artificial heart was a temporary fix, a bridge in fact to carry Chad over to another major surgery. This was not the end, but in fact the beginning of a very long and widely unknown road. How in the world could this be our life? What exactly was God's purpose in putting us through this trial? The lack of immediate answers to my questions was such a major source of frustration for me that before I knew it, red hot tears were running down my face. It was just the first of many silent and sporadic cries for the day. I'm so grateful my family was versed enough to allow me my space in those moments, not make a big deal and just keep Amare occupied.

We got occasional updates throughout the day and things seemed to be going well and definitely headed in the right direction. As the afternoon got later and later, we finally convinced my parents to go ahead and get on the road headed back to Phoenix with Amare. Chad's parents had arrived back into town that morning and joined in the waiting, along with a host of other friends and relatives as well. Having been all too familiar with days like this, we all knew that it would be well into the night before we actually laid eyes on Chad.

Sure enough, around 8PM, we received an update that the surgery was complete, Chad was in recovery, and we could head up to the waiting room outside of the unit and possibly see him in an hour or so. We said our good-nights to some of the group and the rest of us headed up. When we finally did have an opportunity to go back and see Chad, it was

We have troubles all around us, but we are not defeated. We do not know what to do, but we do not give up. We are persecuted, but God does not leave us. We are hurt sometimes, but we are not destroyed. 2 Corinthians 4:8-9 ICB

a frightening vision at best. They were literally uncovering his face and body from under what looked to be an air-mattress, and Chad was extremely swollen. The number of machines and hospital staff was overwhelming and I knew I needed to excuse myself as quickly as possible. Dr. DuBois' was pacing outside of Chad's room intensely watching the staff's every move. I was confident that they were all over the entire case and clearly, it was best I give them space. I just made sure that the nurses knew I would be in the waiting room just outside the door should anything whatsoever come up.

After a very long day of traveling and waiting, Chad's parents needed to go home and get some rest. Thank God, my angel Jessica joined me at the hospital that evening as the hallways could get pretty scary once everyone went home. I will never forget the hysterical and perfectly timed laugh I got that evening when Jessica changed into her nightwear, which so happened to be an adult onesie in leopard print. I could not have asked for a better best friend in that very moment. This was a prime example of the kind of totally selfless gestures that kept Chad and me going on this journey. Though the road seemed unending and we were often weary, we were never ever alone.

Jessica and I survived the night in the uncompromising waiting room accommodations, and bright and early the next day, I could not wait to see Chad. As I headed back to his room mentally prepping myself to be strong, my eyes instantly saw a miracle. Chad was propped up in his hospital bed, wide awake, glasses on and everything. Still on the breathing tube, he was clearly trying to express his discomfort to the nursing team of three for the day. He kept gagging and seemed frustrated. The nursing team was in the middle of discussing medication options to help with the gagging when an extremely high-energy and outspoken doctor came in to assess the situation. He asked the nurses for a status report and without hesitation said in a very obvious manner, "Take the tube out." Chad immediately nodded his head and began clapping his hands. What normally took multiple positive encounters to

We have troubles all around us, but we are not defeated. We do not know what to do, but we do not give up. We are persecuted, but God does not leave us. We are hurt sometimes, but we are not destroyed. 2 Corinthians 4:8-9 ICB

achieve, Dr. Sharp had accomplished in less than sixty seconds. He was instantly and forever in Chad's circle of A-List team members. He was in the family.

For the remainder of the day and throughout the entire week, Chad received visitor after visitor of nursing teams, research teams, doctor teams, all wanting to catch a glimpse of this new (to UCLA) device. They were all thirsty to learn as much as possible about the device and simply amazed to see it in action. While Chad, of course, was grateful to pave the way that could perhaps save another life down the road, the massive wave of onlookers was beginning to take a toll on him. At one point, he likened his situation to living in a fishbowl. With the glass doors on the hospital units and the constant lookie-loos, privacy was totally a thing of the past.

The visitors that really got under our skin were the groups that entered the room, gathered around the larger device that was connected to Chad but housed at the foot of his bed, and had in-depth training sessions yet never even bothered to say hello or acknowledge Chad's very human existence. Some even had the audacity to push buttons on this device that happened to be Chad's heart at the moment. Clearly, this was unacceptable and did not go unaddressed. When our concerns were expressed, the team made sure that Chad had downtime throughout the day and that those still allowed to enter the room were introduced. At the end of the day, we knew that it was not personal and that naturally being a teaching hospital, everyone was just excited to learn more about a tool that would eventually save additional lives. Yet, at this moment, we had to focus on Chad's life and make sure that his needs (including time to rest) were a priority.

We have troubles all around us, but we are not defeated. We do not know what to do, but we do not give up. We are persecuted, but God does not leave us. We are hurt sometimes, but we are not destroyed. 2 Corinthians 4:8-9 ICB

THE HOLIDAYS OF 2012

Kara

Although being the first to receive the totally artificial heart at UCLA came with a daunting level of responsibility and vulnerability, it also came with its share of perks too. Just a couple days after the big surgery, Chad was visited by the President and CEO of the UCLA Health System. The doctor and leader of the life-saving institution thanked Chad, wished him well and left his card with instructions to contact him should we need anything. For better or worse, this again reminded us of the magnitude of our situation.

The Wednesday after the surgery was Halloween so we were a bit disappointed that we would miss our little Transformer Bumble Bee who was back in Phoenix with my parents. My mom was a real rockstar, though, and made sure that Amare was able to attend the Halloween festival at my job, which doubled as Amare's preschool as well. They also joined Tiffany and family so that Amare could go trick-o-treating with his cousins. In the grand scheme of things, if we had to miss a holiday with our little pride and joy, we were okay that it was this one.

After spending the week with Chad in the hospital, I flew home Saturday afternoon so that I could spend some time with Amare before jumping back into our Phoenix routine. It was imperative to us that during these times of high stress and separation from each other, Amare still felt the love and presence of his parents. Still in disbelief and not having fully processed everything that had been thrown at us in the last week, I desperately needed to find myself in a church on Sunday morning. Not particularly interested in attending the church that Chad and I had previously attended, I decided to finally try the big church just two miles from our house that we had driven by for the past five years and always noted to one day give it a try.

The church was called Christ Church of the Valley (CCV) and it was like no church we had ever attended. From the second we arrived on the campus, there were friendly faces every step of the way to help navigate us through parking, Children's Church registration, and claiming our free welcome lunch. The service started at 10:30AM and lasted for one hour. I picked up Amare from his church and we headed to the cafe for our lunch. After lunch, Amare and I hung out and played in the courtyard until past one, when the noon service was letting out. I could not believe that this entire experience was nestled in a beautiful campus literally walking distance from our house. This was exactly what we needed and Amare confirmed it when we reached the car and he informed me that we were never going back to the other church. Literally and figuratively speaking, to be in the desert, and have found this fountain of joy for both me and my son, was truly a Godsend and has been life-changing to us ever since.

As we entered the month of November, we inherently knew that the upcoming holiday season would be unlike what we had envisioned. Having spent the prior Christmas (2011) away from our home, as Chad was settling into his parents' house and newly listed as a transplant candidate in UCLA's program, we had appreciated and enjoyed the accommodations but looked forward to Christmas in Phoenix again the following year (2012). Yet, here we found ourselves entering the 2012 holiday season away from either home and in the hospital instead. Thankfully, Chad was not on the original "Big Blue," which weighed in

Rejoice always, pray continually, give thanks in all circumstances; for this is God's will for you in Christ Jesus. 1 Thessalonians 5:16-18 NIV

at 418 pounds and was at one point the only FDA-approved driver for powering the Total Artificial Heart. Instead, he was on the Companion 2 Hospital Driver which artificial heart transplant patients remained on until they were deemed stable enough for the Freedom Driver. The Freedom Driver was a much smaller and portable version of the Big Blue, which eventually gave Chad independent mobility and allowed him to be released to his parents' house. At this point, there had been discussion of the Freedom Driver being ordered for Chad, but no firm dates had been set. This was the first time in our marriage that Chad's condition had threatened to land us in the hospital for a major holiday.

We had wrapped our minds around the fact that it would be a long time before Chad returned to Phoenix. We had even succumbed to the fact that Thanksgiving 2012 would be celebrated in our Westwood hospital home. But how would we pull off Christmas for our four-year-old son, who had already clocked more hours hanging out at a hospital than many people will clock over the course of their entire life? With each day that passed with Chad still on the smaller version of the Big Blue, this question inched its way to the forefront of our unspoken thoughts. Yet, we were still holding out hope that the Freedom Driver would be delivered and Chad would be transitioned to it in time for a cozy Christmas at his parents' house.

On Wednesday, November 21, Thanksgiving Eve, the Freedom Driver was delivered to Chad's room and we, along with Chad's parents, Dr. Angel and her husband Russell, all underwent training on this device. The amount of information downloaded to us that day, and knowing that a slight mishap in any of the steps could cost Chad his life, all but took my breath away. Again, was God sure in His selection of participants on this particular trial? After all, I had studied numbers in school and never once held an ounce of interest in science. Yet, here I was thrown into the medical scene desperate to do anything that I could to support the one and only man that I intimately loved.

The training had covered how the artificial heart works, an example replica of the same plastic instrument that had been implanted in Chad's

Rejoice always, pray continually, give thanks in all circumstances; for this is God's will for you in Christ Jesus. 1 Thessalonians 5:16-18 NIV

chest, the importance of Chad's blood pressure remaining in a very specific range, the distinction between the various warning alarms, how to charge and change the device batteries, and the scariest of all, how to switch out the devices in the event of a malfunction. After the training, we were informed that a 100-question test would be issued to us all and upon passing, we would be the chosen ones to care for Chad once he was discharged from the hospital. Given the upcoming Thanksgiving Holiday weekend and availability of key staff members, it was decided that Chad's transition to the Freedom Driver would be more feasible the following week. Although we were inching closer to December at this point, we were still hopeful that Chad would be released in time for Christmas.

The next day was Thanksgiving Day and, boy, did we have a lot to be thankful for. Sure, things had not turned out how we would have elected but Chad still had an amazing team of doctors, nurses, and an entire medical facility walking with us every step of the way. The Freedom Driver was in process so the vision of Chad being released from the hospital was in our direct line of sight. Chad's body and the artificial heart seemed to be working well together and there had been no major complications. Despite the designated city, address and unit number, we were still physically together here on earth, and grateful for every moment.

Thanksgiving Day 2012 turned out to be a beautiful day. Charlotte had gotten permission to use the lower lever of the main hospital for our dinner location. She prepared the most exquisite type of chili that one could imagine and a host of accompanying sides of course. In addition to the buffet table, Charlotte decorated round tables to replicate that of a fine dining experience. Were it not for the presence of Chad's dedicated nurse for the day, one might have thought he had already been discharged and we were all guests of Fleming's Steakhouse. In the company of Charlotte, Michael, Dr. Angel, Russell and our nurse for the day, Chad, Amare and I ate, laughed, played card games and watched Amare check Chad's vitals and try to discharge him multiple times with

Rejoice always, pray continually, give thanks in all circumstances; for this is God's will for you in Christ Jesus. 1 Thessalonians 5:16-18 NIV

his play plastic medical gear. Despite Amare's failed discharge attempts, Thanksgiving 2012 had far exceeded our initially tainted expectations.

Later that afternoon, after returning to Chad's room, we Skyped with my family who was celebrating the holiday in Palm Springs. Amare and I spent the night with Chad and over the course of the weekend, we enjoyed visits with Tiffany and Shawn who drove down and spent the entire day with us on Black Friday. My cousins, Nora and Andrea, also came out for a visit that evening and our good friends, Desiree and Eric, hung out with us Saturday night. Those visits, talks, reminiscing sessions and explosive laughs were like medically-induced boosts to our souls. These were the beautiful moments that restored us in preparation for whatever we would be ushered into next. Again, there was no shortage on our list of people, things and experiences to be grateful for.

After Thanksgiving weekend, the quest to get Chad on the Freedom Driver, stabilized and home to his parents' house in time for Christmas was in full effect. Subsequently, Chad also found himself on the fast track to local celebrity regarding his plastic pump and lifesaving backpack known as the Freedom Driver. It turned out that our grand Thanksgiving Dinner soiree on the lower level had landed us a family article in the UCLA hospital newsletter. Also, the second that Chad was transitioned from the Companion 2 Hospital Driver to the Freedom Driver, he was interviewed by a hospital publicist and featured in the UCLA medical newsletter. The feature in the medical newsletter drummed up even more traction for Chad and his battery-operated heart.

The next thing we knew, there was an entire thread brewing regarding Chad on UCLA's Facebook page. His already super-sized network of supporters and prayer warriors was growing exponentially and making the entire experience even more surreal. To have complete strangers wish you well and root for you out of the pure goodness of their hearts is about the most organic medicine that one could ever receive.

Rejoice always, pray continually, give thanks in all circumstances; for this is God's will for you in Christ Jesus. 1 Thessalonians 5:16-18 NIV

All of the publicity surrounding Chad and his artificial heart eventually led to a full fledge media day on Wednesday, December 5. There was very little notice and given that it was right in the middle of the work week, Amare and I were unable to attend as we were in Phoenix. It was a very exciting day for Chad and I just encouraged him to take it all in and enjoy. At this point, he was just days away from being released from the hospital so there was excitement all around amongst our family. The morning started bright and early with an interview in his hospital room by NBC. After the in-room interview and a few stops along the way, Chad was ushered down to the lower level of the hospital where an entire news conference was set up for Chad and a very large representation from his extensive team of doctors. There were representatives from ABC, NBC, Fox, and even Telemundo. The doctors spoke very highly of Chad and I specifically remember enjoying Dr. Hart's interview later that evening on the news as I watched via Skype with Chad. He spoke about Chad's overwhelmingly calm response upon hearing that he would need the artificial heart and how impressed he was with Chad's pre-existing knowledge regarding the device.

Chad, of course, effortlessly answered every question fired at him. The formula that makes Chad who he is came shining through: his calm, cool demeanor with a splash of humor at the least expected moment. Still, by the end of the day, Chad was exhausted but I hung on to his every word as he recapped the experience for me. I was so proud of him, and happy that after all that he had been through, his story was finally being shared with the world. What an unusually exciting hospital experience and a great way to culminate this particularly tumultuous stint. Chad was released from the hospital two days after media day. However, the media team did not let him escape without an additional broadcast. They interviewed Chad and his dad as they gathered his belongings from the room, walked out the front of the hospital, secured Chad and his precious backpack in the backseat, and drove off into the sunset (also known as Westwood traffic).

Rejoice always, pray continually, give thanks in all circumstances; for this is God's will for you in Christ Jesus. 1 Thessalonians 5:16-18 NIV

In the days to come, we enjoyed reading all of the encouraging notes that were generating on NBC's Facebook page for Chad. He was featured on the home page of Syncardia's (the artificial heart manufacturer) website, and we even later got word that there was a write-up about Chad in Jet magazine. Friends and family from near and far would randomly reach out to let us know that Chad had appeared on their local news. Out of all of the things we anticipated we would face as a result of Chad's condition, media had never once crossed our minds. This was all exciting and a fantastic twist that had totally caught us by surprise, but the overarching victory at the end of the day was that Chad was doing well enough to be released to spend Christmas outside of the hospital at home (in Los Angeles) with his family. The Freedom Driver had delivered and provided the flexibility that we desperately needed to endure this chapter in our lives. Despite our concerns at the onset of the holiday season, it was suddenly beginning to look a lot like Christmas!

Rejoice always, pray continually, give thanks in all circumstances; for this is God's will for you in Christ Jesus. 1 Thessalonians 5:16-18 NIV

Amare's Anecdotes #4

Now Wait A Minute!

There were many drawbacks to Amare and me traveling between Phoenix and Los Angeles week after week. But one thing I could always count on was entertainment at the airport. On one particular weekend, we were catching the first Saturday morning flight out of Phoenix to Los Angeles. We had cut the time a little closer than normal for some reason and of course, ended up being assigned to one of the furthest gates in the terminal. Much to Amare's delight, we hopped on the first motorized cart available. Our driver was probably about my age, a cool friendly guy, just trying to enjoy his Saturday morning at work. Amare, on the other hand thought otherwise.

Driver: "What gate are you headed to today?"
Me: "C19."
Driver: "Oh, you're headed to LA."
Amare: "Yep, to see my daddy!"
Driver: "Hey, hey, don't be talking to me about another man."
Amare: (at the top of his lungs) "NOW WAIT A MINUTE, HE'S SICK!"

CHRISTMAS 2012

Kara

The CBS network had somehow missed the boat with Chad's first media day, so shortly thereafter, they scheduled Chad for a holiday-themed in-home interview with his family. This was to take place on Monday, December 17. Amare and I would be there. Careful to not press the envelope too far with my job's flexibility, and needing to preserve vacation time for the holidays, we were unable to make it to Los Angeles on Friday, December 7 for Chad's joyous hospital discharge. I absolutely hated that we weren't there for this pivotal moment, but in the end, it was probably best to give Chad space and time to get adjusted to life outside of the hospital with his new life dependent backpack. Despite the device being named, "Freedom" Driver (which we will explore at length in the next chapter), Chad's well-being would still require diligent care, attention and twenty-four-hour adult supervision. Having already visited Chad's parents' home to ensure that the set-up and environment would work, Chad's device coordinator, Michelle, stopped by again on the evening of Chad's discharge to confirm that he was settling in smoothly.

Although we were unable to be there with Chad physically when he was released from the hospital, it was still very rewarding to watch via

Skype, as his spirits began to rise as a result of his newfound freedom. By the time Amare and I headed to Los Angeles the following weekend, Chad and his backpack were like two peas in a pod. He and his parents were veterans in the new routine, and I was still a bit shell shocked and feeling a little overwhelmed as I thought back through the training that we had undergone just before Thanksgiving. Nevertheless, there was no battery switch, bandage change or backup device that would intimidate me from spending time with the love of my life.

On Friday, December 14, after work and school, Amare and I flew to Los Angeles to spend a highly anticipated weekend with Chad outside of the hospital. We had not been together under a non-hospital roof since that dreadful Sunday evening in September when Chad had found major difficulty catching his breath. Although excitement by far outweighed any other emotion, I could not help but harbor some concern over Amare's reaction to Chad at home with the backpack. Would he see Chad differently? Would he understand and respect the severity of the tubes connecting Chad to the device housed in the famous backpack? How would this all play out?

Of course, in the end, our reunion was truly joyful. Amare saw one thing and one thing only, and that was his amazing daddy! Sure, he might have had a question or two regarding the fact that Chad had left the hospital but not the backpack; however, at the end of the day, we were together again and the holiday season was in full effect.

The biggest adjustment that I had not anticipated was the bedtime experience. Super-excited at the opportunity to simply lay down and sleep next to my husband, I had grossly underestimated the effect of our new soundtrack. The fact that a ten-pound backpack was constantly working to supply life to Chad was every bit of amazing. However, this ten-pound backpack did not carry out its beautiful task quietly. The life-sustaining sound could be likened to a symphony of about twenty swing sets, all moving in unison, all needing to be oiled. Nonetheless, I was in bed again with my husband, headphones and all.

I pray that the God who gives hope will fill you with much joy and peace while you trust in him. Then your hope will overflow by the power of the Holy Spirit. Romans 15:13 ICB

Although we stayed close to the house, with a walk or two around the block, the weekend flew by faster than ever, and before we knew it, it was Monday morning and time for our family interview. Chad being an old pro with the media by now, was unfazed of course. I, on the other hand, began to get a little nervous as the clock inched closer to 10:30am. I just didn't know what to expect from the newscaster, and even scarier, from Amare. Chad's parents had graciously opted out of the interview and left the three of us to share our story. Knowing that we were spending another Christmas away from our own home, Charlotte had gone out of her way to set a magical atmosphere. The house looked even more amazing than usual and if you did not know better, one would have thought that Chad and I were living large.

Once the journalist and cameraman arrived, we said our introductions, signed a few papers and they scoped the house for scenic options. The interview started out with Chad only. They covered the scientific basics of how the Freedom Driver worked and the lifelong medical journey that had led Chad to this miraculous backpack. Next, they taped a scene of the three of us playing Nintendo Wii as a family. Amare did fine and if the mission was to convey the love and bond that he and Chad shared, then it was by far achieved. The interview ended with Chad and me in the living room sitting by the Christmas tree describing what this particular holiday season meant to us. For us, it meant a season of miracles, a season of togetherness, a season that we would cherish for the rest of our lives. Chad's backpack being securely plugged in and gently placed under the Christmas tree, was the perfect pictorial representation of what this Christmas meant to us.

That evening, Amare and I flew back to Phoenix and the following Friday, we returned to Los Angeles for what proved to be a truly spectacular Christmas and New Year's holiday. Over the course of our twelve days and eleven nights visit, we connected with a host of family and friends. Chef Chad, with his backpack in tow, was back in action, cooking gourmet pizza, fancy omelets and his famous prime rib for Christmas. Our friends and family came over for visits and fellowship

I pray that the God who gives hope will fill you with much joy and peace while you trust in him. Then your hope will overflow by the power of the Holy Spirit. Romans 15:13 ICB

and they always left amazed at how graciously Chad was adapting to this chapter in his now legendary life.

Our holiday visit was off to a great start and having arrived three days prior, I remember feeling so relaxed on Christmas Eve. Both Amare and Chad's presents were wrapped and ready to go. No one ever looked for me to cook anything, so I was off the hook in that area. Everything was in order and I even had the privilege of getting a manicure and taking an extra-long nap that day. Chad and his dad secretly worked in the garage putting together Amare's Transformer bicycle. After all of my anxiety surrounding Chad being stuck in the hospital for Christmas, seeing the two of them execute such an ordinary pre-Christmas fatherly duty, struck an extraordinary cord in my heart. We watched Amare's excitement grow by the minute as the day progressed and he knew Santa's arrival was getting closer. We were all overwhelmingly grateful to be out of the hospital and in the company of pure love.

That evening as Chad and I got ready for bed, we heard a suspicious sound coming from his backpack. Upon closer review, sure enough, one of the indicator lights was on and Chad immediately referenced his handbook. While it was not a life-threatening emergency, one of his measurements was trending higher than normal. As we saw our miraculous holiday potentially fade to an emergency room visit, Chad dreadfully called Michelle, his device coordinator on call for the week. I began to think through what we would say to Amare when he woke up on Christmas morning and found out that his dad was back in the hospital. Had we really come this close to the holiday, only to have the carpet yanked just before the clock struck midnight? Fortunately, the answer was no. Michelle instructed Chad to drink a glass of water, wait thirty minutes, re-check the numbers and then call her back if they had not improved. Thank God, there was no call back necessary, nor did we have to disappoint our baby boy the next morning.

To our surprise, Amare slept in a little on Christmas morning. I was up at the crack of dawn, as usual, and spent the time checking in and

I pray that the God who gives hope will fill you with much joy and peace while you trust in him. Then your hope will overflow by the power of the Holy Spirit. Romans 15:13 ICB

catching up with my parents and siblings who I missed dearly during this season of our lives. When Amare woke up, Chad and I thoroughly enjoyed watching him open his presents and respond to each one with an exaggerated, yet authentic level of excitement that only a child could pull off. The finale gift for the year was his bicycle. Chad had slipped out to the garage, rang the doorbell and when Amare and I answered, he was there with the Bumble Bee bike. Amare was on cloud nine as he rode his new bike down the street with me playing paparazzi in front of him, while his dad protectively walked behind him. Later that afternoon, we shared dinner and a beautiful evening at the house with family and friends. Christmas 2012 did not disappoint and it was a special time that we would never forget.

Over the course of the rest of that week, Chad and I managed to pull off an afternoon date at a restaurant in the Marina Del Rey, which was near and dear to us, as we had shared many special moments including our wedding reception in this area. Also during that week, Amare, Chad and I sipped hot chocolate and enjoyed an afternoon walk along the marina, followed by ice cream sundaes at Cold Stone Creamery near Venice Beach. We simply enjoyed spending the time together and did our best to intentionally cherish every moment.

New Year's Eve was low key by some people's standards, but spectacular in our paradigm. Chad rested up for a good portion of the day while Amare and I went to lunch and spent the afternoon at the Century City Mall. After our mall excursion, Amare took a mandatory nap so that he could attempt to bring in the New Year with us. Later that evening, my parents along with our family friend Joyce Henderson, stopped by for dinner before they headed to Watch Night Service at church. We talked, laughed, ate and took pictures with them before they left. It was a heartwarming good time. Next, my friend Jessica came by for what she thought would be an hour or two visit, prior to heading to her outing for the evening. After talking and laughing with Chad and me, she unexpectedly found herself on a date with Amare as he had lured her into watching his favorite movie at the time, *Puss In Boots*. By the

I pray that the God who gives hope will fill you with much joy and peace while you trust in him. Then your hope will overflow by the power of the Holy Spirit. Romans 15:13 ICB

time the movie was over, Jessica had succumbed to our quaint and cozy countdown scene. As the clock inched closer to midnight and 2013 was in clear sight, we poured apple cider and Chad, Amare, Jessica and I gathered around the couch for a toast. Charlotte rushed in from her room with seconds to spare, as we counted, toasted and Chad and I kissed in the New Year.

Twenty-twelve had started on the frightful note of Chad's first temporary relocation to Los Angeles and his admission to UCLA Medical Center on the third day of the year. This was shortly followed by Chad's extremely triumphant first heart transplant in February. We had spent March and April making the best of our weekends in LA, but all the while counting down to Chad's return to Phoenix. From May to August, we had the ultimate best time of our lives as Chad was back in Phoenix. We had survived what we thought to be the most difficult test of our marriage and we were literally on cloud nine. Yet, in September, we had found ourselves back on the see-saw and arguably at our lowest point yet. By October, we had hit totally new and petrifying terrain, as we suddenly found ourselves in the realm of life with an artificial heart. November was about education and adaptation, as we prepared for Chad's next hospital release. Finally, December had been about celebrating and sharing Chad's story with the world. Twenty-twelve had been a roller coaster of colossal twists and turns, but by the beautiful grace and mercy of our God, we were able to end that year and usher in a new one on a very memorable and joyous note that will be forever engrained in our hearts.

I pray that the God who gives hope will fill you with much joy and peace while you trust in him. Then your hope will overflow by the power of the Holy Spirit. Romans 15:13 ICB

THE FREEDOM DRIVER

Kara

Chad and I always made a conscious effort to maintain our gratitude for the Freedom Driver. We constantly acknowledged the fact that it was essentially buying us time outside of the hospital, while Chad's antibodies settled down so that he could be listed for another heart transplant. Nonetheless, this recollection of our journey would not be complete without a closer look into what life with the backpack was really like.

One major adjustment that sounds simple but was far from normal was the need to always have the backup equipment available, charged and ready to go at any given moment. Chad's dad had diligently packed a roller luggage that housed the back-up freedom driver, batteries and charger, emergency blood pressure medicine, and the device manual. Just to be clear, "available" meant, if Chad was up for the day and hanging out in the kitchen, the luggage was in the kitchen and not the bedroom. If we went to CVS to pick up medicine for Chad, the luggage and Chad came in the store as he could not be left alone, nor be without the backup. If we took Amare on a bike ride around the neighborhood, the luggage would go for a ride as well. If Chad was in the car, the luggage was in the back seat with him and not in the trunk. Once, Chad and I went to Trader Joes just so that he could relish what it was like to grocery shop again, and yes, the luggage came in with us. After endless stares and a few double takes as we did our shopping, the checker finally asked us, "Are you going on a trip?"

"Nope," we responded, "just a back-up for his artificial heart." Silence of course was the most common response to this news.

Another major adjustment for Chad was his indefinite subjection to sponge baths, as showers and complete submersion into water were out of the question for obvious reasons. Chad was also banned from driving during this time and in fact was not allowed to sit in the front seat at all, because in the event of an accident, the airbags could do serious damage to the plastic pump that currently served as his heart. This made for really a peculiar dinner date that Chad and I had at Fleming's for my 34th birthday. Having already called ahead to reserve a booth with an electrical outlet for Chad to plug up, we were all set on that front. The battery in the Freedom Driver had a two-hour life span, but out of caution, we would always make sure that Chad's device was plugged in whenever possible. So even in the car, there was a car adaptor for Chad's device to continue charging. What I had not thought about, was the awkward scene as we pulled up to the steakhouse with me driving and my husband exiting from the backseat. Oh, well! We had to do what we had to do and, clearly, we were taking weird to a whole new level but not letting it stop us from enjoying life.

At this point, we had grown oblivious to what people thought about our situation. We had most definitely learned to simply live in the moment and cherish each memory as it was created. Luckily, that evening, the normal sounds and buzz amongst the popular steakhouse, more than masked the noise of the Freedom Driver at work. Chad and I had a lovely date, enjoying delicious rib-eyes and Fleming's famous mashed potatoes. We talked and laughed about our crazy lives and fantasized about our future. Our evening ended in hysterics as we stood outside the restaurant waiting for our car to be pulled around. The valet

Always give thanks to God the Father for everything, in the name of our Lord Jesus Christ. Ephesians 5:20 ICB

attendant that was there curbside as we waited, began to inconspicuously look up and around trying to identify the source of the sound—the whirring of Chad's artificial heart. He seemed so sure of himself when he finally concluded that the sound was coming from the heat-lamp that doubled as part of the outdoor ambiance. He turned the lamp off and appeared confident that the problem had been resolved. Yet, when the noise continued, the dumbfounded look on his face was priceless, and he began to frantically look up and around as if a UFO was about to land. As our car was approaching, I finally told him the true source of the noise as Chad climbed into the backseat. We laughed the entire ride home and chalked up the experience to just another day in the adventures of the Washingtons.

Not really wanting our date-night to end, but not wanting to press our luck out and about either, Chad and I decided to head home and continue our evening by watching a movie. As we snuggled up in the bed together, suddenly, there was an elephant in the room, also known as normal sexual desires shared between a husband and wife. Sadly, though, we had already made room for the elephant, because that was easier to accept than running the risk of indulging ourselves, only to have Chad's blood pressure rise, the "freedom" driver alarms sound, and instantly find ourselves in the awkward company of his concerned parents. Given that our shared living arrangements with Chad's parents was a necessity that we so far had no end in sight for, we opted to air on the side of caution and spare ourselves from that particular Washington adventure.

The following weekend, we attended church for the first time with the Freedom Driver. Chad's dad had already been in contact with the deacon in charge so upon our arrival, he welcomed me, Chad and Amare with open arms. Not wanting to cause a scene or be a distraction, Chad and I inquired about the overflow room, but the deacon insisted that we join the congregation in the main church. We picked a row in the back and off to the side and everything was all good, until the music stopped and it was the Fleming's outdoor patio scene all over again. A couple of ladies a few rows in front of us began looking around trying to decipher

Always give thanks to God the Father for everything, in the name of our Lord Jesus Christ. Ephesians 5:20 ICB

the source of this odd noise. When one of them finally voiced their concern to the ushers, Chad and I took it as our cue to go ahead and find the overflow room. In fact, one usher politely volunteered to show us the overflow room and as we filed out of our pew, the head deacon again appeared and insisted that we stay put because the pastor wanted to pray for us.

Needless to say, despite the thick skin that both Chad and I had developed, this scene was growing more and more uncomfortable by the minute. At last though, after the praise and worship, meet and greet session and other opening rituals, the pastor literally came to our pew himself and over the microphone asked us to stand and come down to the altar for prayer. He briefly told the congregation about Chad's story, anointed our foreheads with oil (Amare included) and with outstretched hands, all of the saints prayed for us. Though the experience had started out on an awkward note, through the fault of no one, just a symptom of the situation, it more than made up for itself in the end. While Chad, Amare and I did politely retreat to the overflow room after the prayer, we left there feeling loved and absolutely covered by the blood of Jesus with an additional army of prayer warriors and well-wishers in our corner.

Although the need to perpetually roll a piece of luggage around town was not our favorite thing about the Freedom Driver, if I could have changed one thing about the device, it would have hands down been the noise. Like most couples, I suspect, Chad and I had a few television shows that we watched together. Watching these shows together was literally a bonding experience for us, especially having to spend so much time apart. We would forego watching the shows live as they aired, and instead catch up on the episodes together during our weekend visits, whether in the hospital or at his parents' house. The Freedom Driver very quickly threw a wrench in our ritual and before we knew it, Chad and me watching TV together was on the same list as intimacy, pleasures of the past. The volume needed to truly enjoy the dialogue in our shows, was just enough to make television viewing undesirable for us.

Always give thanks to God the Father for everything, in the name of our Lord Jesus Christ.
Ephesians 5:20 ICB

In the end, despite the quirkiness and lack of true freedom in some areas, we were undeniably grateful that Chad was alive. Chad longed for some normalcy as an individual, and we as a couple, desperately worked to embrace our new norm. When one of us was having an off day or letting the frustrations of the predicament get the best of us, the other would quickly point out just how bad life could really be without God's grace, mercy and protection. In this moment and time in our lives, the Freedom Driver was an extension of God's grace and mercy. Our UCLA family, blood family, and extended family, along with their friends and families, were our protection and God's perpetual illustration of hope, throughout a journey that could easily feel like a hopeless situation. Without the Freedom Driver, none of the experiences above such as the Fleming's date, church service, and father-son bonding time, would have been possible. The Freedom Driver had delivered the irreplaceable opportunity for our family to make beautiful memories that will be treasured for a lifetime.

Always give thanks to God the Father for everything, in the name of our Lord Jesus Christ. Ephesians 5:20 ICB

THANK GOD WE WERE FRIENDS FIRST

It is January 10, 2013, and as I reflect back on 2012 I realize that Chad was home in Arizona for only four months of the entire year. Granted those were four of the best months ever, but the good times seem like a distant memory as we face the present separation that has knocked at our door yet again. I miss Chad so much and I am finding it significantly harder to keep a smile on my face this time around. I have finally come to the resolve that I am not happy right now. I have enjoyable moments and I am definitely grateful for all that God has done and is doing in our lives. But, I cannot honestly say that I am happy. I can however say that life without my son is unimaginable. He is definitely a true source of happiness and I would love nothing more than to give him a sibling or two or three. Yet, with this stalled state of uncertainty that we've lived in the last few years, Amare remains an only child for now. I am still holding out hope that Chad and I will be able to add to our family in the near future, but sometimes I can't help but get frustrated as I daydream about being a "normal" thirty-something couple building a family and legacy together. Don't get me wrong, I have grown to love our struggle and the amazing perspective that it has given us on life. But, I am starting to wonder when we will be able to get back to at least our version of normal.

> *Marriage, ultimately, is the practice of becoming passionate friends.*
>
> *- Harville Hendrix*

When I reflect on our current predicament, there is really nothing "normal" about it. This is the first time that I am actually beginning to feel the strain on our marriage. Chad has been gone again for almost four months now. That translates to four more months of single-motherhood. Four more months of strained finances. And four months of zero physical intimacy. In all honestly, I am not an extremely sexual person. Actually putting these thoughts in print for others to read is pretty frightful even as I type. But four months of high stress and zero activity can really take a toll on even me. On New Years Eve, before we went to sleep, I tried to kiss Chad a little longer than our most recent pecks, and he all but pushed me away. For a split second I took it personal, but then I quickly realized that he was genuinely afraid of what would happen to his blood pressure and the freedom driver if he were to get aroused. In all of his illnesses, Chad has never been the type to want to forfeit sex, even when he felt his worst. So for him to resist a mild kiss, really brought home to me just how far from normal we are.

I have always been grateful and prided myself on the fact that Chad and I were friends first long before we dated. I truly believe that makes a huge difference in a relationship and has proven to be a great asset in our marriage. But now more than ever, I realize that if our relationship were built exclusively, or even predominantly on physical intimacy alone, we would be in a world of trouble. Instead, our friendship and genuine concern for each other's happiness and well-being is what has kept our relationship afloat during this time. So yes, times are really rough right now, and unfortunately the end is not exactly in sight; but thank God our marriage was built on a strong foundation of friendship, love and respect.

BIRTHDAY SURPRISES AND MORE

Kara

On January 15, 2012, my birthday, Chad was in the hospital waiting for a heart so my girlfriends and family went out of their way to make the weekend special for me. On Saturday the 14th, Jessica and Janice came to the hospital and we all visited with Chad for a few hours. We played cards, reminisced about high school, and Chad and the girls had their usual in-depth discussion about hip-hop, comparing the greatest with the latest. Eventually, the girls kidnapped me for a night of painting, food and movies, ending with a sleepover at the W Hotel closest to UCLA. Amare was with Robyn for the night so I truly had an evening off from caretaking. Jessica, Janice and I conversed with frequent eruptions of gut-wrenching laughter until we all fell asleep. I remember feeling so blessed that they had taken the time to plan this evening of surprises for me.

On Sunday, my actual birthday, the girls returned me safe and sound back to Chad's hospital room. He had written me the sweetest birthday letter to accompany an all-star playlist of love songs that could not have been a better fit for us. Chad's playlists never disappointed and this latest Bday Love compilation was no different. That afternoon, my parents who were in town, along with Amare, Robyn and family, came from Orange County to take me to lunch at California Pizza Kitchen down the street from the hospital. After lunch, we all visited with Chad and had the traditional birthday cake and song in his room. The next day was Martin Luther King Day, so Amare and I were in town for one more day. Chad's Aunt Ginger and Uncle Darryl had offered to take Amare to the Children's Science Museum, so I was again a lady of leisure. Once Amare was squared away, I made my way to the hospital with a few short shopping stops along the way. TJ Maxx seemed to be a nice compliment to an already great weekend. I also stopped by Trader Joes to get the popcorn that Chad and I both loved. I spent the rest of the day at the hospital with Chad hanging out and watching movies. Amare was dropped off later that afternoon so that he could visit with his daddy before we headed back to Phoenix. My 33rd birthday weekend had far surpassed my expectations and I returned to Phoenix feeling extremely grateful and recharged for whatever the next episode would bring.

Kara

Lights, Camera, Almost No Action

One year later in January 2013, Chad was again waiting for a heart and required to remain in Los Angeles at his parents' house. In this particular year, my birthday fell on a Tuesday which meant that I would be in Arizona. Instead of succumbing to the depression that this scenario could so easily allow for, I decided to be proactive about my own happiness. I took a vacation day from work and went to my favorite spa on earth. I enjoyed every minute of the day and to top things off, my parents, sister and her hubby and my nieces and nephew came over to celebrate that evening. My dad cooked my favorite meal, fajitas, my sister brought me some amazingly bright flowers, and my mom brought some adorable cupcakes. Chad also attended the party via Skype, so for the second year in a row, my birthday really superseded my initial

Fill us with your love every morning. Then we will sing and rejoice all our lives.
Psalm 90:14 ICB

expectations. And just when I thought that my birthday was over, Chad told me the ultra-exciting news that he and his surgeon, Dr. Hart, were invited to be on the television show, *The Doctors*. There I was thinking that the day could not get any better, and it did!

Over the next couple of days, Chad was interviewed at his parents' house and I was contacted by the producer who wanted to pitch the idea of Amare and me surprising Chad by walking out on stage during the show. As exciting as this sounded, I had reservations about flying to Los Angeles and Amare and I not spending as much time with Chad as possible. They initially mentioned us flying out Thursday night, staying in a hotel and having a driver pick us up to take us to the studio. My concerns were, one, that's a whole night gone from our weekend with Chad. Two, how would we do our nightly Skype session and not reveal our location? And three, what if the reunion did not go quite as planned? Well, none of my concerns had to be addressed because the reunion idea got tabled anyway for circumstances beyond our control. It probably didn't help that I was completely honest when the producer asked me if I thought Chad would cry and I told him I could pretty much guarantee that he wouldn't.

So things kind of went downhill from there. After the final decision was made, the producer got back to me to say they were still doing the segment, but given the complexity of the heart and having the doctors explain it, there was not enough time for the reunion piece. That was perfectly fine with me, given my initial concerns anyway. He then proceeded to tell me that there would still be a seat in the audience for me. When I asked about a seat for me and Amare, he said that there were no kids allowed in the audience. This is when I began to question whether or not I would make it to the show. The idea of paying for a last-minute ticket for both of us, but Amare not being allowed did not sit too well with me. For him to miss out on such an exciting experience did not really seem fair. So I told the producer that I would have to talk to Chad and see where to go from there in terms of who would be accompanying him on set.

Fill us with your love every morning. Then we will sing and rejoice all our lives.
Psalm 90:14 ICB

Well, the next day (two days before the show), I still had no idea what we were going to do. I was on a call at work and my cell phone rang. I let it go to voicemail because I still did not have an answer. To my surprise, when I checked the message, the producer had an answer for me! He had worked it out where Amare and I could be on the front row during Chad's piece and then be ushered off afterwards. Perfect, that's exactly what I wanted all along! Finally, we were set and headed to Hollywood! Except, that night, Amare came down with a fever and said that his throat was hurting. No, how could this be happening right now, really? Of course, we always have to keep Chad's health the priority so I couldn't risk exposing him to Amare's cold. My dream of heading to Hollywood was looking dimmer by the moment.

The next day, I put our luggage in the car before Amare woke up, just secretly hoping that the fever would vanish and we could catch a flight after work. Amare was in good spirits when he woke up. His temp was like 99 and he gurgled and wanted to go to school. I explained the entire situation to Chad and we agreed that it all boiled down to how Amare looked and felt when I picked him up from school that day.

In parallel to this situation was the fact that Chad had been feeling extremely fatigued and just not quite right. As a result, going into his routine Wednesday clinic appointment, we knew there was a big chance they would admit him to the hospital. So this was yet another hurdle that had to be crossed before we could officially head to Hollywood.

After spending the day at UCLA for a round of morning tests, a late breakfast in Westwood, and the afternoon clinic, Chad seemed to be moving right along—at least from what I could gather from his text messages. Then about 4:15PM Arizona time, I was wrapping things up in anticipation of heading over to pick up Amare, assess his status and potentially head to the airport. I got a text from Chad: *Just pulled into the driveway and Dr. DuBois' called and said to come back.* At that point, I'm like WHAT? And for a split second, I thought, or certainly hoped that it was a joke. I immediately called Chad and he explained that unfortunately it wasn't a joke and that his labs showed him being extremely anemic so he needed a blood transfusion.

I was devastated for my own selfish reasons about being excited to do the show, and also for Chad and the thought of him being extracted from the road to Hollywood, and put on the road to Westwood (home of UCLA Medical Center) instead. I knew I had to make another call, but just hadn't got around to it yet and then my phone rang. It was the producer just calling to get Amare's name. Of course, I had to tell him the news that our chances of making it were slim to none at this point. He said he would pray for Chad and for me to just keep him posted.

I was pretty bummed out when I left work that Wednesday, but in the back of my mind, I still kept playing out the best case scenarios. A perfect Thursday for me would look like this:

- Chad would get the blood overnight, feel a thousand times better and be released.
- I would take Amare to the doctor to confirm he did not have strep throat.
- I would work remote from home so that Amare could rest and get better.
- We would catch a late afternoon flight and get to LA at a decent time to prepare for the early call time on Friday.

Well, Thursday came and things started to unfold just like my perfect dream. I was up off and on half the night texting Chad here and there. I woke up around 2AM to a text message that read, *Very possible that I might not be an overnight guest!* The massive size of UCLA and the fact that there were often no beds available had finally worked in our favor. The next text message was: *Last pint of blood is going in and then I should be out.*

Could this really be happening?!? It was like a dream come true. Granted, it was almost daylight now and I had not heard anything since 2AM. I told myself that as long as the next update was not from my father-in-law (which would mean Chad was out of it), there was still hope. Around 6AM, I stepped away from my phone for one second and when I returned, I had a missed call from Mr. Washington, Jr. (my father-

Fill us with your love every morning. Then we will sing and rejoice all our lives.
Psalm 90:14 ICB

in-law). My heart sank because I immediately thought he was calling with an update that did not go along with my dream plan. Then, upon second glance, I noticed that the call was from Mr. Washington Jr. (home), not cell. Could it be, could Chad really be home? Disregarding the fact that it was 5:30 in the morning Cali time, I could not help but immediately call back! And sure enough, Chad answered and we were golden! He felt ten times better but still wanted to get the doctor's clearance before committing to do the show.

Chad

January 23, 2013. We pulled into the driveway and the cell phone rang. On the other end is Dr. DuBois' explaining that my hematocrit level had dropped to 5.8, which is considered to be extremely anemic. I was told to report to the ER for a blood transfusion. I remember walking through the foyer of the ER thinking how much I hated the place. Every time I have to go to the ER, I end up getting admitted to the hospital. After the lab was done with the cross type and matching process, I received three units of blood and was discharged several hours later and feeling much better.

Kara

On Thursday morning, I proceeded to work remotely, got dressed, took Amare to the doctor, and thank God, no strep! I went home to work remotely some more, keeping an eye on my flight time options, and all the while waiting for Chad to wake up and make the final decision. Finally, around 1PM there was contact. I received a text from Chad asking how we were doing. Of course, I fired back five questions, including one regarding his decision. No answer. Oh, well! I didn't want to be a pest and I certainly didn't want to go if Chad was afraid that he would get sick from Amare. But it sure would have been nice to catch the 3:30PM flight.

Fill us with your love every morning. Then we will sing and rejoice all our lives.
Psalm 90:14 ICB

Finally at 2:05PM Arizona time, Chad called to say that he had been cleared to do the show and to top things off, Dr. DuBois' was calling in a prescription for some antibiotics that would guard him from Amare's cold. How cool is that? God is so good. And Dr. DuBois' is the best! Soooooo, seeing as how our bags were still in the car from the day before, I immediately decided to make a mad dash for the airport. Amare had just opened his eyes from his nap and I asked him if he wanted to go see Daddy. Of course he did, so he immediately made the switch from pjs to clothes and we were out the door. By the time we parked and waited for the airport bus, we had less than twenty minutes to spare before our flight took off. I decided we would give it our best shot, and if we didn't make it, then we would have dinner at the airport and catch a later flight.

As the bus approached our terminal, at what seemed like a snail's pace, I gave Amare a quick pep talk regarding our very limited time. Everything worked in our favor and he was a champ. We got dropped off right by the escalators closest to security, and only steps away from the kiosk to print our boarding passes. Security was almost a problem— as they had to test the children's Advil that I had thrown in my purse for Amare. But for once in my life, I had picked the right line; and the girl was nice and speedy after I told her we were about to miss our flight. Once passed security, we sprinted to the gate as I heard the final call for the flight to Los Angeles. With God's grace, we boarded the flight just seconds before they closed the door. Our perfect day had come to fruition and we were on our way to Hollywood!

Amare and I landed in Los Angeles before 5PM. We were excited to see Chad one day earlier than our normal routine would have allowed for. After dinner, we began to sort through our clothing options for the show, based on the producer's color and pattern recommendations. Blue seemed to be the preference and no stripes or wild designs. I had packed two dresses to choose from and once a clear winner was identified, I had an absolute blast sorting through jewelry options with Charlotte. I was ready and relieved that my ensemble was complete. Both Chad and Amare were ready as well, with two wardrobe options to take to the set.

Fill us with your love every morning. Then we will sing and rejoice all our lives.
Psalm 90:14 ICB

We made sure that Amare was in bed on time that evening, as the next day would start unusually early and likely be long. Although the normal excitement of our reunions threatened to interfere, Chad and I tried to get to sleep at a reasonable hour as well.

I woke up at five the next morning in order to allow time to flat iron my hair and do my makeup, not realizing that these services would be provided to me on set. We did not have to report to the studio until 8AM, but with Los Angeles traffic, you could never be too careful with time. We decided to stay in regular clothes and take our dressier clothes with us to change into. Michael, Chad, Amare and I left the house around a quarter to seven and headed to Hollywood!

We followed the instructions that we had received and before we knew it, we had entered the iconic gates of Paramount Studios, parked, and the four of us were riding a golf cart to the set of *The Doctors*. Next, we were escorted to our dressing room, with our name on the door and a few refreshments inside. Little did we know, we would spend the next four hours confined to these four walls, in anticipation of our moment of fame.

As always, we made the best of our time together. A hair stylist came to visit me and flat ironed my hair in a way that I have never been able to duplicate. Next was a makeup artist who all but laughed at what I had done and quickly explained the do's and don'ts of TV makeup, as she "fixed" my face. In a nutshell, the goal with TV makeup was to draw attention to either your eyes or mouth, but certainly not both, avoid shimmery shades and go for the matte look instead, and use a lightweight mascara to steer clear of clumps. Throughout the makeover, I was kicking myself for forgoing an extra hour of sleep to only have these services at my fingertips on set. I loved every minute of the pampering service, from the director's chair that I got to sit in, to the final presentation with which the glam squad left me. And to top it all off, they took our outfits away for one final press before we got dressed. I could definitely get used to this!

Fill us with your love every morning. Then we will sing and rejoice all our lives.
Psalm 90:14 ICB

Apparently, I was not the only one enjoying the rare glimpse into show business. Once Amare got dressed in his slacks, dress shirt, tie and shoes, you could not get this guy away from the mirror. Chad's dad and the producer took Amare to the actual show set before the taping began, to help him get acquainted with the set-up and hopefully reduce any potential anxiety. However, anxiety never actually entered the scene because Amare was full of himself that day and not the least bit afraid to let anyone and everyone know that he was "sharp." Whenever there was a free moment or someone new entered the room, Amare would smile at himself in the mirror and say, "I'm sharp." We certainly didn't know what to expect from the kid after being trapped in a room waiting for four hours, but thank God, fear and lack of self-confidence were irrelevant on this day.

Finally, after what seemed like a full day of waiting, things got pretty real when Amare, Chad and I each had a microphone connected to us. They sure were putting a lot of trust in Chad and me as parents, that we would not let this four-year old go crazy on the mic during filming. Wow, here we go, no pressure whatsoever. Chad, the producer and Michael, along with the back-up device, left the dressing room first so that Chad could enter right onto the stage. Amare and I met up with Dr. DuBois' and Dr. Hart backstage and were then escorted to our seats on the first row of the audience. Dr. Travis, the TV show host was already on stage and next entered Chad. He looked absolutely amazing on that stage. They had given him a rather high chair to sit in, but he settled in quite nicely with his backpack sitting safely on the floor. Amare and I both whispered to each other with twinkles in our eyes.

Dr. Travis opened up the show asking everyone to put their hand over their heart and feel the beat. He then went on to explain the story of Chad and his totally artificial heart. In a rather dramatic fashion, they rolled the footage of Chad at his parents' house being interviewed about his condition. I had to refocus my energy multiple times during the playback, for despite the sniffles that I heard across the audience, I was determined not to cry. Once the video ended, Dr. Travis threw Chad

Fill us with your love every morning. Then we will sing and rejoice all our lives.
Psalm 90:14 ICB

the first question about life with the artificial heart. For a split second, I could tell that Chad was nervous, but after his first couple of words, he snapped out of it and even cracked a few jokes. Next, Dr. DuBois', Dr. Hart, Amare and I were thrown a question or two. We all survived and represented UCLA and the Washington Family very well. Amare was reserved (by Amare standards) but super-confident, even when invited onstage to join his daddy. I exited the set so very proud of both Chad and Amare. I was also extremely grateful that we had stuck to our needs as a family, who given the circumstances, was desperate to spend every possible moment together—kudos to us for not forfeiting the previous night and morning hours together, all for the potential element of surprise and TV ratings. All and all, it was an amazing, unique and fun family adventure that Amare still talks about and is convinced made us all famous!

Fill us with your love every morning. Then we will sing and rejoice all our lives.
Psalm 90:14 ICB

Amare's Anecdotes
#5

Pilot for a Day

From time to time, honestly more often than I would have expected, a flight attendant and or the pilot would invite Amare into the cockpit as we were boarding a flight. I was able to get some cool pictures and Amare had fun of course, but then he got a little too comfortable. After about the third time, I began to leave him in the cockpit (door open of course), and go secure a seat for us, and the stewardess would escort Amare back to me when he was done playing pilot. A few times as I got comfortable in my seat, I  perked up when the intercom came on thinking it was an announcement from the pilot, and instead it was an adorable voice saying, "Hello, Mommy," or welcoming the passengers and wishing them a great flight.

One time as we were boarding a flight, the pilot stuck his head out from the cockpit and asked Amare if he wanted to look around. Amare quickly entered the arena of lights and buttons and immediately told the pilot, "I want to sit in your seat." I just shook my head as the six-foot plus pilot vacated his seat for my three-foot tall son. Hey, the Bible says, make your request known...

COUNT, DOUBLE COUNT AND RECOUNT YOUR BLESSINGS

Kara

The week following, our Hollywood adventure was a rather odd week. It was the 53rd fiscal week at work, which only happens every five to six years. It was a great week to catch up on projects that always seemed to lose the priority battle, but something about the week was extremely long and seemed to drag on forever. Also, for some reason, every day I woke up during this particular week, I found myself having to pray extra hard and make a special effort to avoid a slight onset of depression. Before we had left the set of *The Doctors*, we had a little impromptu meeting with our doctors regarding the next step for Chad. He had been out of the hospital with the artificial heart for almost two months. We had enjoyed the holidays and the luxury of non-hospital living, but we all knew there was still a huge hurdle, or five, to cross. February was in our faces and reality was setting in hard as Chad was scheduled to return to the hospital on Thursday, January 31, to start preparations for rc-listing.

Despite the obvious stress that had become a normal life element, I couldn't quite put my finger on why I felt this particular sadness. It was very possible that I was feeling a little sad because January had been a fantastic month of family birthday celebrations and an exciting trip to Hollywood, or perhaps my feelings were attributed to the fact that the weather was a little nicer and the family walks in the evenings were grossly incomplete without Chad. But who was I kidding? I had a very strong hunch that I knew the exact source of my feelings. I just did not want to succumb to it. All week long, I could not help but reminisce and think about how this exact same time last year was the weekend that Chad had received his new heart. It was such a celebratory time and we were all so overjoyed by this blessing of indescribable magnitude. We knew we had a journey ahead of us, but we had finally reached the mountaintop, or so we thought.

So as I remembered this time last year, and thought about the present, there were definite feelings of sadness that I was determined to suppress. I had always envisioned that we would be celebrating Chad's one-year post transplant mark surrounded by our closest and most supportive friends and family. I also envisioned that at this celebration, either we would have a newborn baby or one on the way. Out of all of the possible scenarios, what I never envisioned was that I would be sitting here in Chad's hospital room at UCLA typing this particular chapter.

However, over the course of this week, as I struggled to shake off the sadness, I was always reminded that our present circumstances could be a lot worse and they absolutely beat the alternative. We may not be celebrating the one-year mark in 2013, but it had simply been postponed, not canceled. As I thought about all of the amazing families that donated life in 2012 through organs of their loved ones who passed away, I prayed for these families as they approached a different type of one-year mark: the anniversary of the loss of their precious loved ones. Just the very thought that this could be our reality too, really forced me to quickly begin to count, double count and re-count our blessings.

O my soul, bless GOD. From head to toe, I'll bless his holy name! O my soul, bless GOD, don't forget a single blessing! Psalm 103:1-2 MSG

Chad may be on his third heart preparing to wait for the fourth one, but he was STILL HERE. Chad may be back in California, away from Amare and me in Phoenix, but he was receiving around-the-clock, heart-filled love and care from the two people who had been with him from day one of his life, his parents. Chad may be back in the hospital, unsure of his next release date, but he was on the seventh floor, and not, dare I say, six feet under. Life may not be easy, but we still had it, and the breath of life is one blessing that must always be counted.

O my soul, bless GOD. From head to toe, I'll bless his holy name! O my soul, bless GOD, don't forget a single blessing! Psalm 103:1-2 MSG

Amare's Anecdotes #6

My Hands

Amare was born with a bit of a heart condition himself. Thank God, his condition was no comparison to Chad's in terms of the severity. In short, the wall that should have grown between his top two chambers did not develop during the pregnancy. Very shortly after his 1st birthday, Amare had open heart surgery during which the doctors permanently placed a patch in lieu of the missing wall.

During Amare's post-surgery hospital stay, our family friends Desiree and Eric brought Amare an adorable green frog. Desiree told him that the frog was significant because it stood for **F**ully **R**ely **O**n **G**od. What a great acronym!

Well, fast forward almost 3 years and Amare is now approaching Pre-K. From time to time he selects a stuffed animal to accompany him to school for nap-time. On one particular day as I was picking up Amare from school, "Froggio" had gone missing. Amare was very upset and unfortunately, we had a flight to catch and would have to put the search on hold until the following week. Me being stretched extremely thin and running on fumes, proceeded to tell a very distraught Amare, as I strapped him into his car seat, that Froggio would turn up but for now, he would just have to put it in  God's hands. Amare's immediate response, with his hands raised and shaking to emphasize, was: "BUT I WANT IT IN MY HANDS!" Join the club son, join the club. Froggio turned up the following week and has been home safe and sound ever since.

NEVER JUST HAPPENED

Kara

As fate would have it, this would be our second year in a row spending Super Bowl Sunday in the hospital. Both Chad and I were not big football fans so this was really a non-issue for us. However, hanging out at the house for Super Bowl Sunday with good food, friends and family, and the Beyoncé half-time show on the big screen would have been nice. For a split second, it crossed my mind as to why it was necessary for Chad to come into the hospital on Thursday, when the real cleansing process (next phase of plasmapheresis) was not scheduled to begin until Monday. Nevertheless, over the last year, we had grown to truly trust the doctors and the process, so we did not really question minute things such as scheduling.

After a short visit with Chad late Friday night after we landed, Amare and I got a good night's sleep and set out Saturday morning to have a great family day at the hospital visiting Chad. We played games, went to the cafeteria for lunch, watched a movie, took naps and had an all-around relaxing and wonderful day. Amare had been asking me all day if we were going to spend the night at the hospital and my answer was no, we could stay really late and then go home to sleep and come back in the morning.

Amare took a really long nap that day so I was hopeful that we could visit until like 10 or 11PM.

Around 5:50PM, I was sitting on the bed balancing the checkbook and paying bills, Amare was playing one of his favorite games on the iPad, and Chad was sitting in a chair just chilling. The television was on, more for background noise than anything. Amare's game volume was up, but not too loud. And of course the whirring sound of the artificial heart, which we had all grown to know and love since October 29, was present. This was the sound of life—the most important backpack that Chad would ever carry. Then, all of a sudden, there was silence; the loudest silence that I have ever heard, a silence that would replay in our heads as a piercing siren for days, weeks and years to come.

WHAT?!? Immediately, time stood still. "IT STOPPED!" Chad cried.

"HELP!" I yelled and rushed to his side. The Freedom Driver started back up after a second or two, and immediately went into the emergency fault alarm that we had heard during training, but this was clearly not a drill. We immediately got the device out of the backpack and felt that it was hot and so we proceeded to change the batteries, thinking the device had overheated. Well, this did not stop the alarm and by now, every nurse on the floor was in the room and full blown panic had set in. Chad and I worked as a team and did the switch over to the back-up driver—the switch-over, which again, we had trained on, but had hoped and prayed would never be needed. The switch over, where once unplugged, we had less than one second to get hooked back up to the other device. So I retrieved the tool kit to get the scissors to cut the zip-lines that had held the original drivelines in place. We quickly decided who would do red and who would do blue, and we got the job done. But, unfortunately, the back-up device came on and went straight to the fault alarm as well.

This is one part of the training that I did not recall. At home, we only had one back-up device so if that faulted too, then what? Well, thank God, we were not at home. I immediately asked the nurses to page the VAD coordinators and find the 3rd device STAT. Well "stat" turned out to feel like eternity and pandemonium had definitely entered the

It is better to trust in the Lord than to put confidence in man. Psalms 118:8 KJV

room. The underlying and very overwhelming problem was that everyone had "trained" on the device, but no one present had had any real-life experiences with the device. Unfortunately, the veterans in the room were Chad, the patient, and me, his wife. Once this was blatantly obvious by the reaction in the room, Chad and I proceeded to act as a team. While I was repeatedly asking for someone to go get the third and larger device from wherever it was stored, Chad in his ever-cool and forever calm demeanor had retrieved his notebook to review the protocol. Duh! "Someone check my blood pressure," he immediately requested. Of course, it was elevated; his freakin' source of life had paused for a second. At that point, we remembered the emergency pills that were in the magic backup luggage that his father had so diligently organized. One "baby doc" tried to pull rank and say that we should hold off on the pills until further review. However, Chad reading the protocol in the notebook was the further review so he and I proceeded to administer the pills.

Another thing that I could not recall from the training, was just how long the Freedom Driver could stay in fault alarm mode, and if we were in jeopardy of it going out completely? Obviously, not interested in finding out the answer to this, I continued to press the weekend doctors about retrieving the third device and exactly how long it was going to take for them to produce it. And then at last, the larger machine was on the scene. The nurses were on the phone receiving instructions from the VAD coordinator on-call. Once they had the larger device up and running, they were motioning to do the switch over, or so they thought. But Chad immediately halted the room and demanded to know what the coordinator's instructions were and what the nurse's strategy was to do the next switchover. Once everyone was in agreement on the plan, down to the detail of a one, two, three count, with go being after three and not on three, the switchover was done successfully.

Once again, God had ordered our steps and placed both Chad and me in the right place at the right time, together. Oh, and of course, Amare was there too and didn't miss a beat. His immediate recommendation was to "Call Dr. DuBois'!" But after the room was

It is better to trust in the Lord than to put confidence in man.   Psalms 118:8 KJV

flooded with nurses and other personnel, he proceeded to play his game on the iPad and charm the staff members who were not immediately involved with assisting Chad. All and all, it was another day in the Adventures of the Washingtons, and Amare got his wish for us to spend the night after all. This was yet another day that brought everything back into perspective. In the days to come, our anxiety about the next device malfunctioning subsided little by little but never quite went away. At the end of the day, we both agreed and confirmed that while we would be forever grateful for the devices, our ultimate faith and trust was definitely in God, our true and only source of life.

It is better to trust in the Lord than to put confidence in man. Psalms 118:8 KJV

THE CALENDAR – FRIEND OR FOE?

As someone who has been identified as a chronic planner on multiple occasions, the calendar has always been my friend. However, as of late, the calendar has become a constant source of immediate depression. As we continue to chug along in this second wave of the heart transplant journey, it seems as if the calendar has become less and less of a friend. Every target date that we kind of envisioned in our heads has not quite come to fruition. Chad received his artificial heart on October 29, 2012, and at that time it was the doctor's hopes and goal to have him listed for a transplant by January or February 2013. In late January, Chad was re-admitted to the hospital to begin treatments to clean his blood and get him listed. At that point we kind of thought the timeline would go approximately as follows: Chad would be listed by the end of February, potentially receive a heart by the end of March or April, do a six month stay in Los Angeles, and be home in Phoenix by Halloween.

Well, here it is the 8th of March, and Chad has undergone two waves of intense treatments, but unfortunately the reduction in antibodies has been minimal. Chad is not yet listed and the doctors, while still convinced that the treatments will work, have no idea how long it will take. Knowing that Chad will be required to remain in Los Angeles for at least six months post-transplant, it has become abundantly clear to us that he will not be home for Amare's preschool graduation or his first day of Kindergarten. On top of that, 2013 is a year of two big milestones for us. One being our ten year wedding anniversary in July, and the second being Amare's fifth birthday. I have always envisioned celebrating both of these occasions in a rather big way. While I have no problems being totally creative and celebrating these occasions in California, at this point we do not even know if Chad will have received his next transplant yet.

I cannot even begin to describe my feelings about the reality of our current situation. Lately I find myself in an angry state of mind very often and all too easily. I also experience extreme waves of sadness just out of nowhere. The other night during a Skype session, Amare informed Chad that he wanted his fifth birthday party to be at the hospital so that Chad would not miss it. While I find it endearing that Amare would want his dad there so badly that he was willing to have his party at the hospital; it breaks my heart to the core that our four-year-old son even had to think like that.

At this point the calendar is not our friend. Every time I catch myself looking at it or thinking about it, I try to redirect my thoughts. For the first heart transplant back in 2012, Chad was gone from Phoenix for a total of 140 days. This time around Chad has already been gone for 160 days and we have absolutely no clue as to when he will return to Phoenix, nor when we can at least start the six month count down. With each day that passes by we have no choice but to strengthen our faith. We may not know the timeline of Chad's healing, but we have no doubt that God knows. In due time, the master plan will be revealed to us, and one day I will fall back in love with the calendar. But for now, I will just take things day by day, and try my best to not focus on the near or distant future.

Many are the plans in the mind of a man, but it is the purpose of the Lord that will stand. - Proverbs 19:21 ESV

MAY
26
:(

JUNE
~~12~~

JULY
5
???

SEASONS

Kara

If you pay close attention, oftentimes you can feel the seasons changing. The weeks leading up to Easter Sunday 2013 had been rough. Chad was not feeling well at all and it seemed to be one thing after another. The worse part about the whole scenario was that he was still receiving conflicting updates regarding the status of the antibodies and it seemed as if he were no closer to being listed as a transplant candidate, then when he was initially re-admitted to the hospital back in late January.

When Amare and I got to town the Friday of Palm Sunday Weekend, I had no idea that Chad was as bad off as he actually was. Somehow over the phone and Skype sessions, he had been able to mask this. The shortness of breath had returned and he did not want to be left alone. Luckily, Amare and I had been able to catch an earlier flight on this particular Friday, so we got to the hospital around 3PM. Charlotte was there and got me up to speed on how Chad was really doing. As if the scene was not stressful enough, one of the primary doctors and the device coordinators were having an extensive debate in Chad's room, regarding the next best plan of action to address his current issues.

Amare and I hung out with Chad all evening and around 9PM, we headed home (to Chad's parents' house) for me to shower, put Amare to bed and return to the hospital.

The next day, Chad's shortness of breath was gradually getting worse. This happened to be the weekend that my parents were driving from Phoenix to visit Chad and bringing my Aunt Adrienne who was visiting from Chicago, to surprise Chad. All of the company was a nice surprise and distraction for Chad on Saturday afternoon, but unfortunately, the shortness of breath was not subsiding and the doctors were beginning to consider dialysis as the next plan of action.

Around 9PM, Amare and I went home to bath and put on our pajamas. We headed back to the hospital for a good ole UCLA slumber party. When we retuned, Chad's condition had grossly diminished and he could barely talk because the shortness of breath had become so extraordinary. Dialysis was inevitable and the machine and technician were on the way. Chad's parents also headed to the hospital upon learning about the latest turn of events. The dialysis took about two and a half hours and was complete around 2AM. Another episode, another chapter.

In the days following, Chad was pretty weak from the dialysis, but the goal to remove the excess water and resolve the shortness of breath had been achieved. The following week was Easter and Chad was back on the road to recovery. After a few weeks of medical lows, culminating in emergency dialysis, we were convinced that a high season was surely close. Just as we anticipated, Easter 2013 was hands down one of the best weekends in the hospital thus far. Having not spent a holiday with my own parents or siblings since Thanksgiving 2011, it meant the world to me that they joined us for this holiday. And even though they had just visited Chad from Phoenix during the last two weeks, both my parents and my sister and family decided that it was necessary to spend this holiday with Chad.

Charlotte had already begun making preparations early in the week and was more than happy to accommodate the additional guests, so she

There is a time for everything, and a season for every activity under the heavens.
Ecclesiastes 3:1 NIV

and Michael connected with the head of the hospital facilities and secured a beautiful conference room for our private family dinner. The charge nurse for the day even got the doctors to write orders for Chad to be away from his room under my and his parents' watch, for as long as our dinner would last. The nurse came in periodically to check Chad's vitals of course, but it was so awesome to have that free time to ourselves with no external chaperone. Easter Sunday 2013 was truly spectacular. What better way to celebrate the unparalleled sacrifice of our Lord and Savior, than surrounded by the love that we were so fortunate to have. I could not help but get emotional when I looked around and realized just how blessed Chad and I were, and the presence of our amazing family was just a reminder that we serve a God of more than enough.

Chad

Easter 2013 was awesome for me for a number of reasons. Kara and Amare were back in town, which always makes my spirit soar and lightens my mood, no matter the circumstances. My in-laws from Phoenix drove out to celebrate with me. That's a six-hour drive that they made, for what was the second week in a row, with children in tow. My sister, brother-in-law, and nephew were in attendance as well. Of course, my mother and father came. We reserved a conference room, so I was able to get out of my hospital room for about four hours with minimal nursing interruptions. Don't get me wrong, I know that the nurses have a job to do and it is necessary for me to be monitored, and I don't find the nurses intrusive at all. However, to not have the usual interruptions, and being out of the room for such a long time was the most normal thing that I've done in over two months—not to mention that my mom arranged the catering of some delicious Jamaican food! All of these things combined bolstered my endurance and refreshed my resolve for the remainder of the wait ahead. It was a veritable shot in the arm.

There is a time for everything, and a season for every activity under the heavens.
Ecclesiastes 3:1 NIV

Kara

Easter 2013 did in fact turn out to be the beginning of the end for this particular season of waiting. After five long months of being on the totally artificial device, just a couple of days after Easter, Chad was listed as a candidate for another heart transplant. Even before finding out this news, Chad's spirits were riding high after such a special holiday dinner. He described his feelings as genuinely happy, not just in a good mood, but actually happy. Praise the Lord for this new season.

There is a time for everything, and a season for every activity under the heavens.
Ecclesiastes 3:1 NIV

VISIONS OF AN OLD FRIEND

Kara

Disclaimer: *If you are my mother, father, brother, aunt, uncle, niece or nephew, co-worker/boss (in any capacity), please skip over this chapter and rest assured, you'll thank me later.* ☺

It was May 11, 2013. By now, Chad had been back on the heart transplant list for just over a month or so, awaiting his second heart transplant. Amare and I had been traveling back and forth to Los Angeles again every other, if not every weekend since September 2012. While the two week stints between our visits with Chad would always grow long and practically unbearable, I decided to take Mother's Day for myself this year.

My parents offered to keep Amare that weekend, so Saturday was to be a day of shopping and a dine-in movie. I started the day off with a "quick" visit to my favorite Macy's in Phoenix at the Biltmore. I still have the playful voicemail from Chad telling me that they had closed down and were out of business. But in all seriousness, he said that he wanted me to enjoy my day and that he loved me. Enjoy the day was exactly what

I intended to do. After a little damage was done in Macy's, thankfully, I was out of time and my movie was set to start across the street. I saw *Peoples* starring Kerri Washington—cute movie, had some laughs in it. Along with the laughs, I had a delicious Caramel Apple Martini. At some point in the movie, I was inspired to Google the closest Total Wine because I had just got a revelation of what the rest of my day would look like.

Luckily for me, there was a Total Wine less than two miles away. It had not been that long since I had discovered this store through conversations with a co-worker. Not that I am a huge proponent or pusher of alcohol, but for those of you who know how to drink responsibly, Total Wine is the spot. This place is like the Whole Foods of the alcohol industry. I went into Total Wine on this particular day and got all of the necessary items to make a couple more Caramel Apple Martinis at home. On the way to the house, I swung by the grocery store to get caramel to line the glass, and as I strolled through the deli section (because at that point, the grocery store was foreign ground for me), I was instantly inspired to have one of Chad's favorite types of snack plates. I picked up some fancy crackers, fancy cheese, salami and pepperoni.

At home, I made a nice spread with an accompanying cocktail, and settled in to watch one of my favorite movies, *Why Did I Get Married?*

Again, I am by no means an irresponsible drinker, but let's face it, I'm human. The stress that Chad and I and our family had been constantly enduring was getting to be downright unbearable. And on this rare day of downtime and basically no responsibility, I thoroughly enjoyed myself; so much so that I really cannot recall how many homemade cocktails I partook in. Let's just say, enough to allow me to step completely out of my normal box and realm of controlled, calculated and conservative arena.

When that particular happy hour ended, I went upstairs and continued the party. I got this spur of the moment, totally out of

The wife does not have authority over her own body but yields it to her husband. In the same way, the husband does not have authority over his own body but yields it to his wife.
1 Corinthians 7:4 NIV

character notion to send Chad pictures of me that you wouldn't find on Facebook. I did some iPhoto edits and sent them to his inbox with a bolded subject line of: **FOR YOUR EYES ONLY**. By now, having spent way too much time in the hospital and away from our home, privacy between us was a very faint and distant memory. Yet, I was hoping that my subject line disclaimer was enough. What the heck? After a "few" cocktails, even I was willing to take the risk.

I don't remember how much later, but Chad called me almost speechless. Apparently, he had not paid too much attention to the subject and was just chillin' in his hospital room with his dad when he opened the email. Chad said that he was so shocked that he instantly dropped his phone. He assured me that no one else saw the pictures and that they were very safely stored away never to be seen by anyone but him. He was so very grateful for the pictures and could not believe that I had actually done something so out of character, all in the name of making him happy.

So without asking, he returned the favor and by the next morning when I woke up, I had beautiful pictures of an "old friend" in my inbox. I enjoyed the pictures for a while and then deleted them, too afraid of risking anyone else seeing them, and also not thinking it would be my last visual of this old friend in its prime. Well, it turned out that, just six days after I sent that email, Chad was matched for his second heart transplant and that was that. To this day, I am so happy and proud of myself that I sent him that one last present before the onset of pure hell. I am, however, not so happy that I cannot find his returned present to me. I can still see the picture in my head, but I know that it's only a matter of time until it slowly fades away.

The wife does not have authority over her own body but yields it to her husband. In the same way, the husband does not have authority over his own body but yields it to his wife.
1 Corinthians 7:4 NIV

May 17, 2013

Kara

Having taken a week off from Los Angeles and stayed in Phoenix for Mother's Day, by the tenth day of not seeing Chad, I was really beginning to feel the void. I was so tired of our family being separated but I knew I had no choice but to keep pressing on. By Wednesday, the fifteenth of May, our reunion countdown was well underway. I had gotten so used to Amare and I essentially living in two states that we basically had a secondary wardrobe in Los Angeles. This made weekend packing super easy. The staples of our LA wardrobe were jogging suits (deemed as our hospital uniforms), an outfit to wear on our Monday morning flight which allowed me to go straight to work and Amare to school, an outfit for church, and an outfit just in case there was an opportunity to go out with my girlfriends.

On Thursday, May sixteenth, Amare and I were both excited that the next day was Friday and after work and school we would be off to see Daddy! We both went to bed that evening with our family reunion on the brain. At some point later that night, I was awakened by the phone ringing. Somehow, I had missed the cell phone call and did not catch the house phone fast enough before it had gone to voicemail. I saw that it was Chad and tried to call him back immediately but got a weird wireless phone message about circuits. I checked my voicemail and Chad sounded anxious and could not believe that I, the lightest sleeper on earth, had slept through his phone call. I must have tried at least five times back to back to get through to his cell phone, but got the circuits' message each time. I was left with no choice but to call the nursing station near Chad's room. Luckily, it was a wireless phone and the charge nurse took the phone to Chad right away. He was a little baffled that I had reached him via that particular phone line, but oh well, my psychopath ways had finally paid off. The urgent call was of course, to let me know that he had been matched once again and was headed to the operating room first thing in the morning. His parents were already there with him and Chad was in good spirits, ready for the next step. We spoke for a little while longer and then Chad had to go as people were entering the room to prep him for the next day.

After hanging up, I booked Amare and myself on the first flight out the next morning. I also packed a few extra items, not knowing what the following week would bring in light of this latest development. I never laid back down as I knew my mind would not allow me to fall asleep and also, there was no way that I wanted to risk missing our early morning flight. By four-thirty or five the next morning, Amare and I were headed to the airport. Everything went smoothly and we landed in Los Angeles in the eight o'clock hour. Unfortunately though, the plane taxied for an extended period of time because there was another plane at the gate we had been assigned to. Anxious to get off the plane and get to Chad, I had to do something to channel my nervous energy. I called Chad to check in and get a status update. He was still in his room but would be heading down shortly. We decided to Skype really fast since it looked highly unlikely that we would get to see him in person before the operation. I don't know if I have ever been more grateful for technology than in that moment. Seeing Chad's face that morning was such a relief and a pacifier to me as we were stuck on that plane.

He heals the brokenhearted and binds up their wounds [curing their pains and their sorrows].
Psalm 147:3 AMP

We finally deboarded about fifteen minutes after landing. Charlotte was waiting curbside for Amare and me. We dropped her back at the house and made a beeline for UCLA. By now, it was after 9AM on Friday morning in Los Angeles and of course, traffic was a beast. I took the streets and swooped in and out of lanes all the way through Culver City until we finally reached Westwood. Elena had called a few times for status updates on our position as they were taking Chad down to the operating room. She had let the staff know that we were on our way so they were prepared to let us down to the operating floor.

As if in a scene out of a movie, my heart was racing big time as we finally pulled up to the emergency room parking lot, threw the keys to Michael, who had agreed to park the car. Elena, Amare and I literally raced through the hospital down to the operating floor. Amare and I were required to put on operating room attire from head to toe. The staff members were extremely hesitant regarding Amare going into the room, afraid that he would be traumatized. My thought was that he had already seen so much in the last couple of years and we had traveled and come so very close, it would be a shame for him not to see his daddy before this operation. So we agreed on him coming to the door to say hi but not actually entering the room. Amare was pretty somber and maybe a little shaken up, but it was still great that he had been able to see his daddy, wave at him and say hi. I was able to go into the room and spend a few moments with Chad. The scene was a little breathtaking. There was jazz music playing and what seemed like tons of people moving about in preparation for the big surgery. I was so happy and grateful to see Chad and be by his side, but I was nervous as well; so nervous, in fact, that I was kind of afraid to touch Chad. I just did not want to tamper with a sterile environment and put him at risk in any way. At last though, a familiar face entered the room. Dr. DuBois' was upbeat as usual and relieved that we had made it in time. He encouraged me to relax and assured me that it was okay to touch Chad. I spent a few more minutes with Chad until they finally asked me to leave. I kissed Chad and told him that I loved him and would see him in a few moments with his

He heals the brokenhearted and binds up their wounds [curing their pains and their sorrows].
Psalm 147:3 AMP

new heart. And just like that, we settled back into a place that had become all too familiar, Mattie's room, the waiting room for families with a loved one undergoing surgery.

As the morning progressed, more and more loved ones filed into the room to show their support. I was there but not really there. My heart, mind and spirit were all in the operating room with Chad. Many of the UCLA staff members stopped by during their lunch hour or after their shifts to sit with us for a while. One of the Procurement Team members who had actually rode the helicopter and worked to secure the organ for Chad, sat with us for a great portion of the day and into the evening. It was such a long grueling day of waiting, but we were surrounded every step of the way. Dr. DuBois' stopped in at one point and gave us a positive update that tied us over for a while longer.

Later that evening, we received a call from the OR stating that the surgery was complete and Chad would be headed to recovery shortly. Unfortunately, Dr. Hart was out of town on business when the match came up, so we were not familiar with the surgeon this time around. However, we had grown accustomed to a visit from the acting surgeon each time a surgery was complete, so we waited in anticipation. By 8PM, my sister Robyn and nephews, Eugene and Morris, had joined us in the waiting room, as Amare was going to spend the night with them. The waiting room phone rang and the Washington Family was summoned. On the other end was an OR nurse casually informing me that due to excessive bleeding, they had not been able to close Chad up and that he was on his way up to recovery. I thought for sure that I must have misheard her and asked her to repeat herself. Unfortunately, my ears were not deceiving me, and for the first time in his extensive history of operations, they had in fact not been able to safely close Chad's chest. My emotions got the best of me as I hung up and tried to relay this message to the waiting room full of family. We never received a visit from the acting surgeon and we were all completely baffled by the last phone call. Robyn quickly gathered us in a huge circle for prayer and we all cried out to God for Chad's healing. At this point in the journey, we

He heals the brokenhearted and binds up their wounds [curing their pains and their sorrows]. Psalm 147:3 AMP

had had many contending rock bottom days, but this one was by far the worst.

He heals the brokenhearted and binds up their wounds [curing their pains and their sorrows].
Psalm 147:3 AMP

FAITH IS EVERYTHING

Kara

The Longest Week of My Life

Due to the amount of scar tissue from all of his prior surgeries, they were unable to safely close Chad's chest on May seventeenth after his second heart transplant. Instead, Chad was left in an induced comatose state until they could determine the best and most viable remedy for him. The week following this surgery was the longest week of my life. In the entire fourteen years that we had been dating (ten of which married), we had never gone a full week without talking to each other. Sure, there had been stints of long-distance love, but we always connected via telephone, or as of late, Skype and FaceTime.

During this particular week, I experienced a level of loneliness that I had never experienced before. Chad was heavily sedated and on a breathing tube. Since Amare could not have possibly benefited from seeing his dad in this condition, he was back in Phoenix attending preschool and being a kid. So, here I found myself in a waiting room for twelve hours at a time just so that I could be close to Chad and pop my head in every few hours to remind him that someone was always there. The highlight of my day was the 8:30PM bedtime Skype sessions with Amare. It always warmed my heart to see that he was happy and feeling right at home with his cousins and aunt and uncle.

I cannot recall a time in my life where I had spent this much time alone. I almost felt as though I was beginning to sense what life in jail must feel like. Each day, I would make a list of things to accomplish from the waiting room, but somehow I would find myself either mindlessly surfing the net for shows to watch, or chatting it up with other families who had a loved one in the hospital also. To say the days were long would be an understatement. It was during this week, however, that I was challenged to take my faith to another level, for we had found ourselves in uncharted territory, again. Added twists and surprises seemed to be the new norm for us, but never in a million years would I have guessed Chad's chest would still be open seven days after the surgery. Below are the words from a card that I received from my cousin during this difficult week:

Faith is knowing in your heart what you can't yet see with your eyes.
Faith is the substance of things hoped for, believed in, and brought to God in prayer.
Faith is deep. Faith is strong. Faith is real.
Faith is getting out of bed when you want to pull the covers over your head.
Faith is a nudge, a whisper, a shout from the soul.
Faith is sustenance for a moment, for a day, for as long as it takes.
Faith is the answer no matter the question, problem, or situation.
Faith is what it is...
Faith is everything.

The words on the card were a validation of the confidence that we had all carried throughout the week and this entire journey. Now, don't get me wrong, I am the first to admit that this week was not without moments of weakness, fear, discouragement and frustration. But they were just that, a moment or two until I received a perfectly timed text,

God lives forever and is holy. He is high and lifted up, and he says, I live in a high and holy place. But I also live with people who are sad and humble. I give new life to those who are humble. I give new life to those whose hearts are broken. Isaiah 57:15 ICB

call or Facebook post to boost my spirits and remind me that God is still on the throne. The bottom line is, without faith, there can be no peace. And without peace, you are simply one life crisis away from a mental breakdown. Faith truly is everything.

Missing You Already

How is it possible to spend almost every waking moment with someone, yet miss them more than ever? Nine days later, on May 25, they removed Chad's sternum and did a muscle flap to start the process of closing him up and slowly allowing him to wake up. May 17 to May 25 was probably the longest and worse week of my life thus far. It was extremely overwhelming to be in the room with Chad for long periods of time, yet it was just as overwhelming to leave him alone. Jessica and I spent the first night in the waiting room outside the unit, and from there, I had the day shift while Michael took the night shifts. By the end of the week, the waiting room definitely felt like a jail cell and I was positive that on some unconscious level, Chad too, felt like a prisoner in his now further compromised body. Despite my own distress with the situation, I still felt that it was very much my duty to be there. I would go back to the unit once every hour or so just to remind Chad (although comatose) that we were still there and he was not alone.

Even after they were able to partially close Chad on May 25, it was still made abundantly clear to us that the road to recovery was possibly the longest that we had ever faced. The breathing tube was still in and when that came out, there would be a trachea to replace it. When exactly would I be able to talk to my husband again? How was it possible to be by his side almost every one of my waking hours, yet miss him more than ever before? By this time, I had not seen Amare for a week as he was back in Phoenix with my parents, sister and family. I was missing both Amare and Chad and about as close to a mental breakdown as

God lives forever and is holy. He is high and lifted up, and he says, I live in a high and holy place. But I also live with people who are sad and humble. I give new life to those who are humble. I give new life to those whose hearts are broken. Isaiah 57:15 ICB

possible. It was strictly by the grace of God that I did not lose my mind that week.

God lives forever and is holy. He is high and lifted up, and he says, I live in a high and holy place. But I also live with people who are sad and humble. I give new life to those who are humble. I give new life to those whose hearts are broken. Isaiah 57:15 ICB

PRICELESS TALKS

Kara

They say the key to a successful marriage is communication. It's very common that when couples hit a bump in the road, communication is often the first to go, when in reality, it should be the number one focus. But what happens when verbal communication is not an option? Out of all of Chad's operations, illnesses and setbacks, May 17, 2013 was the beginning of the first time since we had begun dating, that I would not be able to verbally communicate in a two-way conversation with Chad for greater than twenty-four hours. Of the one million things going on during the week that Chad was in a self-induced coma after his second heart transplant, one of the weirdest things was not being able to have a conversation with him. That was the first time that I literally felt as if we were on two different planets. Even after the artificial heart transplant, the very next day, Chad was sitting up and talking once the breathing tube was removed that morning. This and the fact that they had not closed him up and I could practically see his heart through his chest with my own eyes, were huge red flags indicating that nothing about this operation or recovery would be the same.

On May 25, when they were able to partially close up Chad's chest, I thought, at last I can finally have a conversation with my husband! Little did I know, that was the furthest thing from the truth. The doctors explained to us that in order to properly manage the pain, they would have to gradually wake Chad up and that removing the breathing tube would be a step-by-step process depending on how Chad's body responded and tolerated the strenuous responsibility of breathing without mechanical support.

When the breathing tube was eventually removed, it was replaced with a tracheal tube. So now we got crash course lessons on the different sizes of tracheas. Once Chad was able to tolerate breathing on a smaller size trachea, they would be able to insert a cover while he was awake which would allow him to speak. At this point, he could even take a swallow test with the speech therapist and be on the road back to solid foods.

Unfortunately, the trachea was never successfully removed for any significant amount of time. Chad's voice never returned to higher than a whisper and he never passed the swallow test or ate solid foods again after the evening of May 16 when the last organ match was confirmed. For someone whose number one hobby was cooking and who would have been totally content if the only channel to ever exist was the Food Network, this had to have felt like an extended vacation in hell. Naturally without proper nutrition, it is very difficult for the body to heal from anything, let alone the major trauma that Chad's system had undergone. But even aside from that ever-looming fact, my heart ached for Chad every day that he had to endure this battle for his life and not even be able to look forward to a plate of food.

For me, one of the biggest factors that caused me to liken this situation to hell, was the fact that Chad could not verbally speak, nor did he have the physical strength to send text messages. This was bad enough in person, but a complete hindrance and source of anxiety when

Consider it pure joy, my brothers and sisters, whenever you face trials of many kinds, because you know that the testing of your faith produces perseverance. Let perseverance finish its work so that you may be mature and complete, not lacking anything. If any of you lacks wisdom, you should ask God, who gives generously to all without finding fault, and it will be given to you. James 1:2-5 NIV

Amare and I were back in Phoenix and unable to be at Chad's bedside in Los Angeles. In all of our entire relationship, I could not remember a time when we had gone even a day without communicating in some form or fashion. Our world had undeniably been turned upside down and I was staring lonely in the face from an angle that I had never imagined. I cannot even begin to fathom how Chad must have felt, and quite frankly, even to this day, it is too painful to try to imagine.

One of the last semi-normal conversations that Chad and I had took place on the evening of Friday, June 14. Here is my Facebook post from that day:

Charles Kara Washington
Jun 14, 2013 near Los Angeles, CA ·

Just had a conversation with my husband after a MONTH of him not talking!!! I am overjoyed!!! He still has the trachea but is being weaned off slowly but surely. In the meantime there is a valve that they let him use when he is not sleep, that allows him to speak very softly. First words to me were "I Love You". I'm good for the rest of the weekend 😊 😊 😊 After chatting with him, now I'm speechless over just how good God is and how amazing Chad's strength and courage is. Have a great weekend all!

80 Likes · 27 Comments

In that conversation, we covered everything from the fact that he loved me, that when he was able to eat again, the first thing he wanted was a burrito and he talked about his days in a special unit of the Armed Forces. Side note: given Chad's very extensive medical history from the day he was born, clearly the aspect of the Armed Forces was not a part of his resume. This was just the result of being heavily sedated for such a long period of time. We were able to joke about it, get a good laugh or two and move on. That particular evening in the hospital was like us being super young and dating all over again. It was awesome, and my hope for Chad's healing and the future of our family was totally reignited!

Consider it pure joy, my brothers and sisters, whenever you face trials of many kinds, because you know that the testing of your faith produces perseverance. Let perseverance finish its work so that you may be mature and complete, not lacking anything. If any of you lacks wisdom, you should ask God, who gives generously to all without finding fault, and it will be given to you. James 1:2-5 NIV

TRUE LOVE

What does it really mean to love someone? I have always associated true love with that feeling you get when you cannot imagine living your life without a certain person. When no matter how excruciatingly tough some of your days together may be, even those days top your best days apart. True love can only exist when both individuals are willing to compromise for the greater good, put their own wants on the back-burner when the other has pressing needs, and always have the other's best interest in mind. Unfortunately, not everyone has the opportunity to experience true love. Some people will settle instead of requiring it. Some people will think they are experiencing it, only to find out later that it was the furthest thing from it. True love is an awesome privilege that should not be taken for granted.

Chad and I had the privilege of experiencing true love for ten plus years. In fact, while the experience has ended in the physical sense, the love will never die. I love that man and I know that he loves me. I am forever grateful to God for showing me my self-worth and sending me a man who valued it from the very first moment we met. I still to this day, feel so blessed and honored to have known what it really feels like to be loved. I would like to urge everyone, men and women alike, do not settle for anything less than true love. The quick or convenient version of love may be appealing at the moment, but true love equals true happiness and there is no substitution for that.

Kara CW III
July 5, 2013 ·

Interesting day as we celebrate 10 years of marriage today. Not exactly how we envisioned celebrating this milestone year, but hey, at least we made it. Our marriage has definitely been stricken with serious health driven lows, followed by extremely victorious highs. God has been so good to us. Our marriage is void of nonsense. There is no room for arguments about non life-threatening matters. We have that love that is scary because there is no end to what we will do to keep each other safe and happy. We'd like to encourage all married couples, especially the young ones, but the more "mature" ones too :-), to cherish each other and appreciate each moment, big or small. Not everyone is so fortunate to have found that special life mate, so if you have, don't take the privilege lightly. Love each other like there is no tomorrow! God bless! - Us (The crazy in love couple :-)

77 Likes 31 Comments

IT TAKES A VILLAGE

Kara

Dollars and Sense

Although our long-distance routine was not the best case scenario, we had found a way to make the best of it and for all intents and purposes, it worked. Until that is, Chad's verbal communication ceased and his trajectory for healing did not mirror any of the prior experiences. My job had been extremely accommodating of our circumstances from day one. However, as Chad laid in that hospital bed unable to talk, with a film of sadness slowly but surely growing in his eyes, it became abundantly clear to me that it was time to take a leave from work. The audacious hope that had fueled us thus far, was beginning to silently fade. I still wanted to believe that Chad would completely heal and recover, but for the first time, my mind began to teeter with the concept of defeat. I will never forget the visit where Chad, in his frustration with the whole predicament, clearly communicated to me with a hand gesture pointing to his chest and doing the swift swipe to indicate "no more," meaning that was the last open heart operation. After two heart transplants with an artificial heart in the interim, it was safe to say that

Chad would do anything to stick around for Amare and me. But even with our crazy faith, we knew there was only so much that one human body could take.

Earning money to keep our household going and maintaining medical benefits was clearly a contending priority for me and usually my first defense when people asked if Amare and I would be moving to Los Angeles. Sure, it would have been wonderful to be at Chad's side 100% of the time, except with no job, UCLA would not have been the location of our visits. Thankfully though, God in His immaculate wisdom had made it possible for Chad and me to receive donations of more than ten thousand dollars. Chad's sister, Elena, solicited donations from friends, family and colleagues, using one of the go-fund me sites that have now become a phenomena. My Aunt Evelyn also solicited donations from various family members. We were all blown away at the immediate generosity received from so many people, many whom neither Chad nor I had ever even met. Not only was this a major boost to our spirits, it also had a tangible impact on our plans because now I could actually afford to take FMLA and really be by Chad's side.

After much planning and scheduling, we decided to make July 12, Amare's last day at the Lil Paws Preschool that he attended on PetSmart's Corporate Campus. On Saturday, July 13, we flew out to Los Angeles both of us overjoyed at the thought of spending four uninterrupted weeks in California with Chad. Upon landing, we dropped off our bags at the house and headed up the hospital to see Chad. He was in good spirits and it did not feel real to any of us that we would get to be together for an entire month. Although Amare loved spending as much time as possible with his daddy and nurse lady friends, and he never once complained about going to the hospital, we had all agreed that we would also find a nice mix of fun outside of the hospital for Amare over the next month.

Michael and I quickly developed a routine where we would take turns spending two nights at the hospital with Chad, so that the person not

Don't burn out; keep yourselves fueled and aflame. Be alert servants of the Master, cheerfully expectant. Don't quit in hard times; pray all the harder. Help needy Christians; be inventive in hospitality.   Romans 12:11-13 MSG

staying the night could get a break and catch up on rest. Chad's last surgery had been on May 17 and so far, we had been fortunate enough that someone from the family was always by his side. As a result of the "event" following his first heart transplant, Chad had implemented a rule/request that someone stay with him post all surgeries until he was able to speak and clearly express himself. On the days that we were not on hospital duty, I would try to plan a fun summer activity with Amare. This was not hard to do given that we were in Los Angeles and skipping out on the dramatic summer heat that Phoenix was notorious for. We had a mommy-mooter day at Venice Beach, visited Disneyland and California Adventures with my sister and nephews and various movie dates, catching all the summer kids movies.

California was treating us well from an entertainment perspective, but there was still the overarching reason for why we were there. Chad's healing was so-so at best. It was like he would take two steps forward in one area of the complex human body, but five steps back in another area. For instance, after a weekend of fun outside the hospital and good updates regarding Chad's progress, Amare and I reported to the hospital on Sunday afternoon to take our post. When we got off the elevator, we were greeted by Charlotte and her sister who quickly warned us that they were afraid that Chad was having a mental breakdown and it was probably best that Amare not visit that day. The nurses had reported that Chad seemed non-respondent to any of them. He was just lying in the bed with a blank stare and the Neurological Team was on their way to conduct a series of test. Amare went home with his grandmother, super bummed that he did not get to see his dad that day.

As I settled into Chad's room, the test had begun. They had stickers all over Chad's head, and he was hooked up to yet another machine. The attendant spoke in a really loud voice hoping to get some type of response from Chad but had so far been unsuccessful. She asked him to squeeze her hand but he did not budge. She asked him to blink his eyes and still nothing. Next, she asked Chad to stick out his tongue, and

Don't burn out; keep yourselves fueled and aflame. Be alert servants of the Master, cheerfully expectant. Don't quit in hard times; pray all the harder. Help needy Christians; be inventive in hospitality. Romans 12:11-13 MSG

as if she had asked the magic question that he had been waiting for all along, Chad quickly stuck out his tongue. It took all of me to not laugh at this very bizarre scene which had become our life.

Later that evening, Dr. DuBois' kindly explained to me that the episode from earlier was certainly nothing to worry about. After spending as much time in the hospital as Chad had, he was sure to develop hospital psychosis which was even more prevalent in the intensive care unit (ICU). This condition was a form of delirium with a combination of symptoms that typically indicated a state of severe mental confusion.

As we were clearly entering yet another new phase that we were all unfamiliar with, I did my very best to encourage Chad to keep fighting and trusting God. It was abundantly clear to me that we had made the right decision and Amare and I could not have come a day too soon. Being able to see Amare in person daily was definitely a powerful treasure in Chad's healing toolkit. But for some reason or another, this particular recovery turned out to be a never-ending onion-peeling experience. And then that dreadful day happened, when the already annoying onion, turned completely rotten.

It was Friday, July 26, 2013. Amare and I were two weeks into our month-long visit and for Phoenix schools, kindergarten would start in August and we would be back to our weekend visiting schedule. On Thursday, I had taken Amare and a family friend's daughter Michele', to the El Capitan Theatre in Hollywood to see *Monsters U.* The day had been a blast. We got to see one of the stage performances that was signature to El Capitan and the kids took a few pictures on the Avenue of the Stars. We also went to Roscoe's Chicken and Waffles, where Amare and Michele' ate every morsel of food on their plates. They were so cute together and even though they were only five and seven at the time, they reminded me of when Chad and I first started dating.

The next day, Friday, Amare and I were preparing to spend the weekend with Chad at the hospital. Michael had called to update us on

---

Don't burn out; keep yourselves fueled and aflame. Be alert servants of the Master, cheerfully expectant. Don't quit in hard times; pray all the harder. Help needy Christians; be inventive in hospitality. Romans 12:11-13 MSG

Chad's morning schedule. There were concerns of infection so they were taking him down to the lab to change his dialysis catheter. Amare and I were about ten minutes from leaving the house when Michael called to let us know that Chad had returned from the lab. I was in the bathroom applying makeup when less than two minutes after his last call, Michael called back. Noting that the timing was unusual, I was slightly paralyzed by fear and let my mother-in-law, Charlotte, take the call instead. Sure enough, my instincts had unfortunately been correct and Charlotte came in the bathroom and said that Michael suggested we get there immediately. Charlotte said that she would be a few minutes and asked if I wanted Amare to stay back with her. Having no idea whether or not this was a final good-bye type of situation, I opted for him to come with me, grabbed our bags and we were out the door.

Once in the car, as calmly as possible, I told Amare that Mommy was super-stressed and that I would not be able to talk, at all, on the way to hospital. Thankfully, he was on his best behavior that day. My mind was racing faster than ever before. Had this been the call that I had dreaded throughout our entire ten years of marriage? What in the world was going on? During a red light at the intersection of Westwood Blvd and Gayley, I posted the following Facebook message:

Charles Kara Washington
7/26/13 ·

Don't know all the details but please pray for Chad RIGHT NOW. Thanks.

The Big Crash

I parked in the parking garage at UCLA and Amare and I ran through the courtyard and Mattie's Room and jumped on the elevator to the seventh floor. When the doors of the elevator opened, Michael was

Don't burn out; keep yourselves fueled and aflame. Be alert servants of the Master, cheerfully expectant. Don't quit in hard times; pray all the harder. Help needy Christians; be inventive in hospitality. Romans 12:11-13 MSG

sitting in the chairs outside of ICU with Chad's social worker. Thankfully, the social worker offered to take Amare on a walk to find snacks so that Michael could get me caught up to speed. Michael quickly explained to me what he had witnessed first-hand. Chad had just returned from the lab and been rolled back into his room and before they had even finished getting his bed parked and situated, Chad motioned that he could not breathe. Seconds later, alarms were sounding, the room was packed with staff and Michael had been asked to leave. When Amare and I arrived, there was a sign by the ICU buzzer stating that no one could enter through that door as there was an emergency underway. After I got the download from Michael, I called my mom to start the prayer chain. Michael's brother Darryl who works at UCLA, joined us as we waited. Amare and the social worker returned with snacks and a toy and he was content.

About forty-five minutes later, a team of doctors that we did not know came to talk with us. As we filed into an unoccupied waiting room, my mind was racing wild, praying all the while that Chad was still alive. They explained to us that Chad had gone into cardiac arrest and had been revived. They were uncertain as to the cause of the crash and would begin to run tests as Chad became more stable. Then they hit us with the ultimate whammy that we had managed to dodge up until this point. It turned out that Chad had undergone almost an hour of CPR and the doctors had felt it was inevitable that he go on the ECMO (Extracorporeal Membrane Oxygenation) device in order to stand a remote chance at surviving the next couple days. My mind immediately retrieved a casual conversation that Chad and I had had with one of the nurses on the hospital patio once about the ECMO device. We were just enjoying a beautiful day and Chad was getting some fresh air. By now, we were friends with most of the nurses so we were just chatting with his nurse for the day who was sharing some of his hospital experiences. Somehow we had landed on the topic of devices and I very clearly remember the nurse saying, as he shook his head, "And oh, ECMO, you

Don't burn out; keep yourselves fueled and aflame. Be alert servants of the Master, cheerfully expectant. Don't quit in hard times; pray all the harder. Help needy Christians; be inventive in hospitality. Romans 12:11-13 MSG

never want that one. Most patients rarely recover from it." As we sat in that waiting room with the doctors after "the crash," my heart sank and my mind tried its best to send the recalled conversation to a permanent archive never to be replayed again, but instead it was like a scratched record that kept repeating and repeating. This was a living nightmare that I began to wonder if we would ever recover from.

The Ultimate Prayer Chain

By this point in our journey, social media (i.e. Facebook) had become a very valuable tool for us. Through this medium, we were able to update our family and friends near and far, about Chad's status. We posted our medical victories, big and small, as well as emergencies where urgent prayers were needed. In the beginning, I was reluctant to post much because I did not want others to feel inundated with our struggles. However, the reality turned out to be quite contrary. If too much time elapsed between my posts, I would actually get gentle nudges and update requests. Later, I realized the obvious, that people genuinely cared and wanted to know exactly what was going on. In fact, our display of faith and endurance had become an inspiration and encouragement to others in their own life struggles. Once this was brought to our attention, it really warmed our hearts and made us even stronger and that much more determined to keep fighting through the tests.

As only God could have orchestrated, the day following "the crash" was the beginning of a 24-hour prayer chain that my cousin, Candice, had facilitated. She had spent the last couple of weeks building a website that would allow people to sign up for a specific time to pray for Chad's healing. The website included some of our family pictures, recent prayer requests, status updates and my favorite, a map of the United States with a marker in each state where someone was praying for Chad. The truth is, by now it felt like the whole world was praying for Chad. My brother was deployed with the Navy at the time so we knew for a fact that there

Don't burn out; keep yourselves fueled and aflame. Be alert servants of the Master, cheerfully expectant. Don't quit in hard times; pray all the harder. Help needy Christians; be inventive in hospitality. Romans 12:11-13 MSG

was a vessel of sailors halfway around the world somewhere praying for Chad's healing. My Aunt Margaret had also informed us that her missionary friends in Israel were diligently praying for Chad. Despite the fact that many had told us, somehow actually seeing the individual states on the U.S. map eclipsed with markers representing our prayer partners, was a precious and timely illustration of the love and support that we so desperately needed.

Don't burn out; keep yourselves fueled and aflame. Be alert servants of the Master, cheerfully expectant. Don't quit in hard times; pray all the harder. Help needy Christians; be inventive in hospitality. Romans 12:11-13 MSG

GOD'S ITINERARY

God's Itinerary: a perfectly orchestrated series of life events which cannot be humanly predicted, yet if accepted, can be regarded as a majestic life roadmap.

Kara

After a month of FMLA, on Thursday, August 8, Amare and I had one of our classic family sleepovers at the hospital. As usual, he had a ball parading about the unit in his Ninja Turtle Pajamas and flirting with all of the female nurses. Both of us were just trying to soak up every moment possible with Chad as our month-long stint in Los Angeles had come to an end and it was time to return to Phoenix for work and the pivotal first week of kindergarten. Chad was still a long way from healthy, but seemed to be stable and his body was showing small glimpses of hope in terms of recovery. The following morning, uncertain about the always volatile traffic in Los Angeles, the plan was for Amare and me to leave the hospital at 8:30AM in order to make our flight back to Phoenix. Around 8AM, the normal morning traffic began to flood Chad's room. The Respiratory Team did their check, followed by the Dialysis Team performing their routine machine maintenance and next, the Wound Team showed up to do their evaluation and change of bandages. Seeing that our window of time alone had quickly closed, I told Chad that we were just going to go ahead and head out. Still on the breathing device and unable to speak, Chad very clearly communicated for us to, "WAIT." The medical team realized our need and gave us a moment of privacy. At that time, we prayed and told Chad that we loved him and we would be back the following weekend to visit him. It was then that he turned this particular goodbye into something very different from the millions of other good-byes that we had said. After Chad and Amare hugged, Chad took his very weak hand and caressed Amare's face in his palm. Although I was careful not to react to this change in scene, it had instantly caught my attention. Was Chad saying goodbye forever? My stomach clenched and I was immediately overcome by a dreadful feeling. In order to physically walk out of the room, I had to quickly convince myself that the depth of what I thought I had witnessed, was just my imagination and typical paranoia. We kissed, finished our goodbyes and headed for the car. I made a conscious decision to bury my thoughts on this in a deep place. For as long as I could keep the thoughts from surfacing daylight, there would be no chance of them coming to fruition.

That day, Amare and I returned to Phoenix just in time to get home, drop off our bags and head out to Back to School Night at his new school. We met his Kindergarten teacher, saw where he would sit, hang his backpack, and have lunch. It was such an exciting time, yet it seemed to serve as a fluorescent highlight to the painful hole in our family. As I held Amare's left hand in my right hand and we walked the campus, I could not help but think about Chad's dream and visualize how he would have given anything to be there holding Amare's other hand. Yet, I pressed on with a smile on my face, determined not to cast any gray clouds on Amare's day.

The first week of kindergarten just flew by. Like many parents, I videoed and took pictures of Amare walking into school on the first day. I took a picture of him every morning that week and when I picked him up in the afternoon, I would ask him to do a quick video clip telling Daddy about his day. At the end of the week, I planned to combine all of the footage so that Chad could experience this monumental week from his hospital room.

A person may think up plans. But the Lord decides what he will do.   Proverbs 16:9 ICB

The Friday of the first week of school was Amare's 5th birthday. Very early on in our parenting days, Chad and I had agreed that we would do big birthday parties on the first, fifth and other milestone years. On the off years, Amare had grown accustomed to really enjoying staycations and week-long celebrations at the fabulous resorts in and around Phoenix. Now that Amare's fifth birthday was here and Chad was in the hospital, I was grossly torn. Surely, Amare had enough friends around the hospital to have a party there. Yet, he was still a kid and deserved some type of normalcy in his already very atypical childhood. Over the course of that week, I would try to gauge Chad's progress and status through reports from his parents and daily calls to the nurses. By Tuesday, Chad seemed to be really taking a turn for the better. I received a picture of him sitting up in a chair looking out the window with a smile on his face. At that point, I decided that it was time to plan a birthday celebration weekend for Amare that included Chad as much as possible. I quickly jotted down an itinerary that consisted of cupcakes from Sprinkles for the nurses that Friday night. Saturday, Amare and some of his cousins were scheduled to go to an arcade where I had reserved a 154-inch screen for them to play their favorite video games. Afterwards, they would go to Chad's parents' house to have Amare's favorite meal from Panda Express, along with Transformers ice cream birthday cake and the opening of birthday presents. Sunday morning, we would pick up donuts from Amare's favorite shop by UCLA and go celebrate some more with Chad and our hospital family before we caught our flight back to Phoenix. That was my itinerary.

Unfortunately, it turned out that my itinerary and *God's Itinerary* were about as far from congruent as one could conceive. On Friday, August 16, Amare's fifth birthday, we went to school and work for half of the day. My parents met me at Amare's school with a surprise flying buddy for Amare that weekend. His cousin Carlton, only three days older than Amare, would be joining us for the weekend of birthday festivities. When Amare was brought into the school office to meet me, he had on a birthday crown and special banner. He was the cutest thing and we were both super-excited to head back to LA to see Chad. Amare was

A person may think up plans. But the Lord decides what he will do. Proverbs 16:9 ICB

pleasantly surprised to see my parents and Carlton in the parking lot. We said our goodbyes and the boys and I headed to the airport. So far, the day was going exactly as planned.

When we arrived at LAX, my mother-in-law, Charlotte, met us and we rode to their house to drop her off before we made a mad dash for Sprinkles and the hospital. On the ride from the airport to the house, Charlotte mentioned that one of the doctors wanted to have another family meeting but that she did not plan to attend. She asked if I would be attending, but not knowing the date, time or specific subject matter, I was quite confused by this question. Something about this conversation was very unsettling and I had a feeling that there were no less than one thousand details that I had missed during the week that we had been back in Phoenix. Just before we pulled off from the house, my father-in-law drove in. Anxious to get on our way to the hospital, we stopped and chatted for a minute. His update regarding Chad's condition and what the doctors were saying was rather vague as well. At that point, I just needed to get there and see for myself what was going on.

On the way to Sprinkles, the boys both took a nap in the car. Curbside delivery had never been so useful. By the time we arrived at the hospital, my excitement to see Chad and celebrate Amare's birthday as a family, had overshadowed my anxious thoughts regarding the riddle-like updates. We parked the car and headed up to the unit. Amare was greeted right away with Happy Birthday wishes from various nurses and hospital staff. The boys and I dressed in our yellow gowns which had become a standard hospital requirement when entering Chad's room. We greeted Chad with bright smiles but I could tell that he was having a rough day. His eyes delivered an immediate indication of pain, overwhelming sadness and just not the Chad that I was expecting to see. Chad's nurse that day was Nurse Lauren, one of Amare's girlfriends. Once I got the boys settled with their games and electronics, Nurse Lauren filled me in with what was going on. One of Chad's lungs had collapsed the day before and the chest tube was not draining as they would have expected. When she finished her update, I tried to summarize what I had heard which seemed to be a ton of issues yes, but

A person may think up plans. But the Lord decides what he will do. Proverbs 16:9 ICB

no one issue sounding terribly severe or irreversible. She also mentioned that one of the doctors had wanted a family meeting and was talking comfort solutions, etc. But she ended her update saying that they were not giving up and that we were all still fighting and in this together.

Over the course of that evening, Nurse Lauren and I chatted about how Chad and I had met, and our extensive history of dating. We talked about how Chad and I had always wanted more kids but it had not seemed to work out just yet. At that point, she asked me if we had frozen any fertilized embryos and my answer was a nonchalant "no." But in my head, I was unpacking this question and wondering if it meant that Chad and I would never have the opportunity to try to conceive again. However, just as I had suppressed my alarm and concern with the nature of Chad's previous goodbye to Amare, I tucked this question in that same dark place. It was as if my mind was determined to protect my heart and would not allow me to ponder on any thoughts contrary to Chad's complete healing.

We got dinner from the cafeteria and the boys and I visited with Chad for about four or five hours. Around eight-thirty, Amare and Carlton said their good-byes to Chad and I took them home to Chad's parents' house. We stopped at Party City to pick up Transformers-themed balloons for the celebration at the house the next day. Once we got home, I bathed the boys and got them dressed for bed. I then headed back to the hospital to spend the night with Chad. Still not showing much movement or reaction to anything, I held Chad's hand and filled him in on Amare's first week of kindergarten. All the while, Chad looked me right in my eyes, but there was an emptiness to his gaze that I had never seen before. He just looked so very sad that I felt my heart breaking in itty bitty pieces right then and there. Still, I attributed his gaze to the pain and discomfort that he must have been feeling, and a much warranted onset of depression from this seemingly never-ending war for life that he had been going through. Around eleven that evening, I turned on jazz music for Chad and got ready for bed myself. As I climbed into the extended chair, I was grateful that it was positioned so that I could see Chad and he could see me. Needing to unwind before falling asleep,

A person may think up plans. But the Lord decides what he will do. Proverbs 16:9 ICB

I pulled out my iPad and pieced together the pictures and video footage from Amare's first week of kindergarten. About an hour later, with the jazz playing from Chad's cell phone and the typical hospital orchestra of beeps, drips and more, we both dozed off to sleep.

I remember waking up around 4AM feeling surprisingly rested. The blood pressure machine was alarming and nurses were entering the room. Next, the ICU doctor in charge for the night entered the room, followed by many more. Um, what exactly was going on here? The ICU doctor, who I had seen around before but was not that familiar with, approached me and started asking me about what Chad and I or the family had discussed regarding resuscitation should the need arise. He went on to say really frankly, "We (meaning the medical team) think we are looking at the end of Mr. Washington's life." I was positive that I had misheard him so I pardoned myself and asked him what he had said. He proceeded to inform me that perhaps they had reached a solution for the moment, but most likely the solution would not be able to sustain Chad for another day or two. Extremely baffled by this conversation with, for all intents and purposes, a complete stranger, I quickly told him that Chad had never indicated wanting to give up and whenever I asked him, he assured me that he was still up for the fight. I also asked the doctor if we could step outside of the unit, as I never wanted to have these conversations in Chad's presence and risk alarming or discouraging him from an already Olympian-style uphill battle.

The ICU doctor let me know that Dr. DuBois' and Dr. Hart had been contacted and asked to weigh in on the situation and make medicinal recommendations for Chad. In the meantime, I called my father-in-law to let him know that the room was filling up, things did not feel right and it was probably best if he came. Next, Dr. P, a familiar resident came in the room to talk to me. She set down in the chair beside me with tears in her eyes. She let me know that they were doing everything that they possibly could to raise Chad's blood pressure, but at this point, he was basically maxed out on every medicine drip possible. I let her know that Chad's dad was on his way and that I was unable to speak to the other doctor again until my support had arrived.

A person may think up plans. But the Lord decides what he will do.   Proverbs 16:9 ICB

When Michael arrived, he was brought up to speed on everything going on. I remember him asking me how I was doing and I told him that the entire thing was surreal to me. I know for a fact that at that moment, my mind, heart and soul were every bit incapable of grasping the reality of the situation. I am certain of this because out of the full gamut of things to be worried about at that moment, I told Michael, "I didn't even get to show Chad Amare's video from the first week of kindergarten." Looking back, I can't believe that that was my concern at that very moment. But I guess that was all that my mind could handle. So Michael said, "Show it to him." And that's exactly what I did. I stood by Chad's bedside holding the iPad while he gazed at the screen watching the twenty-minute recap of his son's first week of kindergarten. Although it may have seemed oddly strange to play the video at that point in time, to this day, I find a sense of joy and gratitude in knowing that Chad did in fact get to see his son go to kindergarten, and Amare's daily narratives to his dad that week did not go undelivered.

Around seven or eight that morning, Dr. Hart came to see Chad. He said that he had received the reports and knew the numbers looked anything but promising, but he just had to see Chad with his own two eyes. As he stood there in disbelief, he just shook his head. He could not believe that Chad looked as good as he did, given the reports he had just seen. Michael asked him what his thoughts were on how the next few hours or days would play out. Dr. Hart thoroughly, yet ever so gently explained where Chad's numbers were at in comparison to where a surviving person's numbers tended to be. Even with this very dismal report, Dr. Hart showed no signs of wanting to give up. He said that if anyone could ever pull out of this condition, it would be Chad. Michael's summation of the conversation back to Dr. Hart was basically that we needed a miracle beyond all miracles in order to pull out of this one with Chad alive. Dr. Hart confirmed that that was correct and with one last gaze at Chad, he embraced Chad's dad and had a breakdown. After a few moments had passed, Dr. Hart quickly gathered his composure and told Michael that no matter what happened, he wanted to be involved. With that, he quickly left the room.

A person may think up plans. But the Lord decides what he will do. Proverbs 16:9 ICB

By now, I had had multiple warnings and major indications that the dreadful moment was most likely inevitable at this point. Looking back, I realize that I read more into the side conversations and actions, than the actual medical reports that were being delivered. I had gotten so used to hearing undesirable news and handing it over straight to God, that it never really shook me to my core—for I knew that God was in control and He had never left us before. So it was not until I had the casual conversation with one nurse about freezing eggs, another nurse slipping me her phone number and my father-in-law telling me to show Chad the video, that my mind even began to scratch the surface of believing that this could really be happening.

After Dr. Hart left, I knew that it was only a matter of seconds before a floodgate of tears would be streaming down my face. I told Michael that I was going to step out to get some coffee. I must have roamed Westwood for a good thirty or forty minutes just in tears and disbelief. Was this really happening? No way could this really be happening. Surely, I would return back to Chad's hospital room and this nightmare would be over. As I was walking back into the hospital, my brother had texted me with a usual check-in to see how things were going. For one of the few times in this journey, I had not even one positive spin on this update. All I could say was that it was not going well and things did not look good.

Still in disbelief, I returned to the room and visited with Chad some more, playing music to him on his cell phone and holding his hand. Around 10AM, I prayed with Chad and told him that I would be back to visit him later. I had made a playlist of four special songs and I asked Michael to leave those on repeat until I got back. When I left the hospital that morning, while I was feeling every bit of hopeless, a small portion of me still had not given up on visions of a miraculous healing in Chad's body. Even though I might have entertained the thought that Chad might not pull out of this one, I never for one split second thought that this would be the day.

Coping with this day the only way I knew how, I proceeded to try to get myself together and pull off a birthday celebration for Amare. My

A person may think up plans. But the Lord decides what he will do. Proverbs 16:9 ICB

sister, Robyn, met me at my in-laws' house and still in a state of shock, I filled her in on everything I could. Even after hearing the doctor's reports, she assured me that it was not over until God said it was over. As I proceeded to get ready and throw the party decorations up, Robyn asked me a few times, "Are you sure you don't need to go to the hospital?" My reply was that I didn't want Amare to think that neither one of his parents made it to his fifth birthday party. But in reality, I did not think I was capable of going back to the hospital to witness my biggest nightmare unfold. So we proceeded to load up the car and head to the Howard Hughes Center where the video game place had been reserved.

Knowing that there was a chance that I would need to dip out early, we drove in separate cars. On the way to the party, which was only like five minutes from the house, Michael called saying that Chad's dialysis catheter had broken and asking if I wanted the doctors to try to replace it. He also said that Chad was motioning for more and more pain medication and the swelling in his hands and feet had gotten worse. Basically, in so many words, I was being told that the end was inevitable and drawing near. I asked Michael if he thought I should bring Amare to the hospital and he said, "Let me ask Chad." At first, the notion was yes, but then it was no. Looking back now, I know that in Chad's ever loving and fatherly way, he definitely wanted to see Amare again, but being the selfless person that he always was, decided to do what he thought was best for Amare. I also did not think that Amare would have benefited from that particular scene and to this day, I stand by the decision. Outside of that conclusion regarding Amare, I know that I was not in my right mind because I asked Michael to put me on speaker so that I could talk to Chad. With tears in my eyes, I proceeded to tell Chad that I loved him, that he was the best thing that ever happened to me, that I thanked God for him every day and that our son would be okay because he has his daddy's strength. I was telling my husband goodbye over the telephone when I was only fifteen or twenty minutes away from the hospital. I was literally out of my mind at that moment. I was scared to death. I had never seen anyone pass away and my only

A person may think up plans. But the Lord decides what he will do. Proverbs 16:9 ICB

reference was the dramatic scenes from the movies and on television. I absolutely did not have the courage to watch my best friend die.

Somewhere between getting out of the car at the party location, walking the birthday boy and his cousins to the arcade, and sitting outside in the courtyard while my sister dealt with the incompetence of the arcade staff, God gave me the strength to do what I had to do. God instantly gave me the courage to do what I needed to do in order to survive the days ahead with no regrets. At some point, Michael had called again and I asked the question that I should have known from the beginning, "Did Chad want me to come back?" The answer was a resounding yes. I proceeded to race up the escalator back to the parking lot. On my way up, I saw Joseph on his way down. He was one of Michael's closest friends and basically an uncle to Chad. As we passed each other, I told him that Chad was not doing well at all. He motioned for me to wait so we could chat but I told him I had to run.

Thank God, there was minimal traffic, especially for a Saturday afternoon in Los Angeles. On the drive over, I got a text from Charlotte telling me that Chad was comfortable and not to rush. I also remember getting a text from my cousin Candice, saying that she had seen my Facebook post from the night before and was checking to see if everything was okay. At a red light just outside of the hospital, I replied, "No and please call Robyn for more details." When the light changed, I parked the car and rushed to the unit. I hit the buzzer and the doors opened right away. A nurse was standing outside of Chad's room motioning for me to hurry. I ran into the room where Chad was surrounded by his family and medical staff. I threw my purse down, skipped the yellow gown protocol, and rushed to Chad's side where the four songs were still playing on his cell phone. At that point, God had very much taken over my body because I boldly and courageously held Chad's hand, not caring who was listening and said, "I'm so sorry, Chad. I didn't come sooner because I was scared." I swallowed hard. "But, that's not the way we handle things, so here I am. I love you. You're the best thing that's ever happened to me." Tears stung my eyes, but I soldiered on, determined to reiterate everything I had said over the

A person may think up plans. But the Lord decides what he will do.   Proverbs 16:9 ICB

phone, only this time, it felt right. "I could not have asked God for a better husband for myself and father for our son," I said. "Amare will be just fine because he is as strong as you are, and as for me, well, I will manage because I have to." I swallowed the lump in my throat as I stood beside the love of my life who was once five foot eight, one hundred and sixty plus pounds and full of life and laughter. "You look at me now," I said to the less than one hundred pound version of Chad as his pain-ridden gaze pierced my soul. Desperate to part on a good note, I calmly joked with Chad saying "Look at my smiling face and don't you dare try to act like you don't know me when I get to heaven." Lastly, I played a video that Amare had previously recorded for Chad saying that he was the best daddy ever and that he loved him so much. I told Chad to play that over and over again on his heavenly iPad. While the song "You Make Me Smile" by Aloe Blacc was playing, I again told Chad that I loved him and I was so grateful for him. Just as I said my last words to Chad, his nurse Linda gently tapped me on the arm and said ever so softly that his heart had stopped beating.

For a split second, I remained calm and gave Chad a kiss on his lips. Next, I turned off the music and threw his cell phone at the hospital chair across the room. I then walked over and collapsed in the chair with both hands over my face and I cried like never before. The gut-wrenching pain and despair that I felt at that moment still sends chills through my body just thinking about it. Sitting in a room full of people mourning the loss of Chad, I have never in my life felt as alone as I did in that very moment. I remember someone tapping me on my shoulder and I looked up expecting to see a relative, but it was a hospital family member instead. The Respiratory Nurse, through a face full of tears herself, told me how sorry she was and that she loved us. Still in a complete state of shock, I do not even know if I was able to respond to her. At some point shortly after, we were informed that they would take all of the tubes out of Chad and give us a chance to come back in the room and see him again. Not really sure if I would have the strength or desire to do that, I again stood by Chad's bedside and told him that I loved him and that I would see him again in heaven. I gave him one last

A person may think up plans. But the Lord decides what he will do. Proverbs 16:9 ICB

kiss and exited the room. At that point, I texted my sister Robyn the dreadful four words: *The battle is over.*

The hospital staff said that it would take about an hour to get Chad all cleaned up and free of tubes and they encouraged us to come back and see him. At some point during that hour, God very gently began to highlight the similarity in pieces from His itinerary versus my itinerary. For if I am being completely honest, in a very deep and dark corner of my mind (never ever verbalized), throughout this journey, I had always hoped and mentally prayed that if Chad in fact did not make it through at any point, I would be able to spend his last night with him and be there for his final moments. So during that hour, God reminded me that even after returning to work for a week, I had still made it back in time to spend Chad's last night on earth with him. Even through my cowardly and very human despair, I had made it back to hold Chad's hand and bid him a proper goodbye. God had even loaned me a big-gulp portion of His strength so that my final words to Chad would be delivered with cheer and not a face full of tears. God had so kindly and beautifully arranged it so that my voice would be the last human voice that Chad heard just as he turned in his keys on earth and watched the Pearly Gates of Heaven swing wide open for his homecoming. So when the hour was up and God's mental slideshow for me had concluded, I knew that there was nothing for me to return to in that room. Needless to say, Chad's departure from earth on that day was not our chosen timeline, because we all know that Chad living forever would have been the popular vote. Yet, when that hour was up, I could not help but admit that God had very graciously given Chad and me an eloquent conclusion to our marriage, which had been blissfully perfect in its own unique way. When that hour was up, I was still very much devastated, in pain and completely absorbed by this emotional shock; yet, I could not help but feel an overwhelming sense of gratitude to God for giving us this nostalgic yet fairy-tale ending that would have never seen the light of day on my calendar. Only *God's Itinerary* could provide such grandeur in the presence of pain, for He truly is the ultimate planner and coordinator of our lives.

A person may think up plans. But the Lord decides what he will do. Proverbs 16:9 ICB

HOW MANY TIMES CAN ONE HEART BREAK?

Kara

After an hour had passed, we, the army of family grieving Chad, headed up to the room where he had spent the last six and half months fighting for his life. With each step forward, internal alarms were ringing in my head as I questioned whether or not I had the strength.

"I can't do this," I said after one baby step into the room and barely a glimpse of Chad.

There was no way that I was looking to replace our "fairy-tale" ending scene with this new one. I all but ran out of the ICU with my emotions back on the rise, and as the double doors slowly opened, I saw Jessica. I immediately broke down in her arms.

"This is the worst day of my life," I sobbed. Reality was rearing its ugly head and all signs were pointing to the fact that I had to deliver this horrific news to our precious baby boy. The "fairy-tale" that I had briefly convinced myself to find peace with had suddenly been reduced to my worst nightmare.

At that point, I wanted nothing more than to leave UCLA and Westwood forever. I had been asked to wait for paperwork to be drawn up so that I could sign. I honestly do not remember what I put my name on that day, but I do recall the paper that I was given to take home. The paper with instructions and the timeline in which Chad's body needed to be picked up by the mortuary, and the dreadful verbiage indicating what happened to unclaimed bodies. I was not ready for this.

As I prepared to leave UCLA, Jessica and Chad's Aunt Ginger were really concerned about me driving. I assured them that I would be okay and needed time alone to ponder how I would tell Amare. I had been in contact via text with Robyn and thankfully, she had improvised after the birthday party gaming session, and taken the kids to the movies in order to buy me time. Jessica finally agreed to let me drive alone, with the caveat that she would be following right behind me. As we pulled out onto Westwood Boulevard, I decided to call my parents in Arizona. Robyn had notified them earlier and by now, everyone had gathered at their house in disbelief. I spoke with each of my parents and siblings individually and we were all a mess, barely able to speak above a whisper. I had to quickly end the call in order to regain composure and focus on Amare. That was just the first of many dreadful calls that I would have to make.

By the time Jessica and I pulled up to the house, I had landed firmly on the decision to give Amare just one more day of life as he knew it. There was no way that I wanted him to associate his birthday with his father's death. Pat, the Washingtons' neighbor and friend, greeted me with a hug in the driveway as she had already received notice. At this point, I was slowly migrating to robotic mode. I had to pretend that everything was okay in order to protect my son for just one more day.

As I opened the door to the Washington home, I felt as though I was leaving the brutal blizzard of reality outside and entering utopia. Amare and his cousins were having a great time playing around in the Transformers party scene. Robyn, my cousin Tamara and friend Janice did a phenomenal job of keeping the scene festive, as I mentally teetered in and out. In this space, parenting almost felt hypocritical, as one second I was smiling and joining in to sing Happy Birthday to Amare,

So do not fear, for I am with you; do not be dismayed, for I am your God. I will strengthen you and help you; I will uphold you with my righteous right hand. Isaiah 41:10 NIV

and the very next moment, I was ferociously trying to wrap my mind around what had just happened and how in the world would I put the pieces of our lives back together.

As the birthday party wrapped up and my mind continued to race from A to Z and back again, the only thing that I was sure of was that I was not prepared to tell Amare. Saving the day twice over, Robyn took Amare and Carlton home with her that evening. Chad's parents had made it home and a few of their friends and relatives were beginning to file in. I headed out to a park in Marina Del Rey with my girlfriends Jessica, Janice and Tara. I just needed some fresh air and space to talk, not talk, breathe, think, and cry as I began to scratch the surface of my new reality. Prior to leaving the house, Michael had asked me to consider the possibility of a more non-traditional funeral or memorial service. I suspect that my initial facial expression most likely said it all, but I vowed to at least consider it.

Once settled in at the park, there was one phone call that I knew I needed to make that day. That call was to Chad's best friend, Aaron. "Hi, Aaron," I said, and then suddenly ran out of words as red hot tears rushed to the forefront of my eyes. Just barely above a whisper, I managed to get out "Chad did not make it."

"No, Kara, no," Aaron said. As I struggled to find words to comfort him, my girlfriends signaled for me to wrap it up fast. That was the last call I made that night. We stayed at the park until almost 10PM when the patrol car started to do its rounds. If possible, I would have stayed all night in order to avoid laying my head on a pillow for the first time, knowing Chad would not be here on earth when I opened my eyes again.

Absolutely not ready to be alone, Jessica thankfully offered to stay the night with me at Chad's parents' house. My sister, Tiffany, was flying in the next morning to be with me so she and Jessica would tag team it out then, while Robyn remained on kid duty in Anaheim. Needless to say, I laid down that night but never went to sleep. I turned on the television for background noise and just stared off into space as tears sporadically presented themselves here and there. I could not stop

So do not fear, for I am with you; do not be dismayed, for I am your God. I will strengthen you and help you; I will uphold you with my righteous right hand. Isaiah 41:10 NIV

replaying the scene from the night before. Between Chad's piercing stare, the orchestra of beeps as his blood pressure tanked, the matter-of-fact doctor followed by the teary-eyed resident, would I ever escape the memory of that night?

Finally, as the sun pierced the sky the next morning, I got up and went to the family room as to not disturb Jessica. I began the dreadful calls once again. The myriad of responses I received was so unpredictable that I dreaded each call more and more. My first call was to Dr. Angel who I assumed already knew, but I had to call anyway. She was stuck out of town for a wedding in which her husband was a groomsman. Otherwise, she assured me that she would be right there by my side. Just hearing her calm and reassuring voice was supportive enough for me. I managed to make one more call before Janice rushed out to the living room to inform me that the news had begun to spread and there were a few condolences posted on our personal Facebook page. While the kind words were appreciated, I quickly deleted each post, as our teenage nieces and nephews could not find out about their uncle's death this way. I mean I had not even told our poor child yet. So adding another title to her name, right behind widow comforter, Jessica quickly offered to be on social media guard. Welcome to the twenty-first century edition of grieving.

The next call I made was to Chad's long-time co-worker friend from his Los Angeles teaching days. She was absolutely shocked at the news and began to cry immediately but offered gracious words of encouragement. Next, I called my friend Tracey from college. In complete shock as well, her first response was, "Did they (UCLA) do all that they could do?" I found myself suddenly offended as UCLA had long since become our family. Thankfully, doubt regarding quality of service received, was not on the list of one million other things ping-ponging in my head. Knowing she had nothing but our best interest at heart, I gently responded that I totally trusted Chad's team with no reservations. That was the last call I made that morning and decided from that point on to delegate as many of those calls as possible.

So do not fear, for I am with you; do not be dismayed, for I am your God. I will strengthen you and help you; I will uphold you with my righteous right hand. Isaiah 41:10 NIV

Tiffany's flight from Phoenix was scheduled to land at LAX just after 9AM. Jessica and I pulled up to the airport curve as Tiffany was coming out. As she quickly approached the car, Tiffany was already beginning to cry and breathe deep short breaths in an unsuccessful attempt to hold back her emotions. No words were needed, as her pain-ridden eyes said it all. Our curbside embrace and slew of tears was like something out of a movie. How in the world was I going to tell our son that our family had been torn apart and would never be the same again?

Gauging by the airport greeting, Jessica determined that perhaps her presence was still very much needed. We stopped at McDonald's for Tiffany to grab a bite to eat. We then headed out to another park in the Marina to connect with Robyn and the kids. I could not put off the inevitable any longer. The time had come for me to break my son's heart. When we got to the park, Amare and his cousins were playing on the playground. We adults sat at a table and chatted for a little while, as I mindlessly recapped the last twenty-four hours. Silently overcome with emotions, Robyn's husband, Carl, excused himself from the discussion.

I finally mustered up the courage to tell Amare. I asked Robyn to join me for moral support. As I pulled Amare aside and we walked hand in hand away from the playground, I told him there was something that I needed to tell him. Once out of earshot from his cousins, we stopped walking and I took a deep breath as I prepared to deliver my script.

"Daddy is not at the hospital anymore," I said.

"He's home?" Amare enthusiastically asked. Alarms immediately fired in my head as I realized the unfortunate fault in my choice of words.

"No, baby, Daddy is in heaven now and he is no longer in pain," I somberly responded.

"Oh, okay," Amare said and asked if he could go back to playing with his cousins. Robyn and I were left dumbfounded, as if we were the ones who had just received the shocking news. Little did I know, Amare and I would have that conversation multiple times in the days ahead, and each time, yet another piece of my heart would crumble.

So do not fear, for I am with you; do not be dismayed, for I am your God. I will strengthen you and help you; I will uphold you with my righteous right hand. Isaiah 41:10 NIV

OUR MIRACLE MAN

Kara

IN THE MIDST OF A BROKEN HEART

Now that the dreadful secret was out of the bag, I needed to proceed with planning a service suitable to honor the life and legacy of the man of my dreams. This was no easy feat by any stretch of the imagination. Everyone was heartbroken, but Chad deserved a proper send-off. Having only by the grace of God, escaped the horrific regret that I would have likely lived with had I not returned to the hospital for a proper good-bye, I wanted to make sure that I got this next step right.

By now, it was Sunday afternoon, and Robyn and her family had gone back to Anaheim, Jessica went home to get some rest herself, and Tiffany and I were back at the Washingtons' house with Amare and Carlton. We were set to fly back to Phoenix Monday afternoon so that the boys would not miss too much school. The goal was to accomplish as much as we could in terms of funeral preparations before we left. The company and condolences were non-stop and it was practically impossible to find a moment to speak with Chad's parents. The overwhelming amount of love and support from relatives and friends alike was appreciated, but after a while, the chatter grew to be way too much for me to bear. At one point, the topic of conversation landed on cooking and how great this person or that person was at it. All that I could think of was that my amazing Chef Chad was gone. As I felt another breakdown coming on, I quickly returned to the bedroom. I missed Chad so very much and my emotions were spiraling out of control. I opened the closet where his clothes were hanging and clung onto them to breathe in Chad's scent. "I miss you so much," I cried out, as if Chad were actually wearing the clothes. I thought there were no pieces left, but my heart was definitely still breaking.

I crawled into the bed and sobbed until the tears finally stopped. I needed to get started but had absolutely no idea where to begin. How do you plan a funeral for someone you don't even believe is gone? According to the final instructions received from UCLA on that dreadful day, I had ten days to arrange for Chad's body to be picked up. This made finding a mortuary a top priority. Even though I did not want to hear it at the time, Chad had told me a long time ago after a relative's funeral that he wanted to be cremated. Initially, I did not think I could follow through on his request, but when the time actually came, my conscience would not hear otherwise. My mind really struggled to get past the concept of cremation. Torturous visions of Chad's body going through the process shook me to my core. I tried to shut the thoughts down as quickly as they came, until suddenly I was able to pacify myself with an online search for urns. If Chad wanted to be cremated, the least I could do was get him an amazing urn. I started at Costco.com and the search expanded from there. The plethora of options available blew my mind. Initially, I thought I would get a heart-shaped urn, but ultimately landed on a custom chef's hat with a heart on the rim.

Somehow, this one decision was enough to propel me into planning mode and from there, the pieces started to come together. Jessica called that afternoon with great news. Her neighbors owned a mortuary and were willing to give me the family discount. I spoke directly to one of the owners and instantly knew that item was checked off. They were so

You're blessed when you're at the end of your rope. With less of you there is more of God and his rule. You're blessed when you feel you've lost what is most dear to you. Only then can you be embraced by the One most dear to you. Matthew 5:3-4 MSG

very kind and compassionate and I knew that Chad's body would be in great hands. At last, the ten-day timeline was out of my realm of concerns.

Monday morning, I was up bright and early ready to tackle the hefty task list. For the most part, I was able to momentarily compartmentalize my emotions and just focus on planning a beautiful celebration for Chad. However, somehow I got side-tracked for a moment and found myself listening to old voicemails from Chad on my cell phone. Big mistake—hearing his voice instantly took me right back to the realm of disbelief that he was in fact gone. I made a note to have the voicemails archived when I got back to Phoenix, but to this day, I have yet to muster up the courage to listen again.

The first call that morning was to the church that I grew up in. I had assumed that holding Chad's services there would not be a problem as long as they were not already booked for the date we needed. I was pretty bummed and surprised to find out that they had recently steered away from conducting funerals on Saturdays. In fact, the news kind of threw us all for a loop, but with everything else going on, we could not dwell on it and had to press forward. Thankfully, Charlotte's best friend's sister came through big time, offering up the use of the church where she and her husband pastored. Dr. Angel was back in town and offered to drive me to the church so that we could check it out. Unfortunately, somehow the lines of communication had been crossed and when we arrived, no one was there. So far, this go get-em Monday was not going so well and it was just about time for us to head back to Phoenix. Dr. Angel assured me that she would visit the church, take pictures and let me know her thoughts. She also assured me that she was here for me and both admired and understood my passion and drive to make sure that Chad's services were no less than amazing.

As Tiffany and I began to gather our things to head back to Phoenix with the boys, a whole new wave of emotions rushed over me. Although Amare and I had been flying back and forth for well over a year now,

You're blessed when you're at the end of your rope. With less of you there is more of God and his rule. You're blessed when you feel you've lost what is most dear to you. Only then can you be embraced by the One most dear to you. Matthew 5:3-4 MSG

this trip home was drastically different. I was definitely not prepared to sleep in our house alone, knowing now that the prospect of Chad returning had been reduced to zero. Thank God Tiffany had flown out to LA, because I was also not mentally prepared to fly alone with two five-year-olds. Basically, I was not mentally prepared for anything. I was a nervous wreck and obviously the sleep deprivation did not help. I gave Tiffany the pleasure of sitting with the boys and I sat one row up and over from them. I attempted to place a beverage order before we even took off, as I needed something to calm my nerves. So far, we had secured a mortuary and a church, assuming the facility was suitable once Dr. Angel saw it. But there was so much more work to do.

The flight to Phoenix was actually quicker than I would have liked, as the moment to finally sit still was refreshing. As we filed off of the plane and headed to the car, I received a text message from a number I did not recognize.

Kara, I am so sorry for your loss and we would definitely like to help in any way possible. I had no idea who the message was from and just as I began to wreck my brain, the next message read, *Oh and this is Bridget from PetSmart.* Wow, I thought, as if PetSmart had not done enough for us already.

Amare and I went home with Tiffany and Carlton that night. We would live at their house in Surprise until after the services. Although sleep was virtually impossible no matter where I was, at least we were not alone. The next morning, in an attempt to restore some type of normalcy, we got the kids ready and off to school. This was only the second week of kindergarten for the boys so everything was still new. Amare's school was less than two miles from our home, but more like twenty miles from Surprise. Tiffany and I rode together for the school drop-offs. We arrived at Amare's school after the bell that day so we were forced to enter the chaotic office scene. I casually mentioned to the receptionist that Amare's dad had died and I would like to walk him to class. She recited the school protocol and said that only the student could go in. Not up for the debate, I began to walk away, but Tiffany

You're blessed when you're at the end of your rope. With less of you there is more of God and his rule. You're blessed when you feel you've lost what is most dear to you. Only then can you be embraced by the One most dear to you. Matthew 5:3-4 MSG

quickly jumped in saying, "Did you hear what she just said? His father just died, and your response was very insensitive." My big sis was simply trying to protect us, but I was not interested in ruffling feathers at our new school. With all of the commotion, it was very possible that the receptionist had not even heard me, so I suggested that we just go ahead and leave, as Amare was already in class and we had a million other battles to face.

Chad's memorial service had been set for Saturday, August 31. My job was gracious enough to allow me to remain off until after the services. This gave me two solid weeks to pull together a tribute that would truly honor Chad's legacy. Now that I was back in Phoenix, with some distance between me and the city where my love had died, I was somehow able to escape a few layers of emotions and go right into planning mode. Tiffany and I left the school and headed to my house. Our friend, Desiree, met us there, and later Shawn too. We set up shop at the dining room table, putting our brains together to sort out everything that needed to be done. The range of tasks included everything from the program to the actual obituary (which I would write in solitude), flowers for the service and even personal business like getting excused from jury duty the following week, contacting the social security office and addressing the Southwest Airlines flights that Amare and I had booked, through the end of the year. I realized that not everything needed to be handled in one day, but just documenting it and knowing that I was not alone in tackling the list, was a tremendous anxiety reliever for me.

Around mid-morning, I received a call from my friend, Bridget, who was the director of human resources at PetSmart, and also on the line was my actual HR representative. They were calling to reiterate the text that I had received the night before. I could feel the intensity of their desire to help through the phone. I honestly had no idea where to begin in terms of how PetSmart could help, as I felt the corporation had already done so much for me and my family. Having already discussed a

You're blessed when you're at the end of your rope. With less of you there is more of God and his rule. You're blessed when you feel you've lost what is most dear to you. Only then can you be embraced by the One most dear to you.   Matthew 5:3-4 MSG

slideshow tribute to Chad, I threw the request out there to borrow a projector from PetSmart. Bridget's response was, "Easy, done, what else?" They made it clear that they wanted to help in a tangible way and in order to do this, my needs had to be documented. The message was finally coming through to my foggy head and so I let them know that we were just getting the ball rolling with the planning, but I should have a better picture of potential needs within the next twenty-four hours. I hung up thinking, *wow, God was certainly pulling out all the stops to make sure I was not alone on my quest to honor Chad.* By the time we wrapped up our planning session that day, we had made amazing progress in setting up the framework for Chad's memorial. I was highly encouraged that the end result would be nothing short of beautiful. The rest of the week would be about executing and delegating until the plan became a reality.

The next morning, Tiffany had to return to work so I was on my own for the day. Having been in contact with Amare's kindergarten teacher via email, I assured her that Amare being late would not be the norm. Amare and I left Surprise Wednesday morning with time to spare. We arrived at the school around a quarter to eight, just as the kindergarten playground gates were being unlocked for the day. As we said our good-byes, Amare broke down crying and did not want to separate. Thankfully, his teacher was on yard duty that morning and gracefully took him into her arms and carried him away. Needless to say, I left the school with a very heavy heart. Was I pushing Amare back to school too soon? Would it be better for him to stay home with me? What in the world was I doing?

Already in a very sad mood, I returned to our house and dived right back into planning Chad's memorial. Today, I would tackle the obituary and my personal letter to Chad. My emotions were already out of their cage for the day so there was no sense in trying to hold back the tears as I typed. Robyn called that morning and every subsequent morning that week to see how she could be of help each day. My sisters and friends

---

You're blessed when you're at the end of your rope. With less of you there is more of God and his rule. You're blessed when you feel you've lost what is most dear to you. Only then can you be embraced by the One most dear to you. Matthew 5:3-4 MSG

were literally carrying me through the entire planning process and without them, I would have been completely lost.

I picked up Amare as soon as school let out and we came back to our house for just a little while before we would head to Surprise for the night. As I pulled into the garage, out of nowhere Amare said, "I can't wait for Daddy to come back home to Phoenix." I immediately froze and my heart dropped as my mind raced for a response. Knowing there was no easy way around this, I looked back at Amare and responded with as much compassion as humanly possible. "Amare, Daddy is not coming back to this world," I said. "He is in heaven now."

"Oh." That was Amare's only verbal response, but his body language deflated as if this were the first time the news truly had been delivered. I was a mess all over again but kept my composure until I could break away long enough to release yet another tidal wave of tears. How many times could one heart break?

That evening back in Surprise, I was not of much company for anyone and after dinner, I retired to the guest bedroom to be alone. Today had not been a good day and I just wanted it to end. Tomorrow had to be brighter, if only just a little bit. Thursday morning, Amare and I headed out to the school again. This time the drop off went way smoother and as if confirmation from God that today would be better, as I turned to walk away from the playground, Amare's kindergarten teacher approached me saying there was something she had been meaning to do. That "something" was to give me a big hug and express her condolences. There is no way that she could have known just how much that hug meant to me, but in that moment, it was everything I needed. I had been so wrapped up and laser focused on planning an amazing celebration for Chad and making sure that Amare was okay, that I had left little to no time to check in with myself. I realize now that I had subconsciously attempted to table my feelings until after the services.

You're blessed when you're at the end of your rope. With less of you there is more of God and his rule. You're blessed when you feel you've lost what is most dear to you. Only then can you be embraced by the One most dear to you. Matthew 5:3-4 MSG

In addition to the planning task list that was thankfully being worked by multiple parties, I did not want the week to close without me finding a counselor for Amare to speak to. Clearly, I did not know what I was doing, as somehow my precious baby boy still thought his daddy was coming home. It was time to seek professional help. I called the church that we had recently started attending and while they did not have a child grief specialist on staff, they did give me a recommendation. Thankfully, I was able to get Amare scheduled to see a therapist the following Wednesday, before the services.

Amare and I took our normally scheduled Friday evening flight back to Los Angeles for the weekend to wrap up any loose ends there, in preparation for the memorial service on August 31. That weekend in Los Angeles was about gathering childhood pictures of Chad to be used in the program, which PetSmart had so generously offered to print at no charge. I also connected with family and friends who would speak or participate on some level in Chad's service. I was able to visit a little more this time with the company stopping by the Washingtons' home, as everything in terms of the service was just about in place. I even began to pack up the guest bedroom that had served as our Los Angeles apartment for well over a year. On the plane ride back to Phoenix Sunday evening, I put the final pieces of the puzzle together to complete the ceremony program and send over to PetSmart to begin the printing process. I definitely felt a sense of accomplishment and a small weight begin to lift in regards to Chad's memorial service.

Amare would attend school from Monday through Wednesday that week and then we would head back to California. Over the next couple of days, I was able to shift gears from less ceremony planning, to making sure that Amare and I were both prepared for the actual ceremony. What would we wear? What about my hair, Amare's hair? And most importantly, did Amare understand what a memorial service was really about? How would this all play out?

You're blessed when you're at the end of your rope. With less of you there is more of God and his rule. You're blessed when you feel you've lost what is most dear to you. Only then can you be embraced by the One most dear to you. Matthew 5:3-4 MSG

OUR MIRACLE MAN

Wednesday afternoon, I picked Amare up from school and we headed to his therapist appointment. On the ride over, I received a phone call from the bank regarding a refinance inquiry that I had made long before Chad passed away. Clearly unable to entertain this type of discussion right now, I quickly told the lady that my husband had died and I had a lot on my plate. When I hung up, Amare immediately asked, "Wait, Mommy, did Daddy die?"

Oh, boy, we could not get to the therapist fast enough. Why had I even answered that call? So here I was, tasked with telling my son for the third time that his dad had in fact died. Later, I would learn that with children and grief, vague statements like "passed away" or "we lost Daddy" left them the hope that there was a chance their special person could be found. The therapist appointment went as well as could be expected. She did not have any immediate concerns regarding Amare's current frame of mind. And as an added bonus, I was able to bounce some ideas off of her and clear up any reservations regarding Amare participating in the upcoming memorial service for his dad.

After we left the therapist, we headed to the airport. This time, we would remain in Los Angeles until after the service and return to Phoenix on Monday, September 2, which was also Labor Day. As we waited in the airport security line, the lady in front of us decided to engage in conversation with Amare. "Where are you headed?" she asked Amare. "To heaven to see my daddy," Amare responded without skipping a beat. The look on the lady's face was priceless and I had no words of consolation for her. Inside, I kind of chuckled and suspected it would be a long time before she asked a kid that question again. On a more serious note though, I was mentally thanking God that we could confidently know where Chad was, and also that Amare was beginning to grasp the unfortunate reality that Chad would not be coming back.

You're blessed when you're at the end of your rope. With less of you there is more of God and his rule. You're blessed when you feel you've lost what is most dear to you. Only then can you be embraced by the One most dear to you. Matthew 5:3-4 MSG

The next couple of days flew by and before I knew it, it was Saturday morning and we were getting dressed for Chad's memorial service. As I dressed Amare in the most adorable beige suit that I had ever seen, I reminded him that today was a celebration of Daddy. I warned him that he may see some people cry, but that it was okay, as they were just remembering the amazing man that Daddy was. I also let Amare know that if the service grew too much for him, he could simply tap me and say, "I've had enough." One of his nurse girlfriends, Lauren, had already agreed to sit within eyesight and was willing to take Amare out should the need arise. Although all of the arrangements had been made and everything was in order, I still had no idea how this day would go, but at exactly 9AM, Jessica arrived at the Washingtons' home to transport Amare and me to the memorial service.

As we pulled into the church parking lot, the sea of orange that we saw was beautiful. Orange was Chad's favorite color, and following our cultural tradition, a large majority of the attendees wore it on this day. We had arrived a good hour before the service was set to begin, and the turnout was already overwhelming. By the time the service was complete, well over three hundred people had gathered to celebrate Chad. The guests ranged from family, friends, past and present co-workers— including the Director of Benefits and more from my PetSmart family in Arizona—as well as an overwhelming representation from UCLA.

The eulogy delivered by Pastor Rogers was both insightful and hilarious. He had visited Chad numerous times in the hospital and spoke of how Chad's consistently calm demeanor baffled him every time. Pastor Rogers described the perfect analogy between Chad and the famous superheroes that we all grew up watching. Chad's superpower was his steadfast ability to remain calm no matter what life threw his way. Even upon learning that he needed an artificial heart after having his transplanted heart for just nine months, Chad's superpower never wavered.

You're blessed when you're at the end of your rope. With less of you there is more of God and his rule. You're blessed when you feel you've lost what is most dear to you. Only then can you be embraced by the One most dear to you. Matthew 5:3-4 MSG

As I prepared for this day, and had asked a variety of people to speak, from family, friends, UCLA nurses, therapists, physicians along with Chad's surgeon, I never once suggested a specific topic or theme for their tributes. Yet, as I sat and listened to the beautiful speeches and recollections of time spent with Chad, I was astonished at the extent to which each tribute weaved into the next. Everyone spoke of Chad's patience and extraordinarily calm spirit. They also spoke of his awe-inspiring selflessness. Dr. DuBois' joked about a time when Chad had turned the tables on him, as he had stopped by Chad's room to check on him, and before he knew it, Chad was inquiring as to Dr. DuBois' well-being. Dr. Hart candidly admitted that even though surgeons are taught to maintain a certain level of emotional detachment, Chad had somehow broken the code and we had all become family. Our friend, Desiree, rendered a powerful poem that she wrote about Chad. She described him as a miracle man for whom God had a plan. With her words, she painted a picture of God placing Chad on a pedestal, like a trophy on a stand.

Chad was absolutely our miracle man and his memorial service by far exceeded even my colossal expectations. Everyone left feeling the call to action for us to intentionally seek the best versions of ourselves. Throughout the day, I smiled and laughed more than I cried, as I listened to everyone describe what their relationship and encounters with Chad meant to them. I had long since known that I was one of the luckiest girls alive to have met and married Chad. But the celebration of Chad's life on August 31, 2013 left me even prouder to be his wife. As the day came to a close and everyone parted ways, I vowed to myself and Chad that there was no way I would allow his legacy to be forgotten. So here it is in print at last, the legacy of a miracle man, my hero and best friend, Charles (Chad) Wesley Washington III.

You're blessed when you're at the end of your rope. With less of you there is more of God and his rule. You're blessed when you feel you've lost what is most dear to you. Only then can you be embraced by the One most dear to you. Matthew 5:3-4 MSG

Malbury, William. *Super Chad*. 2013

September 2, 2013

OUR FINAL ASCENT

As we pull away from the gate at LAX to return to PHX and start the rest of our lives, I have this uneasy feeling in the pit of my stomach. This feels more final than the actual memorial service itself. The inherit pain that was overpowered with joy on Saturday and Sunday is definitely creeping up and settling in. Throughout this entire experience Chad and I knew that our lives would never be the same, but somehow this is about as far from what I had in mind as possible.

My mind is like a flip book right now with flashing images of Chad happy, Chad sad, the three of us together, us apart, Amare happy, Amare sad, me, lonely. I wish I could hit the pause button on the happiest image and stay there forever. Given the current state of our circumstances and the hard cold, gut-wrenching reality that Chad is not coming back to this world, the image that I am going to try to permanently freeze in my head is of Chad in heaven sitting at the throne of God. I imagine him grinning his biggest brightest smile as God says, "Well done my good and faithful servant, well done." Chad is bumping hip-hop gospel on the best most top-notch heavenly surround system. He is cooking in the most laid out 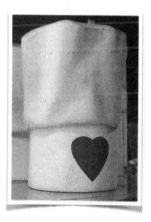 kitchen that you can imagine, with the best utensils ever dreamed of, and the most gourmet ingredients picked from the heavenly grocery village that he visits every single day. His brothers are his suiox-chefs and they are spreading the word about the new chef in heaven. Chad is cooking for everyone, but finding his greatest pleasure in breaking bread with all of his grandparents, as he fills them in on their great-grandson, Amare.

Every morning that Amare and I wake up, Chad smiles down on us and encourages us to make a great day. And every night that we come home, he reassures us that everything is going to be okay. He knows that we miss him like crazy, but he is confident and carries great pride in the fact that he left us with the tools and foundation that we need to lead successful lives that are pleasing unto God, so that we can continue our Mommy, Daddy, Mooter Production in Heaven! Rest in peace CWW3, my warrior, my best friend, my hero. We love you. ♥

EPILOGUE

Bless·ing: God's favor and protection.

Ironically, being dealt seemingly one of the world's worst deck of cards, turned out to be the biggest overall blessing. As a result of Chad growing up battling a serious illness, he was always ever mindful of his blessings. Contrary to many people in the world today, a blessing to him did not mean a gigantic home or a wallet laced with cash. Yes, Chad loved nice things, but nice things did not define him. For Chad, a blessing was a day waking up outside of a hospital or emergency room. It was spending quality time with family, good laughs and great food. A blessing, to him, was being able to help someone out or offer words of encouragement. Once, at a doctor's appointment, Chad was filing out the paperwork for first time patients, and after answering yes to at least 75 or 80% of the listed conditions, he stopped and thanked God for the 25% of boxes that he was still able to check no. Despite everything that Chad endured, no matter what predicament he found himself in, he always made a point to thank God for what was going well in his life. His optimism and astonishing resolve to lead a positive life, was down-right baffling.

Chad's positivity and supernatural gratitude ultimately set the tone for our marriage. His fearlessness in the face of tribulation was astounding and eventually contagious. It was in our darkest hours, when one could naturally be tempted to give up or turn away; that our faith was remarkably ignited and together we soared to a whole new level of trust in God.

In order to hand every aspect of your life, including your own pre-meditated and very carefully crafted timeline, over to God, you will need epic faith. In exchange for this epic faith, you will experience priceless peace that even the world's greatest wordsmith cannot describe. In other words, when you accept *God's Itinerary* for your life, there is no need for "trip insurance," because His will is faultless and cannot be interrupted. When you are traveling on *God's Itinerary*, no matter what challenges are thrown your way, you neither fret nor fuss. Epic faith will give you the confidence to always know that, despite the unpredictable outcome and likely detour from "your itinerary," you can invariably claim a victorious ending with *God's Itinerary*.

PIECES OF A
NEW PUZZLE

5 years later...

Enduring extreme grief is like attempting to solve a jigsaw puzzle, without a clue as to what the final picture portrays. In our early days of bereavement, I often wondered if I would ever have a tearless night or authentically smile again. It was so hard to witness the heart-throbbing sorrow in Amare's eyes, whenever he saw other children playing with fathers still physically in their lives. Some days, I was angry, but most days just sad. I was dumbfounded as to why God saw fit to take Amare's dad.

I struggled to find my identity, outside of being Chad's wife. I didn't fit in with my single girlfriends, still seeking the love of their life. I no longer had a living spouse, so couples events were out. I hated school activities and birthday parties, as they always left me feeling totally singled out. I knew this awkward phase was not sustainable, so I began to search for an escape route.

Thankfully, we learned of Billy's Place, the valley's number one destination for hope to grieving families. At last, Amare and I could relate to others who had lost a great. This was truly the launching pad for our healing. It was a judgment-free zone where we could share exactly what we were feeling. My greatest fear in all of this, was that Amare would forget his dad. But at Billy's Place, my fear was tackled, and we learned a million ways to celebrate Chad.

Now that my comfort zone was changing, I pressed the limits a little more. We joined a CCV neighborhood group, who met practically next door. Our group discussed the Bible, our lives and so much more. My faith had clearly been tested, but I knew that God could restore. We bonded and became a family, and before I knew it, socializing was not a chore. Who knew that so much joy could be found simply by visiting the neighbors next door?

School and work were also huge pillars in our healing. Amare's teachers and supporting staff graciously embraced him, as he sorted through all of his feelings. My co-workers became my brothers and sisters, able to effortlessly gauge good days versus bad. After a while, the outpouring of love that Amare and I received, made it difficult for us to remain sad.

Our family and long-time friends completed our circle. They gave us space as we made strides to find our new normal. And although they served as our compass to all things familiar, when asked to participate in new ways to celebrate Chad, never once did they fail to deliver.

Our life has become the perfect blend of the past and the present. We cherish our old memories, yet welcome new ones too. Our perspective is forever changed, as we intentionally seek joy, peace and happiness in Jesus' name.

Thank you Charles Wesley Washington III for courageously accepting *God's Itinerary* for your life and leaving us with a legacy of Epic Faith.

Acknowledgments

I would like to thank Amare for your constant excitement and genuine interest in this project, despite the fact that I have been working on it for as long as you can remember. Thank you PopPop, for your frequent visits to Arizona to ensure that Amare still experiences childhood with a father, and also giving me time to myself to regroup. Thank you Mommy, for always being willing to help me out at the drop of a dime, so that I can still have a successful career as a single mom. Thank you Karlicia, Kim, Dr. Swilley, and Taletika, for believing in this project before I was even totally convinced myself. Thank you Aunt Nancy and Julia, for thoroughly combing through each and every file that I sent your way over the last five years, and always offering candid feedback, laced with humor, encouragement, and love. Thank you Christy, Karen, Katie, Kim, Monica and Sarah, for reading parts, or all of this book, in its extreme infancy (flaws and all), and still encouraging me to keep writing. Thank you Nina and Gilda, for your precious time and guidance. Thank you Shanara, for instituting our accountability pact, which helped me re-build steam for the final push. Thank you Cara, for challenging me to dig deeper no matter how painful it was. Thank you Kiersten and Kristie, for challenging me on the final details and cheering me on to the finish line. Thank you Kelley and Doug, for giving Amare a second home and family to belong to. Thank you Grandmommie, for instituting Camp Ladera and ensuring that Amare remains connected to his Los Angeles Washington roots. Thank you to Billy's Place for walking alongside Amare and me, and giving us the tools to process our grief in a healthy manner. Thank you to the Berger CCV Neighborhood Group for welcoming Amare and me with open arms, and encouraging me to share our story and continue to seek God's purpose for my life. And last but certainly not least, thank you to our ENTIRE Village of Angels who have given us hope and unconditional love, and have been there for Amare and me every step of the way as we crawled, scratched and clawed our way back to happiness. We are incredibly blessed to have each and every one of you in our lives.

Much Love & God Bless,

Kara

"Random acts of kindness, however small it may be can transform the world."
Amit Ray, *Walking the Path of Compassion*

Made in the USA
San Bernardino, CA
04 March 2019